English Collusion and the Norman Conquest

English Collusion and the Norman Conquest

Arthur C Wright

FRONTLINE BOOKS

An imprint of
Pen & Sword Books Ltd
Yorkshire – Philadelphia

First published in Great Britain in 2020 by
Frontline Books
An imprint of
Pen & Sword Books Ltd
Yorkshire – Philadelphia

ISBN 978 1 52677 370 8

Typeset by Mac Style
Printed and bound in the UK by TJ International Ltd,
Padstow, Cornwall.

Pen & Sword Books Limited incorporates the imprints of Atlas,
Archaeology, Aviation, Discovery, Family History, Fiction, History,
Maritime, Military, Military Classics, Politics, Select, Transport,
True Crime, Air World, Frontline Publishing, Leo Cooper, Remember
When, Seaforth Publishing, The Praetorian Press, Wharncliffe
Local History, Wharncliffe Transport, Wharncliffe True Crime
and White Owl.

For a complete list of Pen & Sword titles please contact

PEN & SWORD BOOKS LIMITED
47 Church Street, Barnsley, South Yorkshire, S70 2AS, England
E-mail: enquiries@pen-and-sword.co.uk
Website: www.pen-and-sword.co.uk

Or

PEN AND SWORD BOOKS
1950 Lawrence Rd, Havertown, PA 19083, USA
E-mail: Uspen-and-sword@casematepublishers.com
Website: www.penandswordbooks.com

Contents

Introduction: The Nature of Collusion

History may be written by the victors but those who write it still only know what they have been told and what they believe. The chroniclers who wrote about 1066 'and all that' were, almost exclusively, not there at the time. At best they relied on other people and those others had reasons of their own for censoring and distorting, or even inventing, their accounts. So these 'historical' chroniclers accepted or invented statistics, had no idea of motivations or outcomes, hated any form of taxation and were part of an elite who were furthering their own careers. They were not historians but institutionalised propagandists, even when ostensibly writing from the defeated side. We would not accept such reportage today as at all 'factual'. It follows that most of what we have been <u>told</u> as '<u>history</u>' is, in fact, propaganda, though not even consistent or uni-directional propaganda. That is why accounts vary so widely. This re-analysis is an attempt to discover the real 'conquest', who conquered whom I wonder?

If we want to recover any sort of 'truth' we need to work with whatever we <u>can</u> recover as surviving 'facts', and not with opinions or inventions. We need to be pragmatic, logical and strategic in our analyses and to remember that the essence of conflict is to win and in the end war is the totality of the means employed to attain a political end. The comprehensive picture, whether we consider attack or defence, is a compound of blood <u>and</u> Bletchley Park, environmental <u>and</u> economic warfare, in the field <u>and</u> undercover, in fact the formation of a comprehensive tool combining manpower, technology and financial resources. Of course, there is also luck but this tends to matter most at the local and incidental level. Overall it is planning and the power of money and resources that most often, maybe always, succeed in the end. Without unity these things are not forthcoming, but did unity involve collusion?

Dynasties are not established, nor yet campaigns won, by skill in battle and its attendant luck. Such claims belong in *Boy's Own* literature.

Ultimately such major achievements are rather the products of good management backed by economic muscle – though, of course, there is also a degree of luck, not least the good fortune to discover the essential resources. From the outset of his invasion we can also say that William the Conqueror displayed acute strategic vision. He was moreover an astute politician, rare in commanders of any Age, while his ultimate grasp of economics marks him out as unique in his Age. In spite of the propaganda cover-story, he probably had no intention of becoming King of England when he set out. The Bayeux Tapestry makes no mention of any such ambition, but events played into his hands and he knew just how to play the hand that fate had dealt. Up to December 1066, we can say, he displayed no interest in accepting the Crown of England and even then seemed at first uncertain. If he was faking his response when offered the throne of England, well we will never know for sure. All we can say is that no reference to him being King occurs anywhere on the surviving majority of the Bayeux Tapestry so all such claims have been and are pure speculation.

The Normans were a race of men, not supermen, who are famous for their special, though not fabulous, horses and neither men nor horses were either legion, invincible or invulnerable. The heavy casualties sustained at the Battle of Hastings and during subsequent campaigning, plus depletions for garrisons and then the need to divide field forces for simultaneous campaigns, placed impossible demands on such a small expeditionary force. It is manifest that no little army could sustain such losses and remain in the field. Very soon it required continuous supplements and reinforcements and though mercenaries always figured prominently, they were a dangerous expedient. When the money resource ran out, as it did, even in England, only English co-operation remained and for twenty years defence of the acquired kingdom necessitated very careful preparation and concentration of all forms of resource in order to meet so many threats. Inevitably the necessary controls then applied by William generated frictions and they become a part of our story and of the problem. Here is both a dynamic and a Machiavellian picture in one man, a man sometimes assisted by capable lieutenants but always in control and such a man tends to make his own luck.

From the outset, from the landing in 1066, there had been English co-operation. It sounds strange today but in 1066 there was no concept of the nation-state or nationality, only of community, often very local community, and by now the English were fatalists. They had grown used to invasion and foreign rulers, they had tasted peace and wished to maintain it and in 1066 their Witan actually invited William to be King, at Berkhamsted, though our history books have ignored this event. In English eyes this made him King, so to assist the appointed King was not collusion, not in any modern sense. He took some time to reply, but then he was not the only leader of the expedition and maybe there was some dispute as to who should accept this role. He was then crowned King, which also made him King to his Norman followers who, like the chroniclers, did not understand the significance of a Witan.

For many years English religious leaders had excused such invasions and destruction as God's punishment for the manifold (and unspecified) wickedness of the English people: they had no other doctrine to offer. In fact it was the very wealth of England that encouraged so many raiders and invaders, including the Normans. No other kingdom in Europe had paid so many and such large ransoms since 991 and obviously they could afford them: '*radix maleorum est cupiditas*', 'the root of [all] evil is the love of money', as the Vulgate said! Now God had seen fit to give victory to William and his Normans were certainly no worse than Danes, Norwegians or Bretons looking for loot. This made 'coming together' – '*covine*' in Old French from Medieval Latin '*convenium*' – a possibility, hence the Witan's decision.

Most important of all, though always overlooked by historians, there were no maps, none at all, no road signs or sign-posts, so a stranger (even a military expedition) could not know where a place was and soldiers could not move around, let alone arrive, without local guides and knowledge. For two decades local help was essential to our columns of supposedly 'Norman' troops. Without local knowledge there could be no strategic concept even if efficient scouts could provide tactical plans. Novelists always forget this evidence, this proof of co-operation, and I also believe England could not have survived but for Anglo-Norman defence forces. Indeed we <u>are</u> often told of English involvement and this helps to explain how King William could continue to field armies for so many difficult years and, sometimes, simultaneously in several places. What we are not given by chroniclers or historians is emphasis on such involvement, but why should we be given such an obvious observation at the time? What we should ask is why historians have consistently ignored such references, for such references do occur.

Today it is easy to dismiss this success by vaguely attributing it to 'feudalism' which, if it was anything, was a military and not a social system. Actually it has no definition among historians or in law, for the term was invented after the 'Middle Ages' had ended and is now pejorative. That is why no one can tell you how it created William's success, including the endless supply of soldiers. Yet 'fealty', from which 'feudum' is derived, in return for a military 'fief' or 'fee', has a great deal to do with our story for it was an essential reality. If 'feudalism' never existed we cannot speak of a 'feudal system' but maybe we can say that if 'feudalism' was ever systematised anywhere it was in England, for here the retention of the military fief eventually came to depend on fealty, thanks to King William.

In the end the actual achievement was security for England, for all her peoples, and a new identity, this was the real Anglo-Norman achievement (though it has been forgotten). Moreover it was (like the Battle of Hastings itself) a 'damn near-run thing', moreover one involving twenty years of fighting in two separate theatres of war, sometimes simultaneously. It was no easy achievement. It really was an astonishing success but also a success only possible in England, and only possible under a man as determined (and I think we can say as skilful) as William for it happened while France and Normandy were falling apart. A Norman accession gave England security, but this wasn't accomplished by an occupying army, much less by destroying the economy.

As we shall see, it was probably England's experience of repeated invasions and attacks which first united those much earlier kingdoms listed in the Tribal Hidage. Then two new opposing kingdoms and forces appeared, a unified Wessex and a Danelaw creation, who in their turn appear to have come under common attack from Viking raiders. These attacks were sporadic but sustained and were not related to settlers or to settling but only with exploitation and terror. Both England and the English Danelaw were rich enough to pay successive ransoms to these Viking pirates until, finally, a Scandinavian king ascended the joint throne. When he died the kingdom, we might say, had been united in adversity and so, in spite of the ethnic differences, the accession of first a Breton and then of a Norman king seem to have created and perhaps even cemented some new feeling of a common group identity. What then remained, after 1066, was the battle for survival in the face of further attempts at exploitation by foreign invaders who attacked in the north, south, east and west. In this final act of the drama the Anglo–Norman culture prevailed and as a result it created a new political structure for England.

Out of military necessity and from unremitting warfare King William created a polity which finally conferred unity and then this newly created national security (in an England which had been in fear of fire, slavers and the sword for so long) went on to secure William's posterity, including the Plantagenet Kings. Its vestiges remain even today, a thousand years after England civilised and thus actually tamed the Normans. Decide for yourself just who conquered whom, did the Normans conquer the English by dynastic change or did the English conquer the Normans through their culture. Was this 'covine' actually collusion or was it co-operation, I think it represented 'novation', mutual self-interest, but I also think we can discern a quite unexpected 'coming together' or 'collusion' which then gave rise to the myth of 'feudalism'. Well now, we must first clear away all the historical debris which obscures both our clear thinking and our 'feudal' records. In the words of Dylan Thomas, we must, 'begin at the beginning'.

Chapter 1

Eliminating Fantasy

In 1066 England was the most desirable kingdom in Europe, and had been so for over a century, yet by 1100 it had become secure from invasion. With the benefit of hindsight it is easy to simply attribute this to the 'Norman Conquest', as if that alone explains everything, but in 1066 there was no reason for Duke William of Normandy to desire to acquire a kingdom rather than collect a ransom. The 'promise of succession' was probably a justification added later as a justification for accepting a throne to which others also had a claim. The Franco-Breton-Norman invasion which he led was just another in a succession of attacks and could well have been followed by others.

England had already been brought to her knees, by 1018, but then she gained a temporary respite; another series of invasions would have ruined her and possibly for good. Invasions do not create security and only good management with strong defence allows a kingdom to develop unity and identity, the essential pre-requisites for what we now define as 'nationality'. These pre-requisites ultimately depend not on military competence alone but essentially on financial and human resources. That is why I am going to propose that out of military necessity there slowly grew what was one day to become constitutional monarchy and it all began when Duke William of Normandy was offered the throne of England.

If historians can agree on anything it is that 'feudalism' was a military system. It is a commonly held belief, to which I do not subscribe, that the Normans brought it with them because its manifestations were castles and knights.[1] This pervasive view of the Norman Conquest is, in reality, a complete fantasy and it is sad to reflect that historians have uncritically accepted a world of 'super heroes' which in all probability has more to do with the French Revolution than the establishment of a Norman dynasty.

In the creation of this fantasy world of invented 'feudalism' we can see the hand of that French republican Augustine Thierry and also our home-grown 'father of historical fiction', Sir Walter Scott, both of them writing at the opening of the nineteenth century in a genre which melded Robin Hood legends, a humanitarian reaction to contemporary right-wing sentiments and a desire to promote the newly emerging concept of the nation-state several centuries before its time, thereby hoping to create its pedigree! Forty years later Charles Kingsley provided his own Fenland super-hero in 'Hereward the Wake'. Such simplistic redactions, reducing everything to a black-and-white perdurable morality, have had an enduring appeal which then lasted through to Hollywood and the action-comics of the 1950s, becoming the unquestioned staple of historical propaganda. It is time such silver speculations and phantoms were given over to folklore so that history <u>can</u> be written.

Outside the realms of nineteenth-century melodrama and Hollywood fantasy, the surviving written evidence we have does not provide conclusive evidence of any sort of 'English resistance movement' opposing the Norman 'supermen'. Indeed if we look at the evidence available from a military perspective, especially as a grand-strategic overview, we find that the period 1066 to 1086 was not marked by the recrudescence of a non-existent nationalism any more than it contained Robin Hood. Instead it was punctuated in England by periodic military problems of the sort experienced before 1066, viz. both attempts at invasion and the internal disruptions evidencing the ambitions of aristocratic entrepreneurs. Without English co-operation (or collusion) and also unification of command to oppose them, these two destructive forces could not be permanently disarmed let alone removed, as became increasingly evident to King William.

The arch-priest of all this supposedly 'reliable' history is Oderic Vitalis who writing, at St Evroult some sixty years after the events themselves, about a secular world he left at 5 years of age and a kingdom he left at 10, being well indoctrinated in the Church view of England by his father (a monk) as well as by his holy auditors and mentors and, perhaps, with his English mother's honour in mind, carefully repeated the old soldier's tales told to him by those who had joined his French Order (in order to die 'in the Lord' and in expiation). These old war-horses (we don't know how many) were not apparently expressing remorse for their own actions nor yet sympathy with Holy Church's views but (we are supposed to believe) were impartially and accurately recounting (many years later) the intimate conversations and strategic decisions they had enjoyed with their commander and King, as (of course) all soldiers can do.

King William, it appears, constantly discussed his strategic objectives, vision and campaign planning with every one of his men, secure in the knowledge that no one would divulge such vital intelligences to the enemy (whoever, pro tempore). This enabled every soldier to see beyond the limited horizon of his own actions and orders and to comprehend the grand-strategic overview and polity of the kingdom to a degree never experienced before, certainly not since, in any army in the world. In the words of an eighteenth-century ballad, 'He cut his throat with a piece of glass and he cut his donkey's after'! And if you believe that is possible, then you can believe anything. Kipling hit the nail on the head when he said, 'Heart of my heart is it meet or wise to warn a king of his enemies? We know what Heaven or Hell may bring, but no man knoweth the mind of a king'. That is just as well, the commander whose mind can be read is likely to be very soon dead. Of course no one knew the King's intentions and he never discussed outcomes, moreover he left no autobiography.

In the eleventh century there was no standing army, yet by 1086 King William had welded together an economy and a military command structure which he could hand to his posterity, as both an effective deterrent and an inheritance. This is how he did it. Pause and consider his achievement. For a period as long as the Napoleonic Wars King William I fought ceaselessly, one campaign after another, protecting both his new kingdom and his old duchy. He fought in two separate theatres and on half-a-dozen fronts without a standing army, leading from the front, knowing that his first failure would be his last, improvising when the money ran out and finally cementing the economy, the law and a system of defence all together. Can we find a parallel? He campaigned over widely separated areas having to learn the tactical details while 'on the hoof' and often in atrocious weather. Somehow he held his expeditions together and the major influence and assistance here was money, though (even in England) the supply was not inexhaustible and so he was then forced to improvise. Nevertheless he eventually achieved something which had previously been unattainable and which then secured his final year and also his posterity. What was it?

Well, if we wish to understand the real evidence we first need to clear our minds of all the misinformation we have been told to believe. We have all heard of something called the 'feudal system' and say that we know what 'feudalism' was and it is easily defined. Well, is it? '"Feudalism" has become an insult even more derogatory than "medieval" ... even historians seldom agree on a date for the beginning or end ... or on what precisely it was', said one eminent scholar.[2] And if there never was a definition of 'feudalism', then how could there have been a 'feudal system'? Another and attractive simplification has attributed its genesis to William the Conqueror by saying that 'William next invented a system according to which everybody had to belong to somebody else, and everybody to the King. This was called the Futile System.'[3] It seems that this has become the most attractive of propositions or definitions for the invariable answer to 'what do you understand by the feudal system' is 'a system where a few lords had lots of slaves who had to work for them'. One feels bound to ask just what the Industrial Revolution did for us or the advent of democracy? Are our modern societies still 'us' and 'them', with a few super-rich over a powerless plebiscite?

Though this loose definition can be applied to any autocracy and to just about any other social and political system, it is not what most people mean when they use 'feudal' as a pejorative. They want it to mean 'we are better off today, democracy is not just a confidence trick'. In fact such usage is meaningless precisely because it fails to separate 'feudalism' distinctly from anything else. Many of us were taught at school that it comprised some medieval social and economic pyramid which, in some unspecified way, was different from any other political system or hierarchy, class or tribal system, though with all sorts of parallel evolutions such as pre-industrial Japan, Islamic States, Romanov Russia and so on. In fact the basic definition of the 'Futile System' is probably a good starting point: everybody belonging to somebody else. What is important is that this should be seen as a military rather than a social structure.

Certainly in 1930, when spoof history-book creators Sellar and Yeatman were popularly rewriting English history in *1066 And All That* (by claiming that it had actually come to an end), 'the Norman Conquest was a Good Thing as from this time onwards England stopped being conquered and thus was able to become top nation'.[4] Well, 'top nation' we are not today but these tongue-in-cheek 1930 historians seem to have hit the nail on the head with their antidote to conquest. Just how did '1066 and all that' end up protecting England, the most desirable kingdom in Europe, from further exploitation and destruction by renegades and invaders? No, it wasn't just the arrival of the 'Middle Ages', if you need a tag, it was (you guessed it?) the much abused and misunderstood 'feudal system', the precursor to later standing armies. More precisely it was the ability to control power within the social system and so ultimately to impose polity. Let us see if we can somehow define it for it played an important part in the development of our constitutional monarchy and our modern society. How could this be?

After all, we have so far established that 'feudal' is a meaningless term employed by (probably) thousands of people every day, and that seems ridiculous. My guess is that these people are using the term in the sense of 'us-and-them', which in older socialist jargon would have been 'toffs-and-workers' half a century ago. This seems to divide medieval history into only two classes or degrees, the 'barons' and the 'villeins' (alias serfs, alias slaves), which simple structure (of course) never existed. Such a proposition is the liquidising of a perceived historical 'fact' called exploitation, an identification which probably had its roots (via Thierry) in the Republicanism of the French Revolution. It is a factoid which reduces 'feudalism' to a political slogan in default of any reasoned progression, making it the ideal pejorative for anything that cannot be defined. Perhaps, instead, it has something to do with military and economic necessity?

Like 'medieval', the term 'feudal' is a relatively recent invention, a word created *c*. 1700 from the Latin '*feudum*' or '*fief*', meaning (in law) a landholding by virtue of some ancient, not well-understood, medieval service contract more recently equated with '*servicium debitum*'. By the time it was invented just about everything had become either an hereditary property right or commuted to a payment in cash, so 'service contract' (let alone 'military service contract') no longer had any meaning. Indeed 'medieval' was invented to convey the idea of a period between the 'death' of Classical learning (and its principles) and the new Renaissance of learning, including Enlightenment, represented by the rebirth of such knowledge and especially of Vitruvian principles. Some of us doubt whether any such gap ever existed outside architecture, making the '*medium aevum*' also into a linguistic nonsense.

Medieval society was based on service contracts for the simple reason that society evolved only very slowly into an intrinsic-value cash (or specie) economy. Most of these contracts concerned the tilling of the soil while some involved praying for divine intervention, and all were contracts made with the minority who controlled the economy by force. A third social group provided this minority with their force, they fought for their masters, and these (if anyone) fall into a 'feudal system' by virtue of the 'fee' they eventually held. Being in all practical senses the power within the power in the land, their fealty to their masters was of prime importance to all parties if they were not to become mere mafias. One other principle should also be understood. Today we pay in cash and not (generally) in personal services, for tax purposes, but the university student is just as much in thrall to his debt as the villein was to his landholding, neither is able to reject their obligation though the one is based on (legal) 'interest' and the other was bound by manual service to his 'feudal' overlord and this represented 'realty'. It is just that times, and structures, have moved on, including the separation of 'interest' from 'realty' in law.

According to influential French historians, it (not unnaturally) first arose in France and then 'feudalism was introduced into England in its French form, more particularly the form which it had assumed in Normandy' (so it presumably had more than one definition?) and this explains why 'feudal relationships were more universal in England than they were in France or Germany' for 'English feudalism therefore shows … characteristics which are quite peculiar to itself'.[5] Right! Frankly the semiotics involved in this elucidation of embodied contradictions are quite beyond my comprehension, no doubt a subtlety of ratiocination that I cannot match, so I have instead chosen to look for the origins of this 'English feudalism' in England, being as it was, apparently, quite distinct from that of France (including Normandy). Moreover it appears to me that the developed form we can perhaps eventually call and truly define as 'feudalism' is one based on its requirement of loyalty or 'fealty', an enforceable loyalty which first evolved in England and <u>then</u> spread to France.

So if we reject as 'feudal' the universal structure of domination by force, the sophisticated protection racket, we cannot claim that in 1066 the Normans possessed any properly defined feudal 'system'.[6] It therefore follows that they could not impart that which they did not possess. When addressing the proposal that Norman feudalism might even have been introduced under King Edward, Stenton observed that every historian inevitably uses the term 'feudalism' in accordance with his (or her) own interpretation of the recorded course of social development and that no process of evolution could have bridged the gap between these two societies (England and France).[7] His definition of feudalism was (of course) largely dependent on mounted 'knights' and 'castles' all organised specifically for offensive war yet this in itself is fallacious for the objective, war, can only be maintained if a state of war exists. Within England itself no general state of war did exist immediately after 1066, only (generally) of defence against outsiders, and defence was dealt with much as it had been dealt with prior to 1066.[8] Nevertheless defence is as much a military matter as offence. As for 'knights', though mounted troops existed in Normandy they were hardly homogenised into feudal 'knights' fees'. As to 'castles' (a general term for all sorts of fortifications in 1066), the specific 'Norman castle' of motte-and-bailey design appears to have evolved in England, not in France.[9] Therefore the process of evolution we seek, such as it was, was rather a phenomenon of English than of French or Norman creation secured, in the end, by combining resources and with the overall determination to permanently secure this kingdom from exploitation.

In the centuries following the destruction of the Roman Imperium in the West, war bands roamed Europe seeking control over defenceless tillers of the soil. These then coalesced into power blocs, even (in France) into 'Comital' blocs, while landholders large and small sought alliances where they thought best, but we have little systemisation of pyramidal power under one ruler with overall control of a definable polity after Charlemagne. In England, rich and cultured beyond her neighbours 'over-the-water', we see some attempt at uniting and focusing regional and tribal power structures in ways which might resemble polity, but these movements towards the creation of a systematic solidarity are largely, maybe wholly, the results of invasions and so of defensive necessity. The realisation that strong monarchical governance was the only safeguard of public order therefore took faltering steps forwards in England when Continental rulers were still only concerned with self-aggrandisement and replication of a lost Imperial Age.

In England exigencies reduced the opportunities for localised autonomy and in so doing helped build what has been termed a loose congeries of the gens Anglorum, a cairn rather than a solid wall but still something positive and cohesive. Inconsistent policies and shifting alliances between powerful magnates were tempered (over here) by the need to acknowledge a supreme leader upon whom to focus resistance to outside aggressions and the barrier of water in particular helped to unify regional resistance. Thus in England there was fruitful soil in which to plant a system subservient to the commands and dictat of one supreme individual power. Whether we should identify this with Offa, Ælfred, Æthelred or even Cnut is not for me to say, though I think it began as a defence against Danish invader-settlers and then converted to a joint or mutual interest in resisting indiscriminate Viking attacks. Without the barrier of nationalism it was not difficult for King William to similarly enlist the co-operation of his new subjects.

Of course, in modern law 'collusion' is a compact between persons who unite in order to prejudice or to commit fraud.[10] In a financial sense this was true of both those English and 'French' landholders who defrauded the Crown. We might also present some of the burghers of Pevensey (in 1066) as colluding with an enemy and perhaps they were fifth columnists?[11] However, to speak generally of collusion in the modern, political sense is quite untrue for to apply such a pejorative we would require nation-state identity and this simply did not exist in 1066 or 1086. We need to remember that the flower of thegndom and their king died at the Battle of Hastings leaving the kingdom defenceless and open to all comers. There was no one capable of organising further resistance to Duke William (or anyone else), no one even competent to raise and offer tribute (by now 'geld'), so it made sense for the remaining English notables to form a 'field Witan' and offer William the Crown of England. After all, both sides were Christians of the same denomination, had similar social structures, no national identities and each side encompassed several linguistic groups. It was hardly a socialist or a fascist invasion, it was not even a strictly foreign invasion.

A king and an army were essential if England was not to be torn apart by rival opportunistic invasions, so this Witan did its duty. From that point onwards those Englishmen who chose to be loyal to the Crown and serve in defence of the realm can only be said to have colluded because they pragmatically co-operated. But I fancy that the proper legal term should be 'novation' – the substitution of a new obligation for an old one. Just as before, some wanted to protect hearth and home (*pro aris et focis*) and others needed a 'good lord' and wages, so being warriors they joined the royal army because that was their trade as select fyrdmen. We must not judge this society by implanting concepts and understandings developed in later and recent centuries. Such revisionism has been the curse of Anglo-Norman historical studies for at least two centuries.

Old French '*covine*' came from the Medieval Latin '*convenium*', a coming together, from which modern lawyers derive 'covin' which, in Latin, as '*collusio*' would give us our modern 'collusion'. We should, I think, view the Anglo-Norman collusion evident after 1066 as this Old French 'coming together'. The new chief lords were therefore providing opportunities for integration through such defensive arrangements, though English stewards on their new estates were, no doubt, helping them with a real intention to deceive (the geld), definite acts of 'covin'. Well these new 'chief lords' did not become outright winners: the unforeseen obligations acquired along with their new estates actually led many of these new lords into real legal 'collusion' against the Crown. Had this not been the case our polity today might have been very different. In the end unity came down to taxation!

The landless miles and mercenaries who came over with the Conqueror in 1066 were not, initially, motivated by land acquisition but by financial gain. Ultimately all that remained available to them, after William's accession and protracted campaigning, was land for the cash ran out. The fact that the invaders did conquer a kingdom was probably more than they (at first) expected and so their individual perspectives changed with the changing ambitions of their leaders. For the magnates whose hearth-troops these men were, there were vast (confiscated) estates available to add to their French possessions, yet these English estates (they were to discover) came at a price, at the price of the geld. Status required magnates to field impressive retinues of miles/milites but the English Crown required impressive (though equitably assessed) proportional revenues.

These were assessed on the amount of land held. It was then that the process began of granting small estates or fiefs to lower vavassours and miles in return for their military services, a sort of reverse-commutation.

So this was directly necessitated by the application of geld (tax) to landholding, allowing a major landholder (magnate) to lay off a moiety of his fiscal liability onto a lower vavassour by granting him a modest estate, someone who was, by definition, a 'free man' (alias, usually, 'Frenchman') and so liable to pay according to the land he held. This man then in turn acquired not only territorial responsibilities but also a place in the money economy by which to acquire specie. Specie <u>alone</u> was acceptable to the geld, so <u>only</u> those in the money economy could meet this liability and military men had to be in the money economy in order to purchase their arms and mounts. A consequence of this was that new markets arose in order to acquire essential specie, simultaneously promoting the adoption of a money economy in accordance with Collis' Hypothesis.[12] The civil, economic and military all dovetailed together in England in a gradual process of evolution towards a new social structure.

So we can see that the post-1066 imposition of geld, for ready cash with which to pay soldiery and usually in order to pay mercenaries (maybe also fyrdmen), stimulated the granting of estates to lesser 'nobility', men 'ennobled' by their military obligations, a process aggravated (or stimulated) by the gradual absorption of existing specie and treasure during protracted campaigning – not only in England but in France. The immediate 'mother-lode' of wealth (to a large degree) 'dried up' in the 1070s. Land-granting to their vavassours then relieved magnates of some of their irksome tax obligations but also ensured that they permanently retained, at no cash cost, the military services and personal loyalties which their status (and the King) required.

Yet such war-band loyalty still remained dangerous to the Crown. Indeed it was more so because a mercenary's (per se) loyalty can always be out-bid and transferred, but a dependent vavassour usually acquires familial responsibilities as well as territorial pride in property and dominium. These things are decidedly effective in deflecting counter-bidding, even by the Crown, for hearth-troop loyalty was sworn to the overlord and not to some abstract. Norman-French miles could plead loyalty to their 'good lord' as their 'essoin', their legal excuse, for what we would now deem treachery to the Crown for they swore no higher allegiance than to their lord and so they had no appeal beyond the will of their lord and his judgement!

What was required was a single clear and legal directive by which to undermine the autonomy of powerful (ambitious) magnates, something compelling their seigneurial power to acknowledge one supreme individual among themselves as representing the common weal. On the Continent there was almost continuous warfare between rival Comital or even castellan factions because of this lack of overall control. We should remember that the young Duke William of Normandy had himself benefitted from such conditions.[13] Ganshof defined a 'feudal system' as a set of reciprocal legal and military obligations among a warrior nobility.[14] However, without absolute economic powers vested in a figurehead there could not be legal enforcement of loyalty to that figurehead let alone to some concept of a 'superior' and, therefore, there could not be any real existence of reciprocal obligations. A strong man could hold what his current military strength dictated, so there was no system there!

'Fidelitas', the faithfulness of the vassal, had to be enforced, gratitude was not sufficient, so the derivative, 'fealty', was generally accorded to a strong overlord rather than to some other social equal representing an abstract such as 'the Crown' or 'monarchy'. In the case of the clergy, they had ecclesiastical lords (bishops) in their hierarchy as well as their institutional interests, yet bishops generally rode with hearth-troops as impressive as other magnates and were war-lords in their own right. Moreover St Benedict had emphasised the autonomy of the Church, which hardly helped establish any central authority of state! Without some absolute legal and economic power it was impossible to act punitively, let alone arbitrarily, against dissident magnates of any sort while senior clergy had the added power of excommunication at their command. Even kings were not proof against this!

We see little in the way of formal restrictions on individual power in pre-Conquest England, though the ruthlessness of English royal authority when dealing with dissentient magnates is usually ascribed by historians to English 'barbarity', thus conveniently ignoring the general sadism of Norman-French magnates when dealing with their defenceless social inferiors. The Norman aristocracy, of course, were more tolerant of their social equals out of regard for self-preservation in their internecine world. It is yet another example of the Norman 'supermen' myth to present them as more 'humane'. The truth is that in England it was possible to exercise more positive control and yet, in spite of precedents, it was only William's eventual extension of central power through the Domesday Surveys (with their cadastral and economic overviews) which provided him with a real basis for a further and final, binding, legal construct, which was the Oath taking at Salisbury. This then granted the Crown real hierarchical authority as *primus inter pares*.

Although we have been repeatedly told that 'Norman' success was due to their genius in castle-building, 'feudal' administration, tactical superiority and superior education – none of which can be proven, none of which claims are true (as we shall see) – it was in fact England's superior cultural and educational achievements which had made it possible for King William to adapt what he had acquired by conquest (and evidently respected) to this grander purpose. True 'feudalism' was only born when he finally made it necessary for all vavassours, both great and small, to acknowledge primary fealty to the Crown rather than to some great lord. From 1086 onwards there was no 'essoin', no legal excuse, for treason, so death and forfeiture of property became Crown options while loyalty to the Crown granted heritability and a right of appeal, even to minor and local lordlings. At last England had a 'coming together' structure which created military forces loyal to one supreme authority, all of them holders of fiefs and so, whether large or small, 'shareholders' in 'the firm', and thus defenders of their monarch's faith.

War has been described as politics by other means but in spite of those writers who have insisted that 'feudalism' was designed simply for war it was (from this perspective), if it ever existed, finally much more than such a limited piece of political machinery, one simply designed to create knights and castles, at least in England. It became governance by fealty to legal authority, guaranteed by sanctions, a polity directed by a single will and, as it then evolved to an abstract in 'the Crown', it moved the kingdom along the long road to nationality. The social cohesion generated by a desire for effective defence then acquired the effective defence machinery it required. It regulated and stabilised the old and haphazard French system of rivalries to establish, as others have noted, an English paradigm.[15] Call this 'collusion' if you please, but if so it was in England actually collusion between the Crown and its real power base. That this supposedly 'feudal' paradigm was a tremendously successful political system is evidenced in its lingering vestiges today which go further than defence. Permit me to explain.

What has been called the English genius for transforming difference into hierarchy is, I believe, one lingering remnant of English feudalism. The present educational divides between 'us' and 'them', echoing our outdated class system, the demarcation between 'degree' and 'non-degree' attainment, the distinction between educational and vocational degrees, are all attempts at hierarchy based on observable difference. The Conquest was as much an acceptance of Divine Will by the English as an English military defeat, replacing a hierarchy of mainly English landholders with an ostensibly Franco-Norman one as a consequence of battle losses.[16] One result of this, given the ethnic and polyglot confusion in either camp, was a very rapid simplification into 'French' and 'English' legal entities, into 'us' and 'them'. Another and parallel result was the absorption of residual English martial cadres into the new Franco-Norman martial class, so that a century after the Conquest we find numerous, small, military fief-holders, lordlings newly enfeofed by magnates, men who have no more determinate pedigree than a French Christian name, names such as 'Richard fitz William'. I have written about this phenomenon elsewhere as well as the participation in King William's campaigns by such men, which has also been noted by earlier writers.[17]

This systemisation of a (covine 'feudal') hierarchy in England, with its supreme power (as well as title) vested in the Norman (and later) kings, restricted the earlier Norman internecine French aristocratic warfare and stiffened communal loyalties. Yes, it relapsed when the opportunity arose, as in the Civil War between Stephen and Matilda when no fief-holder could be certain which claimant to the throne actually held the title to their personal real estate, and it kicked the traces with Magna Carta, a purely selfish aristocratic document which came in useful centuries later, but then it always re-established its fundamental control.[18] In so doing it created a broad class of landholders, landholders both large and small, distinguished by their 'French' connections, with those men without such origins then adopting them in order to become the minor squirearchy of later centuries, even into more modern times, by when '*servicium debitum*' (feudal military service) had itself passed into history. Over the centuries this hierarchy of large and small changed (often through treachery and civil war) to a property qualification, to landowners, the class systems' 'us' and 'them'. In the process it absorbed nouveau-riches and so admixed aristocratic with capitalist values as economics changed, finally becoming no longer dependent on an ethnic or linguistic divide in law but still hierarchically separated by artificial political and class distinctions. 'Feudal' covin is with us today, doing its best to hide in a democracy for without economic resources, and a belief that our united polity is the best, there can be no effective defence against either attack or subversion. And in one other respect it remains, for the members of our armed forces today still swear personal fealty to the monarch and not to the state.

Chapter 2

The Jackpot

I n retrospect the Battle of Hastings was a decisive battle, but on the day after the battle and for weeks, maybe months, afterwards it did not seem so to the victors. We can forget all about them being a race of supermen, they did not possess magical powers, they were ordinary human beings and their horses were (for all their expense) ordinary horses. They had fought a battle which lasted four times as long as it should have done and won it by a fluke just as the sun was going down.[1] Nor should we ignore the English ethic of dying with one's lord so that in the darkness, with all men so resembling one another, the confusion must have been considerable. Even the fortunate survivors finally lay, like the dead, next to them on the ground.

Somehow they had survived the night free from surprise attack, clustered together in tight, comrade groups for security, probably with little if any food and certainly no clean water. Adrenalin-fuelled by the prospect of death and then by the massacre of their enemies, exhausted by unremitting exertions, sound and wounded alike would have been choking mad with thirst. If there was any beer in the English camp lines of the night before it would have gone to their leaders. For the majority of the dazed survivors the only liquid available was in watercourses running with mud, blood, faeces and urine from men and beasts; the same was true for their mounts. By dawn they would be able to ascertain that no English force remained nearby and so they could safely forage and disperse. By mid-morning large numbers of horses and men would have been far from well.

For the men it would be vomiting and diarrhoea to add to the misery of walking wounded and the bone-weary soldiers, then there were the seriously wounded to attend to and there were thousands of corpses attracting flies, kites, crows and ravens. For the horses their 'stand-down', even if attended by superhuman handlers, would have brought on azoturia, serious 'Monday morning sickness' (ERS) with staggers, blowing and sweating and 'boarding' of the big muscles in loins and quarters. Colic would be another major problem, especially if they had been poisoned by water crowfoot, while the shock and stress could well engender incipient strangles, which then becomes contagious.[2] It is doubtful they had anything like the 10 gallons of water required either the day before or the morning after and water shortage and faulty feeding themselves cause 'unthriftiness'. Many would have wounds and lameness and sprains would have been commonplace. Horsemanship takes second place in a fight for survival and the veterinary 'bill' has to be paid after a battle. At least five days of intensive treatment would be required for azoturia, and that is what William allowed.

Nor were the essential heavy horse the only arm incapacitated, the archers and especially the crossbowmen would also have been temporarily out of action. For at least a day there would have been a grisly search among the corpses to retrieve as many missiles as possible, all the more difficult with crossbow bolts (quarrels) because of their high impact. Then would follow the task of creating new ammunition from any heads available. No doubt scouts were desperately seeking news of any enemy, though careful not to get caught in the broken country of the Weald, others would be requisitioning or bringing up supplies from Pevensey. Everyone would be apprehensive: surely if other troops had been marching to join Harold's army they would now be out there, waiting for the right moment, and they had the advantage of knowing the terrain. Now without sufficient heavy horse or crossbowmen the Norman-French infantry, already badly mauled, would need to face English infantry on their own. Gallopers must have been sent back to the royal stud at Eastbourne for remounts, though they could hardly take the place of the lost and disabled destriers and they would have taken two or three days to come up.

Miraculously no army came, but neither did anyone sue for peace or offer 'tribute'. What could it mean? Remember, the story that Duke William was seeking his rightful inheritance and that thousands of men joined his cause in righteous indignation is no more than a story. It is a later justification and an invention and, albeit an invention which can be made to fit the events apparently shown on the Bayeux Tapestry, a source that actually has nothing to say about promises of kingship and makes no reference at all to a 'King William', remarkable omissions had these been the real *causus belli*. The truth is that this invasion was a joint-stock venture by avaricious French super-rich lords and it is more than likely that they would have accepted, at this stage, some sort of tribute payment if it was at least the size of the one formerly offered to Cnut. In the absence of either an enemy or an embassy, the expedition was faced with the problem of what to do next.

Duke William of Normandy, Odo of Bayeux (his half-brother bishop) and Count Eustace II of Boulogne were undoubtedly the chief stock-holders, the wealthiest among the leaders. Eustace seems happy to have passed all risks over to William together with overall command, the bishop could not challenge either his 'cloth' or his brother for command, but between the three of them they seem to have received some critical intelligences. The first of these had been the availability of Pevensey, an impregnable fortress with a port, wharves and harbour roads: we will see as the campaign unfolds just what the other intelligences may have been.[3] Once the surviving destriers had been nursed back to effective strength and remounts brought up the intervening 25 to 30 miles (by circumferential roadways), after five days, the field force moved out eastwards to round up other ports and make for Canterbury. Dover, with its 'castle', and Canterbury, with its archbishop, were essential key points by which to threaten London and any remaining English unity of command. Surely there were other English leaders eager to take on this now battered and depleted expedition? One battle does not win a campaign and William, unlike his enemies, had no reinforcements. Therefore he needed to enforce payment through panic.

Should the Franco-Norman-Breton expeditionary force take the risk of advancing, attempting to force a payment of tribute? If so, where should they aim for, London or Winchester? Should they move back to the safety of Pevensey and wait for an embassy? It would be foolhardy indeed to presume a power vacuum with such a rich prize at stake. What William, as the apparent commander-in-chief, required most of all was time, time for his men and mounts to recover, time to begin training the most promising of the remounts. Time would make his forces stronger so the longer the English vacillated, the better. For perhaps a fortnight William garnered his resources in the Hastings district (later renamed as the 'Rape of Hastings') of East Sussex, an area replete with supplies not only because of the season (and all harvests now gathered in) but also because it supplied the industrial workforce in the Weald with provisions.[4] However, when they then decided that it had become time to act it also became necessary for them to commit an act of terror, the customary prelude to a territorial campaign. The choice William now made seems instructive.

The invaders actually marched on Romney, just over the border in Kent. We do not know whether some of the force had originally landed there by mistake or whether it had resisted requisitioning but the panegyrist, William of Poitiers, tells us that such was the excuse for making an example of the port. Burning it out also made sure that there was no local chandlery or harbour facility to challenge Pevensey or Rye. Then the question remains, how did Rye escape a similar fate, situated as it then was on the Sussex side of the same lagoon and wetlands ecology occupied by Romney on the Kent (north) side? It looks as though there was an element of reward involved: Rye had perhaps co-operated with the invaders, Romney had not. Strategically, with Romney destroyed, Rye would then have dominated this lagoon just as Pevensey dominated its lagoon. It is therefore not impossible that the men of the Hastings/ Pevensey (Sussex) district had an ancient grudge to settle and so co-operated in this naval attack. Kent now knew what to expect if it opposed the expeditionary army.

Dover was a formidable natural obstacle strengthened by its 'castle', which was probably focused on the old Roman Pharos, and we are told that it had a strong garrison but William's advance now put them into a panic and so this port also capitulated.[5] The army halted and there was looting and burning, there was also a serious outbreak of dysentery, meaning that the sickness had reached crisis point. William's army had now secured the Channel coastline, a further incentive for reinforcements to join the expedition. Now (if not before) it seems a plan of conquest began to form as an alternative to tribute. It was obviously a plan based not only on strategic acumen but also on reliable intelligences. If Muhammad would not come to the mountain then the mountain must go to Muhammad.

Romney had provided a positive example, Dover an equivocal one (the damage was blamed not on policy but on indiscipline), so when

Duke William's forces moved on Canterbury, the Ecclesiastical heart of England, the citizens sent out an embassy and wisely submitted. The Archdiocese and the Archbishop's caput were thus secured and the next move was to send a strong flying column to Winchester, now the seat of the dowager Queen Edith. Immediately she and the city's fathers also submitted, thus providing William with the most eligible pawn in the political power game, one he could set alongside control of the spiritual focus of England and one who had perhaps been the cause of Harold's visit to France in 1064, Edith.[6] It also provided him with some highly restricted information which was held in this ancient English capital. Who gave this intelligence to him, that we do not know. What was it? It was that Winchester was the heart of the English administration, what we would call the civil service: here at Winchester were the ancient royal records including the fiscal and territorial records of that unique English specie-taxation, the geld.[7] We will discuss this at length later, but I doubt that William or his fellow stock-holders really knew what a treasure they had just secured or the part it was destined to play in William's lasting achievement. I doubt it because English administration and surveying were pre-eminent and unique in Europe and so not something any Frenchman could possibly comprehend. Once we have dealt with the invasion we will return to this secret information but, for the moment, I suggest William's concern was for money, tribute from the legendary geld. He had a mercenary army to reward.

The next thrust had to be and was a big one. Leaving the sick and dying to fend for themselves (under the tender mercies of English citizens), the army made for London, the commercial heart of the kingdom. Here was money indeed: when England had paid tribute with geld of £72,000, London had paid a further £10,500. A mere square mile called London was as valuable as 14–15 per cent of England. The Franco-Norman army entered Southwark, then separated from London proper, only to find that the citizens of the city had destroyed London Bridge. Here were the 'horns of a dilemma': London must be secured but London must not be destroyed. Its wealth was critical to both sides. Moreover the heart of the City still lay behind massive, ancient walls, impregnable if defended. William pulled back and moved on westwards leaving Southwark in flames. The Southwark Strand, its wharves and warehouses were lost, but the value goods and bullion lay secured within the City. It only remained to arrange the capitulation of the City with its treasures intact.

The Ætheling Edgar had by now been elected by many of the Witan but only a weak sortie was made before the bridge was destroyed. So William had now secured the south coast, contained the Weald and its armaments industry, divorced the Archbishop from his See and from his power and confined Edith so that she could not offer marriage to any challenger.[8] With the ruthlessness of the age, William set about a reign of terror ravaging parts of Sussex and Kent, Hampshire, Berkshire, Hertfordshire and Middlesex in order to 'make the pips squeak'. He stopped briefly at Wallingford, no doubt strengthening that ancient fortress, larger than nearby Oxford and so the key to the river crossing, which in the Burghal Hidage had contained a circuit of 3,300 yards and so 140 acres (by its formula).[9] Here Archbishop Stigand came to make his peace and to renounce any allegiance to the Ætheling. One wonders what was passing through the minds of the expedition's leaders now, William, Odo, maybe Robert, certainly Eustace? In the words of the Afghan proverb, 'me and my clan against the tribe, me and my family against the clan, me and my brothers against the family, me against my brothers'.

Swinging north-east, the army now continued with a secure flank to Berkhamsted where there was an English burgh or 'castle', probably on the site now covered by the later Norman motte. The Earls Eadwine and Morcar, who should have led the English, apparently deserted London for their own lands in the north of England leaving the citizens and English refugees to defend the boy-king Edgar and their city against this terrifyingly vengeful alliance army. Accepting necessity 'after most damage had been done', a delegation of English magnates escorted Edgar to Berkhamstead to submit to Duke William, the French army's supreme commander.[10] This was a Witan, though never named. What had started as a joint-stock venture, almost certainly for tribute and loot, had become a conquest of a kingdom by default. And so there arose a problem. Edgar had not been crowned and so, in French (though not in English) eyes, could not be King yet there was a kingdom and it required to be governed, defended and administered. It required a 'strong' man. Norman sources tell us that the English magnates begged William to become King, the obvious source of stability, but he was not the best, the pre-eminent, candidate in French eyes. Count Eustace II of Boulogne, of the Carolingian line and dynasty, married to the late King Edward's sister Godgifu, was the man on the ground, King Philip of France, the nominal (if juvenile) overlord to all the joint stock-holders, was the theoretical 'loyal' choice.[11]

There clearly followed considerable discussion, William (we are told) hanging back, Eustace in a weak position when faced with Bishop Odo of Bayeux and by Robert of Mortain, both of them William's brothers. The subordinate commanders and the soldiery wanted their rewards, traditionally handed out by the supreme commander as 'gold-giver', so wasn't a big chief and gold-giver 'the King'? It would have been foolish for Eustace to protest (especially if his son was Odo's hostage) but, no doubt, he was given promises of extensive estates and ample treasure.[12] For the English magnates and Witan it was essential to stop the devastation and restore some sort of order and William was the only power, or the only one as yet. Given the recent problems in the north of England, in Harold's reign and before that in Edward's, the English needed a protecting army. Quite accidentally, William had pulled out the plum, now he needed to find a good reason to accede to the Crown. Meanwhile he had a major problem: the mercenaries who comprised a good part of his joint forces had to be brought under some sort of control and that required cash.

William's advance guard seems to have run into resistance from some of the survivors from Hastings who had filled the City, though the ensuing conflict does not appear to have had disastrous results. Immediately the invaders set about building a secure fortification, a 'castle', outside the city walls on the east side. William himself seems to have felt secure and to have taken up his residence in Edward's new palace at Westminster, so his forces were controlling both ends of the City and no doubt his ships were in control on the river. The City was now 'battened down' and we have no evidence that William feared its citizens. This last point has relevance to what followed.

On Christmas Day Duke William went to the new Westminster Abbey (St Peter's) to be crowned by Archbishop Ealdred of York. He went wearing his helmet and a mounted escort stood outside but there does not appear to have been a major military parade, so no especial security against an English attack was deemed necessary. Rather, one suspects,

William was taking precautions against his own followers when he wore his helmet? Herein, it seems, lay the root of the trouble that followed for while he was within some of his soldiers began looting and burning the City, which quickly dispersed the crowds in terror. If it seemed a bad omen to all who remained, including King William, what was notable was his respect for and adherence to the traditional and legal ceremony: he took the English Coronation Oath and was acclaimed by all. Now he was not only elected by some sort of field Witan, he was also crowned. God had sanctioned his nomination and succession.

What are we to conclude from the evidence before us? Well the pro-nationalists have spent two centuries repeating that a shout of acclamation within the Abbey Church caused William's troops outside to conclude that maquisards were attacking him so, rather than entering and clearing the church, they began to burn down the houses around it, just to teach the English a lesson. Is this logical? Well, fortunately they did not set the City on fire. Let us instead place our evidence together piece by piece. The English had already offered William the Crown so this Coronation ceremony was just that, a ceremony, one designed to impress William's followers with the fact of kingship. In spite of the City being filled with Englishmen, William had chosen to take up residence at the western end (Westminster Palace) while his troops built a 'castle' at the east end of the City. This was not evidence of insecurity. On the river was his fleet. On the south bank Southwark was destroyed. Next, William went to his Coronation wearing a helmet but we are not told of any great assemblage of his forces either inside or outside the Abbey, we are just told there was an escort waiting outside. We should remember that William was a vassal of the King of France and not a free agent and that he had taken some time before accepting the Crown from the English delegation. Maybe his brothers were loyal to him, as yet, but Eustace of Boulogne himself had a better claim to the throne of England and he was also a partner in this enterprise which should have been on behalf of the King of France.

It sounds as though William was apprehensive that someone among his own coterie might attempt to sabotage his coronation, this being rather more likely than an English suicide squad breaking into the Abbey. If such a group of zealots had been feared, where then were the security forces and why did no one clear the Abbey? Let us instead consider that

William's polyglot and heterogeneous army had been in cantonments, in transit and in the field (now) for four months or more and, as yet, remained unrewarded, unpaid. The majority of them were not his tenants, only his hirelings. The royal escort would have been derelict in their duty if they had left the Abbey when William was supposedly under threat and still inside, so we should assume that they held their ground, on parade, ready for action if required. That only leaves us with renegades, mercenaries, 'making hay while the sun shone', indulging in the fruits of victory, in looting, murder, rape and arson, now that their commander had been installed as King. One way or another, William's dangers lay within his own forces, either among dissident elements, envious plotters or, most likely, the presence of too many mercenaries.

Quickly he took steps to pay off his uncertain soldiery and to assure his new subjects of his respect for their laws. Always canny, he took immediate steps to bestow treasure (no doubt from English sources) upon French monasteries and upon the Papacy. In English eyes the fact of victory was confirmation that God had willed it, yet the added confirmation of such piety and gratitude ensured that Mother Church would also discern the hand of the Lord at work in his victory. As for the English, this was the price of peace: they paid a heavy tribute, made their peace and then had to buy back their lands. Eadwine and Morcar made their peace. From the vast real-estate forfeited by landholders who had died at Battle William distributed vast estates, particularly ensuring that Odo of Bayeux and William fitzOsbern held the vulnerable coast and hinterlands from Kent to Hampshire. It reads as though King William was reassured by the quiescence of his new subjects and by their native fatalism and now wished to pay off and disperse his less trustworthy followers.

What of Eustace of Boulogne? He is one of the prominent figures on the Bayeux Tapestry, though apparently libelled by the panegyrists.[13] A very rich man and principal stockholder, controller of much of the cross-Channel trade, he had undoubtedly hoped for at least the Earldom of Kent as recompense for not being King, yet this plum went to Bishop Odo. Eustace was left with extensive estates, probably in Wiltshire, Gloucestershire and Surrey, and he apparently cared little for them. Keeping a low profile, he waited for King William to go to Pevensey in March; there William discharged many of his 'knights' to enjoy their rewards and himself departed for Normandy with a vast treasure and all the suspect English notables as 'guests'. The kingdom was now left to Odo of Bayeux (at Dover) and William fitzOsbern (in Winchester) and either they were complicit in Eustace's schemes or they were plain negligent, for Eustace slipped away back home by himself and there he began plotting and preparing.

Chapter 3

'Blood, Toil, Tears and Sweat'

The birth of a concept of nationhood is often conveniently attributed to the Treaty of Westphalia in 1648 but the concept of the nation-state is usually placed in the nineteenth century. Arguably the republican movement of the French Revolution also saw the inception of nation-statehood, though most of Europe waited until the mid-century to follow suit. So what is the relevance of this? Well, the concept of the nation-state was immediately so attractive that nineteenth-century historians, in their enthusiasm, sought to apply it to every preceding century: even back to the Roman Empire where there had actually been some concept of 'the nation'.[1] The nineteenth-century historians began to speak of national identities and national consciousness opposing empires and invaders in the distant past! Such speculations justified national claims, national pride and xenophobia: each nation superior in its own culture.

The relevance of this to us is that Augustine Thierry wrote of 'Anglo-Saxon' (when he really meant English) resistance to the Norman yoke and tyranny, further elaborating his personal Republicanism with the new nationalism by accepting the leadership of Robin Hood on the English ('Anglo-Saxon') side! For those who remember the 1950s' comics and Hollywood films this association of Middle English with Old English, Danish and Norwegian will come as no surprise, it is the stuff of fantasy. You see, in the 1950s we had just lived through another world war where national identities and stereotypes had been actively promoted: Flanders and Swan could sing, 'the English, the English, the English are best ...'.

Of course there was no such 'national' consciousness in 1066 and no unification concept, other than as a kingdom formed from other kingdoms, among the polyglot thirty-four shires which comprised England (and excluded the kingdoms of Wales and Scotland). As I have already hinted, the borderlands between these 'outside' Kingdoms were extremely fluid and often semi-autonomous, the 'North' (especially Northumbria) being particularly antagonistic to English sensibilities. King William did not have to deal with any single linguistic or ethnic group among the 'conquered', though he apparently made some attempt to learn Old English.[2]

Indeed in Domesday Book we encounter regional and not purely national expressions of quantity and also arithmetical groupings which actually encompass more than one shire and so seem to mirror the ethnic identities of peoples and sub-kingdoms found centuries before in the Tribal Hidage, unless they had been displaced by later Danish incomers (with their own distinctive units and social practices).[3] Sometimes these indicators even survived in spite of such Danish intrusions in what we might call a palimpsest of usage. The agglomeration of such separately distinct groups under unifying 'English' monarchies did not create either a national identity or a nation-state, at best England was a congeries of the gens Anglorum, as yet without any firmly mortared and integrated identity. It did, however, have very troublesome borders to both the north and the west which did not acknowledge this broad gens and so a mixture of ethnicities within a given area was united by the need for self-preservation.

King William, apparently somewhat overcome by his good fortune, took an extended triumphal leave in Normandy during 1067. Under new, white, sails he set out from Pevensey with booty and an entourage. With this new figurehead thus removed from the kingdom it is not surprising to see other opportunists now stepping forwards. In Herefordshire a thegn known as Eadric the Wild joined forces with a couple of Welsh petty-kings and raided the borders to acquire whatever the Norman mercenaries had not plundered, but with no claims to make on the English Crown. He was simply assuming that nature abhors a vacuum. The standing down of much of the invasion force made it impossible to apprehend him. Meanwhile in the troubled North, earl Copsig (who seems to have ingratiated himself with King William), who had been appointed as the 'strong man' required to pacify ever-troublesome Northumbria, proved incapable of the task: he was ambushed and killed. Having thus forfeited legality the area sank (not for the first time) into general lawlessness. Over the waters Eustace of Boulogne was secretly making his own preparations.

Where, in all this, were Odo of Bayeux and William fitzOsbern? Well their task was to secure the Channel coast and to administer the south but they both appear to have been busy enjoying conquests elsewhere for when Eustace slipped across the Channel with his own expeditionary force, Odo was nowhere near his caput of Dover. The panegyrists try to tell us that the people of Dover were so abused by Odo and his hearth-troop that they 'invited' Eustace to liberate them, a theme which has supplied so many historians with visions of English nationalism discarding the yoke and shackles of novel oppression, conveniently ignoring Eustace's French identity! In point of fact when the Boulonnais forces arrived there was no evidence at all of collusion and the remaining Norman/French garrison of Dover put up a spirited defence, aided by Englishmen, then sortied, drove off the attackers and pursued them into the night. As most of the Boulonnais expedition had no knowledge of the area, they were, it seems, easily cornered; some were driven over cliffs and others swamped and drowned as they attempted to re-embark. Count Eustace and some of his hearth-troop escaped, but then he knew the territory: in 1051 he had fallen foul of the townsfolk of Dover, which probably helps explain their eagerness to help the Norman garrison in 1067.[4] Here we see no clear 'nationalist' distinction between the forces.

It can only be speculation, of course, but my evaluation is that Eustace did not do his homework, he did not prepare. If he landed at Dover he cannot have found it easy to land his destriers and it may be that he was seriously lacking in heavy horse? He was certainly crossing against prevailing winds and currents, making for a very difficult passage, and his fleet cannot have been large or elaborate, otherwise advanced news of its preparation would have spread. Maybe he anticipated Odo's assistance and a cosmetic siege rather than a battle but he clearly had not remembered the tactical formula which had benefitted Duke William the year before. As a 'castle' Dover would have had a strong contingent of crossbowmen as well as a heavy horse garrison. A deadly discharge of quarrels followed by a charge of the heavy horse would easily have broken besieging French infantry, especially if in the open. As to Odo, well he could take the credit either way, for preventing the coup (as happened) or for not opposing it, the garrison was his. As I have speculated elsewhere, it may be that he was in collusion with Eustace, William being out of the way?[5] One possibility for the Bayeux Tapestry is that it was intended to celebrate a joint enterprise by Eustace and Odo.[6] If this was it, failure would account for the Tapestry being quickly hidden away and then lost for some centuries.[7] Odo would have needed to destroy such evidence. Maybe some of the garrison were William's men, not Odo's, and so he needed to act with circumspection, only committing himself when the case was certain? Maybe he reckoned without English loyalty to the Crown?

Later in this same year Harold's mother, Gytha, appeared on the scene with sons of the Godwine house and an Irish mercenary fleet. She had massive estates around Dartmoor and probably felt safe in the West Country, which seems to have been settled by English incomers under a novel security system not unlike the Anglo-Irish 'plantations' of Elizabeth I's reign.[8] If so there would also have been a discontented Damnonian residual population susceptible to promises of loot and revenge against both English and Normans, so Gytha set up her caput at Exeter and there appear to have been rumours of a massacre (said to be of 'Normans', if there really were so many of them in residence) early in 1068. Intelligences had by then reached Normandy and in spite of the dangers of the season King William took ship early in December 1067 to be in London during Christmas. The Norman-French writers assure us of a conspiracy, so that may well have been the tale told to William by his half-brother Odo, in order to excuse his absence from Dover. Meanwhile the Godwines were certainly sending envoys to the Danes and invitations to other towns to join the insurrection: they needed allies, which in itself tells us they did not have English support. King William imposed a heavy geld on England and set about raising an army. This army also included the English fyrd, so it was an Anglo-Norman army that marched on rebellious Exeter in 1068 in order to save the English settlers of the West Country and a few Norman nobles.

At first the surviving citizens of Exeter sent a delegation to humbly offer surrender but on arrival William found the walls manned and defiant, explicable if Damnonian elements had united with the Irish invaders.[9] The siege which followed was apparently bitter and bloody but when the Godwine faction circumspectly deserted it came to an end. To their surprise the now helpless citizens were reasonably well treated (it had hardly been their fault) and the King then moved on into Cornwall, a further indication of the ethnic and regional nature of the support obtained by Gytha and her Irish mercenaries. So that is how the English and Norman colonists presumably regained control of their estates in Devon and Cornwall. Disbanding his army, William celebrated Easter at Winchester, distributing those lands now forfeited by Gytha and her followers and also selling Northumbria to a petitioner (Gospatric) for a handsome sum. Already the Crown was in need of ready money having taken so much loot to Normandy in 1067. At Whitsun Mathilde, William's consort, was crowned Queen in England, a further indication of settled conditions.

Along the Welsh border he now created a buffer zone with William fitzOsbern at Hereford and Roger of Montgomery at Shrewsbury, but this may have eroded the former territorial powers and revenues of Eadwine and Morcar for they now apparently began to conspire with one of the Welsh kings on their own account. They were joined by Máerleswein in Yorkshire, also the ungrateful Gospatric and the Bishop of Durham as well as the well-treated Edgar Æthling. The North was living up to its record and reputation for autonomous aspirations regardless of who was on the throne of England, just as the Welsh Marches always troubled the adjacent English shires when opportunities arose. These regions were the fluid borders of the English kingdom and their inhabitants were always vulnerable.

King William advanced northwards with characteristic forethought, in spite of his speed erecting fortifications (popularly voiced as 'castles') at strategic points, in effect hammering in pittons as his harriers climbed ever northwards. He had no intention of slipping or retreating: a later age would have said he advanced on his foes 'par industrie'. The revolt quickly collapsed on his appearance, some rebel leaders suing for pardon, others fleeing to Scotland. With King William at York, King Malcolm of Scotland quickly took stock of the situation and himself swore fealty and obedience. Meanwhile three Godwine youths landed in Somerset (from Ireland) to plunder and, no doubt, take slaves, moving westwards and perhaps besting local forces before retiring to Ireland with their profits. Hardly a glorious 'nationalist' demonstration, especially for those 'liberated' by slavery!

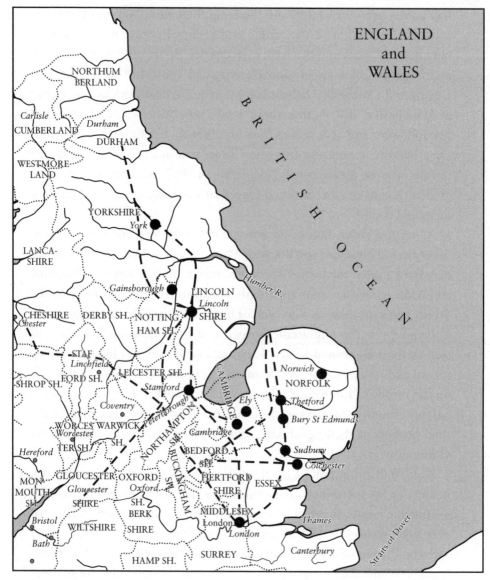

Map 1: 'Highways, *c*. 1070–80.

Yet the nationalist fantasy has been implanted onto the past with such fervour that every aspect of these troubled years (whether in the north or the west) has become evidence of the existence of 'English' national consciousness and its maquisards. In an attempt to put the bare bones of the actual events into an alternative and credible perspective I am now

Map 1: Highways, *c.* 1070–80

Contrary to popular superstition major roads (and, of course, waterways) connected important centres of population as Map 1 shows. The major Anglian centres (as recorded in Domesday Book) were London, Norwich, Thetford and Bury St Edmunds. London and Maldon were important ports. The Icknield Way and then Ermine Street ran from the edge of the Wash in north-west Norfolk right round to Lincoln, the Peddar's Way from the same source to Sudbury and Chelmsford, Wool Street ran from Colchester to Cambridge and so all were strategic routes. Warships stationed on the Thames, Blackwater and Colne could protect vital routes inland. The Wash, of course, stretched far inland, even down to the Isle of Ely. Watling Street ran from London to Chester and the Fosse Way from Lincoln to the West Country. By using such established routes King William could exercise a fair degree of control over events.

going to present an entirely novel picture. It is not pro-Norman, though I do not doubt that some will try to represent it as such for it challenges the comforting romantic web of misrepresentations which enables what we might call pro-Saxonists, as well as the Norman supremacist faction, to rejoice in senseless and ruthless brutality. War is always brutal and uncivilised yet sometimes the age dictates peculiarly unpleasant responses. So it was here and then, but that is not evidence of genocidal conflict between ethnicities and we do not need to revel in and promote misery devoid of historical proof.

I think we can assume that by now King William had advanced his claim to be the 'nominated heir' of King Edward to his own followers; as for the English, the majority seem to have accepted the 'Will of God' and also the evidence of William's Anointing by Witan and by Crowning. Mercenaries are, by definition, of doubtful loyalty and are always difficult to control, added to which many of the King's loyal followers had now been in the field for almost two years, when normal obligations probably already required no more than forty days. Of course there was no such thing as a proper feudal structure as yet.[10] Each member of a hearth-troop was actually serving the lord who fed and housed them and was not strictly part of any 'royal army', but William had given out lands and estates to many lords and they, by promising rewards to their hearth-troops, could keep several loyal forces in the field. We should ask what need there was for the real mercenaries, or for a mass of infantry, or for those who wished to return home? To both the King and his magnates it must have seemed that at last some stability had been attained and so the more dangerous (mercenary) elements could be discharged and voided from the kingdom.

Some historians now speak of 'desertions' but this is pure fantasy based on supposed English resistance under every hedge! There were numerous garrisons to maintain, which spread the essential miles and crossbowmen around, but clearly the under employed soldiers-of-fortune were now a liability as the King looked forwards to a period of stability and recuperation. So he paid off those who wished to go (or whom he wished to go) and himself returned to Normandy. It is not impossible that some of his barons had already realised that they were liable to pay geld for their enlarged hearth-troops (on their English lands), after all, the King was levying heavy gelds on all 'free men' in order to pay for his mercenary contingents. His chroniclers hint that among the loyal troops were those who did not 'feel secure' enough to bring over their wives and families (a not unknown and sometimes convenient complaint by soldiers on foreign service) and there were other married men who were apprehensive for their wives' loyalties 'after so long alone in Normandy' and these milites wished to return home. After all, at the level of the humble knight or sergeant-at-arms, many were still retained in hearth-troops and without lands of their own in England or, if they now had land, still without the resources to 'up sticks' and establish a new domestic centre in this country. All the indications are that King William had been lulled into a feeling of security and was now 'winding down'.

He had, however, appointed a new earl in the North, Robert de Comines, possibly a Flemish mercenary captain, who took with him a hearth-troop of perhaps 700 men, probably a sensible precaution with refugee earls still sheltering in Scotland. That said his force was true to its mercenary principles and once north of the Tyne set about pillaging and destroying the equivocal lordlings and their essential peasantry. They were certainly heavy-handed and probably arbitrary in their actions. They entered Durham and its cathedral by force, settling down for an easy winter and then came a heavy snowfall which rendered them not only disinclined to patrol but incapable of easy deployment, for snow never favours cavalry. The angry and apprehensive Northumbrians took advantage of this (and presumably of negligent guards), entered the city and massacred the Flemings, then (emboldened and knowing that they now had nothing to lose) they moved south and on to York. Now the opportunists Máerleswein, Gospatric and Edgar re-appeared together with Archil, a Yorkshire thegn, but they were premature in their expectations for the 'castle' at York held out, in spite of the ambush and murder of Robert fitz Richard, the city's governor. King William, though having now returned to England, immediately turned around and (no doubt weary and angry) marched north to its relief. We are not told whether he called out the fyrd, but it seems impossible for him to have acted so decisively otherwise. On arrival he set about erecting another 'castle' and all resistance melted away. By Easter he was back in Winchester leaving fitzOsbern in charge of York. Sporadic attacks continued but were no match for the wily fitzOsbern.

Down in the West Country, at midsummer, the sons of Harold returned from Ireland with pirates in over 60 ships, perhaps 2,000 or more men, only to be beaten off by local forces. Once again we should expect these locals to include many Englishmen for there would not have been enough Normans to go round. At the same time other powerful men elsewhere had larger and more subtle ambitions, for there is nothing so sincerely flattering as imitation. Thus King Swein of Denmark now put it out that he too had been promised the throne by the late King Edward (not an impossible claim for he seems to have made several such promises) and in a duplication of William's own process in 1066 he began assembling an invasion force.[11] Like William, in order to acquire a fleet of sufficient size he must have commenced building and fitting out two or three years before 1069.[12] Late in the summer of that year he despatched perhaps 300 ships, under a lieutenant (his brother Osbeorn), himself remaining circumspectly at home. Arriving in the Channel this fleet must have met some effective opposition for it then turned north to join the northern rebels at the Humber rather than fighting through to the rich prize of London or along the lucrative south coast. This gave William warning but York's garrisons now panicked at the prospect of meeting a large army and in an attempt to fire the houses adjacent to the 'castle' (to provide open ground without cover) they set the city on fire. Caught in the streets fighting these fires, they were massacred and the city was sacked, and the victorious Danes then retired to their ships. They were not going to make the mistake of fighting a pitched battle, their objective was plunder. As long as they could live off the fat of the land they had no stomach for a real fight. Nevertheless they were a formidable force and although their shipping was probably mixed, with a number of massive warships and some much smaller vessels, if we only average out at 40 men per ship that was still a possible 12,000 men! If you think that excessive, well no less than 9,000 men.

Yet again King William set about creating an army, hiring and coercing, both Normans and English, sagely identifying the North as his primary objective. Now, if not before, he must have begun to experience serious remount problems for it was a war of movement over rough terrain and ice and attrition would become real problems, something to add to hampering snowfalls. The Danes, true to Viking form, made (as they thought safe) camp and strand on the very large and marshy Isle of Axholme, in north-west Lincolnshire.[13] There William caught them unprepared for his onslaught and drove them clean out (no mean feat) and over the Humber to York. Things looked bad for the pirates and then the news of their arrival reached other ears, in Wales. In the West County trouble was still rumbling around when Eadric the Wild and his Welsh allies on the Marches decided to attack Shrewsbury, only to scatter when an Anglo-Norman column sought to engage them. As this column next moved on south-westwards to Exeter, to assist the locals there, so the Welsh and Eadric's renegade English emerged from the Marches to harry Staffordshire, and here it was that King William's own column now caught them. This was an astute strategic coup, though sadly under-recorded. But the North was still in peril and despite losses he briefly returned to Lincolnshire and Lindsey, only to have to pursue the Danes once again, in winter weather, to York, where they also disappeared and returned to their ships. It was obvious that if he retired again they would immediately recommence their harrying, plundering and slaving.

We will return later to the wealth of England and her economy but here it is essential to give a brief outline if the subsequent events are to be understood. In the first place, contrary to popular fantasies, the peasant population did not pay the royal tax, also known as the geld, for the simple reason that they did not have the requisite pennies.[14] These subsistence farmers provided food and services for local lordlings who alone had the resources and opportunities to market such commodities in return for specie.[15] The geld was (at this time) a unique specie-only tax and it was assessed on the land that a man (lord or lordling) controlled, the land he was 'lord of'. It was therefore in everyone's interest to protect the peasant and his ox-plough for they were legal and financial assets. As yet the separate concepts of (legal) realty and interest were not discerned and so commuted payments and cash (alone) escaped taxation.[16] When one powerful lord wished to dispossess another he generally had some regard for his own interests and tried to preserve the peasantry, but if he simply sought loot, without dominium or proprietas, as Viking pirates did, then wiping out peasant assets beggared an opponent and rendered him defenceless and friendless. When looting included slaving, as it did to Vikings, then the essential peasantry were further endangered and when mercenaries got out of hand, general pillage and rapine destroyed whole communities and made the land worthless. An understanding of these things is essential to our comprehension of King William's dilemma at Christmas 1069–70, sitting in burnt-out and destitute York with its plaintiff citizens and an army to feed, responsible as he was for the defence of the entire kingdom. King Harold's mantle had fallen on King William's shoulders, it came with the Crown.

The city and its hinterland had been plundered by the Viking horde and so it would certainly have been brought to the verge of starvation before the spring. Now the Anglo-Norman army (or the quartermasters of each troop) were also clamouring for food as they arrived and they also needed shelter. For its own safety this defence force cannot have been insubstantial and it needed to mount coastal patrols in several places as well as holding in reserve in what was left of York. With the Vikings occupying the Humber they could not send for a supply fleet, they had to live off the land. The choice for William was a stark one, either to retreat southwards and requisition elsewhere, losing troops and abandoning this territory to his (and the kingdom's) enemies, or to requisition what remained (as the Vikings would certainly do before spring if he left) and so himself destroy whole populations in order to support his troops. These desperate peasants, though they looked to their new King for succour and relief, were also and moreover assets legally belonging to rebel earls and the Church's teaching, as exemplified by the Venerable Bede in his 'Ða Domesday' treatise, was that on the Day of Judgement whole families would be held responsible for the behaviour of each of their members, each lord for his people, peoples for the actions they had condoned of their lords' doing.[17] The territory of Yorkshire and beyond had certainly failed to check the treachery of the several rebel lords. Was there therefore a contemporary legal or moral justification to add to awful military necessity? Well, the dictum *'cuius regio, eius religio'* would seem to cover any royal action and besides, what strategic choice was there? The rebels and the Viking army had already decided the issue by their plundering and requisition, now they needed to be exterminated.

King William took a terrible decision, one as callous as an atom-bomb and one which would deprive him of much territory-in-gift, many peasant assets and so (especially) of future geld (over a significant area) for many years to come. He decided to stay and to actively stabilise the territories around York, even south and into Derbyshire and Staffordshire. The districts of Selby, Harrogate, Ryedale and southern Hambledown seem to have been most affected by this policy. The Danes could either come ashore and fight or they could starve in the winter gales, but he would be waiting for them and his army would have the only provisions. With luck and determination the King's enemies would perish miserably of cold and sickness out on the winter waters. Incidentally so would the essential peasantry deprived of food, seed-corn and livestock but (one can argue) the country needed such a sacrifice and the outcome, for the weak, would have been the same whoever held the land.

Leaving aside the counter claims of the Welsh, every Yorkshireman knows that he lives in 'God's own country'. The windswept moors and moorlands, sudden defiles and woodlands, stony roads and stonier uplands with rushing torrents and generous rainfall make much of Yorkshire a tourist paradise today, in summer, but in 1069 habitations were fewer, supplies scarcer and an enemy could usually see you coming for miles. Combined with fortuitous places for ambush this would have made it an easy terrain in which to defeat an expedition, provided the resistance was local. Such an appreciation was obviously not lost upon the Vikings, who vacated these wilds for the Humber as soon as they heard of professional soldiers, so it follows that William's Anglo–French force was not at first unwelcome to the locals. However, to the weary cavalry and footsore infantry in their bivouacs and shroughs, and following such tracks as they could find (or were shown by local guides), 'God's own country' only differed from the Devil's, as winter set in, by virtue of its lack of warmth. To most of William's army hell must have seemed a welcome mirage. Nor should we forget the influence of superstition on those medieval minds, now confined to bleak moorlands and fells, with little shelter or fuel, straitened rations and, as the winter drew on, harbouring starving locals with nothing to lose by murdering in the night. Horror stories must have been very real, the protection of each individual military unit imperative, discipline almost impossible to maintain. Each side was imprisoned, but only the one had access to food and fuel. Soldiers who left their units would have been as vulnerable as Viking pirates when alone among the desperate, the vengeful and betrayed peasantry and the marauding brigands from the wildlands further north.

Yet we must move, or think, with circumspection, with reflexion, rather than with the hysteria so often encouraged in reviews of this event. There is real evidence, outside the joyful utterances of religious chroniclers, in Domesday Book itself of the dreadful consequences for the civilian populations of this harsh strategic plan, but would they have fared any better for a retreat, for abandonment of the North, by the Crown? No military commander can compromise his mission for humanitarian considerations, for to do so would be to betray the political objective and the lives entrusted to him. Yorkshire, Lincolnshire and shires even further inland depended on his protection and he could not cover them all simultaneously, he had to destroy this enemy army while he had the chance. William was, therefore, faithful to his Coronation Oath, that is faithful to all the shires and people in England. How hard would the (consequent) renewed campaign have been, how long would it have lasted if he had retreated and, we should ask ourselves, did the moorland peasantry really favour one side rather than the other? Surely such speculations as 'affinity' with Viking culture and pirate activities are no more than sentimental affectations of ethnic and nationalist affinities? They are intellectual afflictions! These peasants required quiet security not slavery, sex and theft!

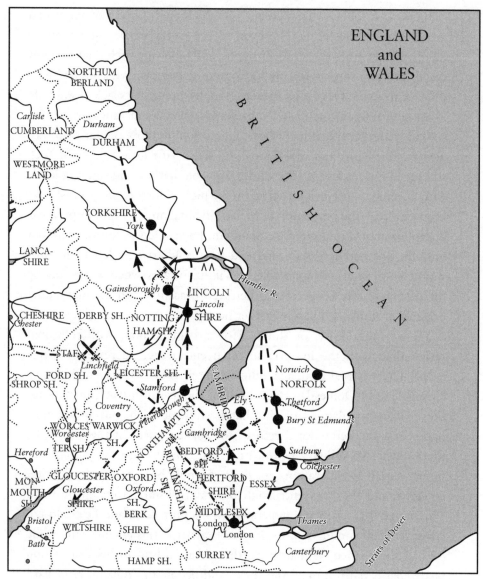

Map 2: The campaigns of 1069–71.

Then again, if the whole of Yorkshire had been reduced to a frozen desert, could the Honour of Richmond really have sustained, provided for and equipped so many milites immediately afterwards? When Domesday Book tells us that its Earl had 199 manors in his CASTELLATUS, of which his men held 133, and that he also had 43 manors in this castelry,

Map 2: The Campaigns of 1069–71

Looking at Map 2 we can see that the royal army took Ermine Street northwards to Lincoln but instead of ferrying over the Humber took the route to the west of Gainsborough, so encircling the Isle of Axholme and so the Viking army camped here was driven back by an astonishing victory, eastwards into the Humber, and William occupied York for his headquarters. Setting watches to either bank of the Humber (the small arrows) he then dispatched two field forces at intervals south-west to Watling Street via the Trent valley. The Welsh raiders were surprised as one force passed them south-westwards but, as they reformed behind it, they were caught and defeated at Stafford by the second force, which then retired to York and the Humber leaving the Viking army imprisoned on their ships for the winter; stragglers were then chased northwards and perhaps southwards by royal foraging parties.

of which his men held 10, do we really suppose that they sprang like dragon's teeth from the totally barren soil of only 16 years before, or did these armoured and mounted warriors pluck hauberks and helmets from local stones and sustain themselves with bilberries? No, the response to literary enthusiasm for fiction has, to some extent, been remiss and uncritical. The truth, the reality, has been erased in order to provide a 'good' (dramatic and saleable) story. In some places the essential tillers of the soil must have survived, it was not one homogenous winter desert. Monkish chroniclers further south would have had no knowledge of such residual populations when they saw wretched refugees streaming past them. That winter must have been a hard one even for all who remained in that place, including the Anglo–Norman 'exiles' imprisoned by the season in and around York, but for the would-be invaders on their ships, afraid to come ashore, locked in by winter gales, starving, freezing and dying of sickness, it must indeed have been terrible. Our pity should go to their prisoners, what happened to them?

What can Domesday Book tell us about the longer term effects on this area or about the conduct of these campaigns? Well, it has a great deal to say and we can only sample its evidence here. It confirms that continual fighting, on and off, starting before the Norman Conquest and involving Viking and Scottish incursions, had a very serious long-term effect on Yorkshire. King William's expeditionary force of 1069 was concentrated on York itself, so we can expect its influence to reach up into the North Riding, the Howardon Hills and North York Moors, predictably the districts of Selby, Harrogate, Ryedale and into Hambledown. The 'wasted' entries in Domesday Book (North Riding) figure large on the west against the Pennines, also the northern part of the Vale of York and north of the city itself, the Vale of Pickering and the east coast and, of course, in the East Riding, severely along the River Humber and its estuary, where the Vikings spent their winter in one of the most dangerous estuaries in Europe.[18] In itself this was a brilliant strategy, for the established Viking pattern was to find some island where they could make camp, bring requisitions and fuel, careen and maintain their ships and be safe from attack during the winter months, but now they were imprisoned by the weather, on the water and denied access to the land having been driven out of Axholme and not daring to return.

However, the least ravaged area of the East Riding was Holderness, an area part marsh but partly good quality arable land. While others have attributed this safety to the 'affluence' of this area (which, if anything, should have encouraged spoliation) I interpret it as a tactical phenomenon.[19] This Holderness coast, from Flamborough Head to Spurn Head and Point, has an evil reputation, not only for storms and currents, but for dramatic coastal erosion of its cliffs resulting in unpredictable rocky hazards close inshore. Battered by winter gales it would make a miserable beat for defensive patrols yet it had to be secured, both for its provender and as a precaution against flank attack on York.[20] If, true to form, the Viking fleet had included massive drakkars, designed for sea battles and long voyages, then they would now have been immobilised in the estuary and only the smallest craft could have possibly attempted a landing on this coast for it would still be unpredictable and dangerous lee shore to approach. Remember, their best speed under oars would not exceed 5 knots, insufficient to combat winter wind and wave on this coast (even when crews were fit) and sailing would be out of the question among the rocks. With watchers and flying columns on the shore to catch any survivors as they clambered up the cliffs, such foolhardiness would have been suicidal. King William had no need to risk his English fleet in a sea battle, even had the weather permitted: this unwieldy, battle-designed

Scandinavian fleet was effectively imprisoned in the estuary. All he had to do was ensure vigilance and sufficient force while the poor devils on the ships died from disease, exhaustion, cold and starvation, praying to Wotan for the spring to come so that their warships could safely leave the Humber. Perhaps they ate the slaves they had taken?

On the opposite, the Lincolnshire, bank of the river we also see 'wasted' entries in Yarborough, Bradley and Morley Wapentakes and further south in Louthesk Wapentake and inland along the valley of the Trent.[21] William's forces no doubt requisitioned here as well but the Vikings may have done the same before they retreated from Axholme. Now this 'Ageland' and Lindsey coastline was then (and in places still is) marshy, salt-marsh and estuarine mud and I have no doubt that patrols were also established here, so that any 'seamen' floundering ashore could be cut off before they could escape. At Grimsby the ferry seems to have had a special guard as only a single, tiny, 'wasted' entry was listed (at Little Grimsby) in 1086 and the other 1,875 acres of arable land seem to have remained untouched. A Dane is said to have founded Grimsby, but I doubt its inhabitants welcomed the Viking pirates. As to the Viking opinion of the place, Kali Kolsson wrote in his *Orkneyinga Saga*:

> Much slime, mud. We waded
> For five mired weeks, reeking,
> Silt-fouled bilge-boards souring
> In Grimsby Bay[22]

Many of these Vikings were not shipmen at all but mercenaries from Poland, Saxony and Frisia and Máerleswein and Waltheof had also provided ships.[23] This was not what any of them had anticipated for even if they did not perish now King William did not intend to give them an opportunity to service their ships for a seaworthy return journey. As Viking resources were finite, if one could now eliminate as many as possible it would be long ere they returned to England and many would never return to their homes. Economy of effort (and resources) as well as maintenance of the aim are Principles of War.

That William later regretted his necessary actions we know from his deathbed confession, if report be true, but he sent out his flying columns

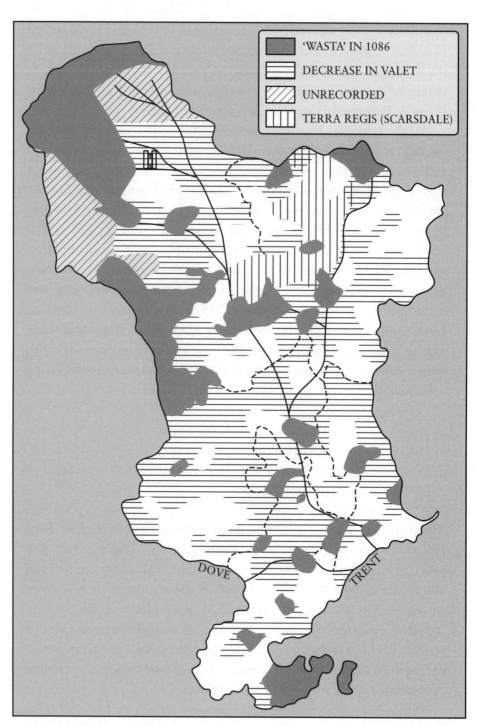

Map 3: 'Wasted' areas of Derbyshire.

Map 3: 'Wasted' Areas of Derbyshire
As recorded in 1086 Map 3 shows those areas entered as 'wasted'. A larger area also recorded decreases in values, while the 'unrecorded' areas conform to the millstone-grit moorlands which in the adjacent Staffordshire (grit) moorlands extended to 30–40 square miles similarly unrecorded. The most heavily populated and farmed area, in the south of Derbyshire, was less affected and the 'terra regis' estates also seem to have been defended. Incursions seem to have followed the valleys of the Dove and the Derwent and to have come from the desolate Staffordshire uplands, possibly fugitive brigands dispersing after their defeat at Stafford. This suggests that William had made his attack on these Welsh and renegades from south of Stafford, via the Trent valley, so driving them north into the uplands.

across Yorkshire, requisitioning, burning and murdering, as mercenary armies will.[24] There was little he could do to control them, isolated as they all were by the season and with little money to hand with which to buy compliance. The wretched peasantry fled southwards, those who could, with the devil on their tail, begging food and shelter, selling themselves into serfdom, down to Leicestershire and even into East Anglia. I have tracked these refugees elsewhere through the record left on the pages of Domesday Book, an apt (though still inadequate) record of an apocalyptic event long before envisaged by Bede in his 'Domesday'.[25] Yet for all the horror and mayhem displayed there was some control, at least on the margins. In Derbyshire we see clearly that the retributive hand fell heavily on some places and some districts but <u>not</u> on others. Mapping the Domesday Book entries discloses that 'terra regis', the royal estates, were certainly respected in this shire.

At the same time the King sent to the leader of the Viking army in the Humber offering a 'large ransom'. Well, it was believed to be large but escape was what these pirates needed now. Contemporaries professed disgust at this man's 'greed' in accepting it but, in truth, there was little left for him to do but wait for better weather and then try to go home, unless he wished his starving pirates to face an army which now not only had a formidable reputation but was much fitter than his own. Of course, contemporaries, half in admiration, represented this scorched earth policy as a salutary act of ruthlessness, the sort of thing which, in this brutal age, tended to mark out a monarch as a terrible lion and as vengeful as God. Educated clerics understood such things better than they understood peasants, let alone the exigencies of war and 'if you're looking for a stick to beat a dog, you'll find one'. The Church hated the King's taxes, so why not discredit him and 'teach him a lesson'? No one else was writing 'histories', that is what I have observed time and again. This was a God-sent opportunity to belabour the King without actually committing treason.

This 'harrying of the North' has, therefore, been represented as one of the most notorious acts in English history but we should ask ourselves what alternative the pious declaimers would have chosen, what could they have advocated? As to claims of 100,000 perishing at Norman hands, just who was capable of making, much less keeping, any such record?[26] Also which army was most to blame, and surely the 'Norman' forces included Englishmen as well as foreign mercenaries? The consequences of warfare are invariably deplorable. Would Harold have fared any better had he remained as King and faced yet another Viking challenge? Orderic Vitalis (who wasn't there) created a livid account of wanton destruction in Yorkshire as rebels were pursued, but Yorkshire thegns had joined the Vikings and there were, no doubt, brigands from the wildlands of Northumbria 'freelancing' as well. With these in mind and a large force to provide for, is it any wonder that William pursued others to Durham and into that ancient and festering political sore, Northumbria. Undoubtedly his Anglo-Norman force committed atrocities and senseless vandalism during December and January but did he order such acts and, if so, was he only following his Coronation Oath to defend English society from its enemies? The trail we observe sixteen years later, in Domesday Book, as we have seen, does not suggest a desert landscape, neither does it represent genocide. It could, however, represent necessity combined with unenforceable discipline.

Symeon of Durham, very wisely and safely writing long after the King's death, showed his disrespect by calling him 'William the Bastard' in his *Historia Regum* so, as a Norman by birth, he demonstrates that not all Normans were pro-William. Just as well to wait until he was dead to call him that![27] In fact Symeon's task was to further Durham's claims in the North, especially by promoting St Cuthbert and (like all religious) by condemning taxation (of the Church) by the Crown as immoral and unjust. Once again, the geld lay behind all this unrest and the geld affected the rich, not the peasantry. Then again, Symeon seems to have largely plagiarised Florence of Worcester, who (in turn) seems to have copied from Brother John! Whichever one of them it was wrote the *Chronicon Ex Chronicis* the pair of them were English by birth and vehemently pro-Harold.

When William's chroniclers speak to us vividly of the horrors of this short period and the burden upon the King's soul we have to remember that <u>they</u> had no perspective on the campaign, no experience of military matters, no strategic grasp (being sheltered and protected monks) and some may have thought it (theologically) partly deserved. Yet had it been possible to act in some ameliorated manner, the fact remains that mercenaries and hearth-troop contingents could never be properly disciplined and controlled, even by their own lords. As yet the power of constraint which true 'feudalism' is said to apply was absent from Anglo-Norman polity. This world was not dissimilar to Italy under the Condottieri.[28] Neither mercenaries nor hearth-troops could be properly disciplined and obliged to obey all commands, especially those of the Crown, much less when under rewarded, hungry and isolated, and such formations do not attract the finest of human natures. England's new King was demonstrating that he would keep the ancient oath he had taken, to defend the kingdom, and events were to show that not even family ties would make him break it.

Chapter 4

Strategic Acumen

Although King William returned to York early in 1070 and found it secure his labours were certainly not yet over and so he next turned his attention to the Welsh borders and raised the siege of Shrewsbury.[1] Do we imagine that the inhabitants were unhappy about this? Nevertheless, at this point some nation-state historians like to proclaim that the 'English revolt' was over (now that Northumbrians, Danes, Welsh, Irish and bandits had all been bested) but assuredly William's problems were not yet over.[2] He could and did appoint trusted lieutenants to commands over the (now) desolate lands on his borders to the north and to the west (so there were some local survivors, some sizeable human assets able to support such lieutenants and the garrisons they commanded) but his stood-down mercenaries required money and he was broke. He was now both desperate and vulnerable. He had to discharge the least trustworthy elements in his forces if he was to survive, remembering that he might, one day, need them again. As with so many monarchs after him, the sinews of defence had to be made paramount. He therefore ordered searches to be made of all monastic houses, searches for both secular stashes and religious treasures secreted therein which might be converted to cash and so was finally able to dismiss his army at Salisbury.[3] At Easter he was at Winchester where he was joined by Papal legates. They now reinforced the penances already declared for all who had participated in the immediate conquest.[4] Yet for the King they had an especial 'essoin' to help him expurgate all his sins committed in the course of conquest.

The Papacy had long been vexed by the insular independence of the English Church, especially their lax attitude to celibacy and (to a lesser extent) plurality. As a Duke, William had undertaken to promote Papal interests and so now the legates proposed wholesale 'reform' of the English Church, blackening the old order with a will and suggesting that overall control should now be placed in the hands of imported, pro-Papal clerics.[5] It was the quid pro quo, assisting the 'true Church' justified the invasion. This presented William with no problems, rather with familiar opportunities, and he happily agreed to a purge of bishops and abbots, anyone (like the Bishop of Durham and his St Cuthbert alter ego) whom he suspected of sympathies with foreign or English lords, or of opposition to his policies (which would include taxation).[6]

He had been astute enough to invoke the Church's blessing on his original enterprise, which endowed his victory with the 'divine retributive' aura so long presented by English churchmen (such as Wulfstan) as the reason for English military disasters, an association with God which had made William's victory in 1066 even more credible to the credulous English. It should, then, have come as no surprise to the English Church that they, in turn, were to be purged for a new order of new men, dependable (and of course predictably grateful) Norman clerics. No doubt this also helped him prise their treasures from them. It was William's personal affirmation of political piety in this age of such declarations, being yet another astute secular, political, move by him. He no doubt reasoned that he would not be bound to treat these religious incomers as custom required the old order to be treated and so he could reasonably expect some fiscal gratitude, at least for a while. What form should this gratitude take? This king was an astute politician and he knew exactly what he wanted.

Of course, the question of penances posed a real problem for ordinary men, but not so for the greater lords who had an established formulaic response. It was to be another two centuries before the concept of Purgatory was introduced by the Church and so, as the world was then, in Benedictine eyes at least, irremediably sinful, this made the pains of Hell (pending the arrival of Domesday and the Last Judgement) inevitable. In short, whatever you did you were damned for a long time, maybe forever as doctrinal matters were so tricky, but at least the wealthy did not need to suffer. Although even 'resting in the bosom of Abraham' does not seem to have been devised as yet, there was a sort of '*refrigarium*' (it was understood) for those who gave generous endowments to Mother Church. For the King as for his magnates, land posed no problems and they could all afford to generously establish new Conventual houses to the

Glory of God and in expiation of their sins on earth. For King William this took the form of a generous grant of an abbey (and lands) at Battle, where prayers could be permanently offered for the soul of its benefactor and his family, which was the intercessory role of the Benedictine Order in the Opus Dei. There is no evidence that William ever visited his new establishment and given the paranoiac ecclesiastical horror of bloodshed on Holy premises it is most unlikely that Battle Hill, the site of the abbey, was the actual site of the battle.[7] Even years later the scattered bones of the slain must still have been visible on Caldbec Hill to the north where the grass grew green on blood and bone meal. Of course the financial loss to William, in revenues, was negligible, the new abbot would pay tax on his lands, just like his fellows. I doubt the Papal legates had foreseen this for outside England no one had to face a land-based 'income' tax. It is yet another example of King William's political acumen.

But William was nothing if not pragmatic. He had proved himself to be a great planner and now he had perceived the solution to yet another problem.[8] Even the resources of England, which we will explore in due course, had been strained to breaking point by four years of mercenary armies and the secret rivers of treasure, loot, were drying up for King and magnates alike (as his recent desperate measures to find the means by which to discharge mercenaries had disclosed) leaving even hearth-troop miles discontented with their unremunerative service. In return for the generous concessions made to Mother Church (and with little censure to fear from the ecclesiastical 'new arrivals') the King now imposed on Her the secular burden of military service imposed already on many bishoprics and Conventual houses.[9] It is likely that temporal estates held by bishops and abbots were already, like those held by lords temporal, required to supply quotas of miles at their own expense for they all had hearth-troops but now King William was extending the concept of the hearth-troop (as an additional financial burden on top of the geld) to the spiritualties of such lords spiritual. To men like Odo of Bayeux, a keen warrior and reluctant cleric from birth, this was irksome but no problem, he already kept and enjoyed his own hearth-troop, though it was a further expense to add more 'knights'. For the more spiritually inclined clerics this was a fresh financial burden <u>and</u> a difficult disciplinary one: costs of horses, armour and living, and with bonuses for commanders. Of course it is impossible, in the absence of lists, to quantify these additions to the royal host, but it would have provided a significant increase in the quantity of heavy horse available in the future and at a reduced cost to the Crown. For the present the actual heavy horses also posed a separate problem, which we will return to in due course.

Not only did this measure dispense with the expense of hiring some mercenary miles it also tightened compliance with discipline, for now a miscreant brought to book had nowhere to run and hide as mercenaries did. He must now submit to his lord's will in judgement. It also, at a stroke, solved the problem of garrisons for the Conqueror had been building burghs, or 'castles', and disbursing defenders from his strike forces on a liberal scale. It is always assumed that this 'castle'-building programme was a Norman innovation though, in fact, the English had been building burghs since the Burghal Hidage and then added to them under Edward the Elder, so there were already earthworks in many places.[10] It also seems that, contrary to popular mythology, the concept of a tower on a hillock or promontory was also an English innovation, one commenced just prior to the Invasion, a form of strongpoint increasingly adopted (if not universally adopted) by William's armies after 1066.[11] But garrisons ate up soldiers and strongpoints were not invulnerable to attack, therefore they were only useful if one also had a mobile field force. The tactic of the 'hammer and the anvil', by which to trap raiders, is as old as Hadrian's Wall and still useful today.

Often called 'the bones of a kingdom', these strongpoints were more the nails by which the patchwork of the landscape were held together and rather than symbols of oppression, designed to incarcerate and interrogate English maquisards, they probably functioned as strategic links for flying columns, posting stages for strategic gallopers, secure domiciles and lodgings for minor lords and also secure repositories for the treasure trains of the essential geld. By impeding and also simultaneously tempting raiders these gave relief forces time to arrive and to make contact with the besieging enemy. Moreover each 'castle' became a service-industry provider, requiring local services to focus and support it and so it acted as a stimulus to the establishment of markets and then an encouragement to increasing numbers of suppliers to join the money economy. Of course, initially, 'castles' were almost exclusively

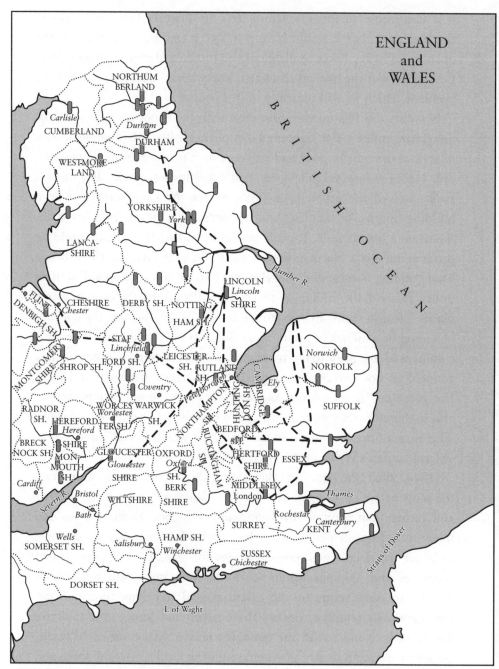

Map 4: 'Castles' securing England.

> **Map 4: 'Castles' Securing England**
> Map 4 shows strongpoints and castleries established *c.* 1080 (or before)
> in order to secure all the routes south and the Wash and east coasts. This
> was because Anglia included the most populous towns and important
> commercial centres outside London. Note how these 'castles' covered main
> roads and river valley routes.

built in earth and timber and often in the form of small burghs, except
in stone-building uplands, so local labour was readily available in all
cases and the expertise used in vernacular construction was necessarily
reproduced in military architecture. Needless to say, there was no Robert
fitz McAlpine force of 'royal engineers' trailing after Norman armies,
we have not a single shred of evidence for such a corps. 'Burgh-bote'
was a traditional English obligation on local inhabitants.[12] The idea that
'Norman' supermen built such structures in their 'off-duty' hours is
equally ridiculous.

In one important respect, however, these 'castles' differed from the
old 'burghs', for whereas many of the latter (though not all) had been
large and so capable (in need) of admitting a number of civilians, the
new 'castles' were of a more compact design, intended only for a few
soldiers and horses. Still, the fact remains that this was the first new
system in 150 years to offer impeders to invaders, for not all could be
bypassed, there were too many, and so they were a remarkable and
necessary development. By *c.* 1070 the larger, older, Alfredan burghs
had developed into towns, to the advantage of hereditary tenants and the
negation of their military value.[13] 'Castles', being more compact, could
also be made stronger, for the weakness of the old 'burghs' was that they
aggregated refugees and so became even more attractive targets for slavers
unless, like Portchester, they were actually impregnable.[14] William's own
attempts to build impregnable stone castles at London (White Tower)
and Colchester were, however, thwarted by falling geld revenues (as we
shall see) and were not completed until Rufus' reign. In this ambition he
failed, there was only so much revenue to be had by the 1070s, which was
the economic problem. Unremitting warfare was draining the kingdom
of resources even though initiative was now supplying men.

King William's strategic vision was not confined to strongpoints and the means of recruiting garrisons, however, for when King Swein of Denmark finally arrived off the English coast to lead his army in person, no doubt in the belief that it was ready for success, he found it on the verge of starvation with many crews battered, debilitated, sick, demoralised or even lost, drowned in winter gales. The combination of scorched-earth policy and strategic strongpoints had prevented them from obtaining provisions and flying columns had dissuaded them from attempting to forage further afield. If King Swein had now been drawn to his expedition by report of the ransom, he was now sorely in need of an army – and the ships to carry it home. In an attempt to retrieve the situation these Vikings sailed southwards, as the season improved, plundering the coast as they went.[15] They finally entered the Fens (the one available landfall), there commandeering the island community of Ely, a weak spot in the chain of defences. Claims that the inhabitants were enthusiastic about their arrival do not sound like 'nationalism' but, instead, as though a desperate pragmatism prevailed, especially as the pirates were now joined by a wolf's-head named Hereward.[16]

This brigand has enjoyed a largely fabulous history created by nation-state adherents and ballad-mongers which is probably a very long way from the truth. Taking a force to Peterborough, Hereward razed the town and sacked the abbey before retiring onto his Viking friends at Ely, hardly the act of a patriot fighting for his country. This suggests that he may have moved southwards out of Lincolnshire or the Midlands, ahead of the royal army marching south from the Humber to drive the Vikings into Ely. The response of the new and incoming Abbot of Peterborough, Turold, who rode with a hearth-troop of perhaps 160 men was certainly 'church-militant'.[17] He not only arrived first but he now made Peterborough secure and the position of the brigands and raiders very uncertain. When King William arrived and offered them terms the Vikings readily decamped, taking all the treasures they could find with them and probably slaves as well, then sailed away in their now unsound ships and into a great storm, which deprived them of the main part of their loot. It would be many years before others of their countrymen would be tempted to come to England. The inhabitants of Ely now began to wonder how their new King would view their apparent collaboration with his enemies and (of course) Hereward still remained there with his brigands. There was no welcome in the fjords awaiting him and maybe there was no space left in the partly unserviceable fleet. He could fend for himself.

In 1070 Ely was an island at the south end of the Fens and through that terraqueous wilderness it connected to the Wash and the North Sea. The Abbot of Ely held the island and a surrounding district to south, east and west, with outliers at Whittlesey (far to the north-west) and at Wisbech (4–5 miles to the north and on the Wash), and these estates were recorded all together, in Domesday Book, as the 'Two Hundreds of Ely'.[18] The island itself comprised 2,400 acres of arable with an equal amount of 'meadow' and an eyot of 120 acres called Hainey Island and, to the south, a separate estate and island of 360 acres (arable) called Stuntney. Most of these hundreds comprised a 'mainland' to the south-west and west of the Isle of Ely with a 'port' at Haddenham (Hill Row). Although it is not exactly certain how the waters and fens should be calculated from the eels and fisheries recorded in Domesday Book, I have made an attempt based on earlier research.[19] So it seems that the landmass then involved came to about 32,800 acres or 51 square miles (including some 28 square miles of geld of which 23.7 were historic or established arable) with about 38 square miles of fens and perhaps 42 square miles of meres and enclosed waters which rendered fishing rents, in all perhaps 132 square miles recorded, apparently over a total area of 300 square miles. About 56 per cent of the landscape here was entirely open water by 1086 and therefore an inland part of the Wash.

This, of course, made a very convenient anchorage within the protection of the land on either side, stretching down 30 miles from the North Sea. Ely, at the southern end, was a secure refuge that Viking expeditions had used in the past, an island 'fortress', a strand and safe harbour with rich estates on either hand and, thanks to reedy fens, eyots, marshes and meres, also providing ambushes for those who knew the local terrain if other shipping should enter the open waters. Although seclusion had long ago appealed to the religious who went there (or so they claimed), its greater appeal to them was probably its fecund habitat of fertile arable, lush grazings, astonishing fish stocks (96,283 eels each year are recorded as 'renders' in 1086) and enormous flocks of passage and sedentary birds together with reeds and rushes (for use and for sale) and revenues from port dues.[20] Only its location deep inland and the fresh waters of the Ouse seem to have prevented it from exploiting salt production as well. In a world and economy of self-sufficiency and subsistence this was a very attractive and a very valuable environment.

Before 1066 these estates had been set at high values and although the 1070 occupation does not seem to have affected Ely as badly as it did other places, the deficient totals in 1086 (Domesday) records show that to the south and south-west, and also across towards Peterborough, there had recently been serious damage. Not surprisingly this included the 'port' of Haddenham which had, no doubt, been plundered for chandlery by the desperate Vikings. Cottenham and Waterbeach, on the edge of Cambridge, and Exning (Newmarket) were also mauled though adjacent Burwell, Fordham and Chippenham and even Southery and Littleport on the east side of the Fens, were not. It seems that the Viking army had mounted raids to the south of Ely but that local resistance gave a good account of itself on the Norfolk margins. Clearly Danelaw Norfolk felt no affinity with these pirates and outlaws and was stout enough to deter them.

As we know only too well today, through recent examples and tragic events, the lack of central power and consequently of stability which results from prolonged and indecisive conflicts itself breeds opportunism and lawlessness. Peripheral to any attempts at stabilisation there occur lawless individuals and groups intent on flouting legal authority and such elements melt into landscapes to re-emerge elsewhere. Regaining the rule of law is, in such circumstances, never easy for lack of identifiable and restrainable targets. The situation in 1070–1 was no different from today, remove one major security threat and there will still be minor 'mopping-up' operations to pursue against less formal elements and survivors. Ideally these lawless elements need to be attracted to and then cornered in one area and King William's policy now seems to have been to round up as many social threats as possible in order to eliminate them from the heart (at least) of his kingdom. The north and the west, flanked by alien kingdoms, would remain troublesome but the English heartlands and the east and south, bordered by waters, needed to see and to enjoy the benefits of strong kingship. They, at least, could and should expect peace and relative security.

Under Hereward Ely now seems to have acted as a magnet for all remaining outlaws and rebels for leagues around, both lay and ecclesiastical.[21] It was, after all, seemingly impregnable in its isolation, which left the inhabitants no choice but to co-operate with any and all occupying forces. Besides, the surrounding Fens (as I have said) were rich in fish, eels and fowl of all kinds and provided splendid grazings while only those people with local knowledge could traverse the treacherous waterways. William, however, still had politics to pursue over the waters and left this problem on hold as there was probably little the now self-isolated brigands could do outside the island itself. It was as much a prison as a refuge now that the main force had departed and local defences around them had been organised. They were largely contained. Once William was gone, across the Channel, Eadwine and Morcar slipped away from the English court, no doubt in some sort of an attempt to regain power over their devastated lands in the North, though these were now part of a military zone and closed to them. Their defection was therefore pointless and hopeless: Morcar finally elected for Ely while Eadwine travelled on to Scotland. Early in 1071 William returned to take personal command.[22]

The one thing the rebels on Ely could not have known was that the King had had experience of fenlands in 1066, when he landed at Pevensey, though for some of them the Viking experience on Axholme should surely have been a warning.[23] Whether he next built a pontoon bridge, as later legends claim, we do not know but personally I suspect that he once again recruited local 'fen tigers' to assist his passage through reeds, meres, bogs and backwaters. The obvious route would be from Stuntney and Soham, especially as adjacent Fordham, Freckenham and Chippenham appear to have been strongly defended royal properties now offering a base for further operations, roughly along the modern A142. Obviously this was not cavalry country, though light horse might have been able to swim from Stuntney, and my guess is that William also used light craft from further back on the Ouse to row or pole from Haddenham and so ferry crossbowmen and infantry to the Isle of Ely in a pincer attack. Meanwhile, now that the Viking fleet was gone, Anglo-Norman ships could safely enter the Wash and Fens and so seal off any northerly escape route as well as themselves landing troops on the north side of the Isle.

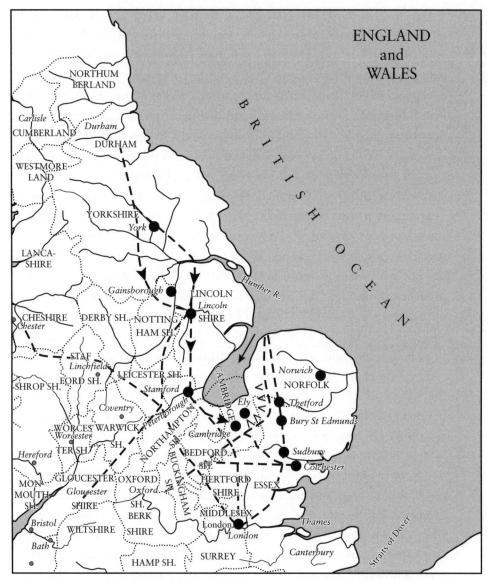

Map 5: The campaigns of 1071–2.

William, it seems, had a shrewd grasp of local possibilities. First, that a largish force of brigands would soon be in difficulties for provisions and from the morale effects of ennui, second, that local resistance would stiffen and strengthen surrounding key points, third, that once the enemy fleet was gone encirclement was possible and also it seems, fourth, that

Map 5: The Campaigns of 1071–2
The astuteness of this strategy is shown on Map 5. The royal army left York to shadow the retreating Viking fleet by marching southwards along Ermine Street. With the improved weather it smoked out fugitives from Staffordshire and Derbyshire and drove them south. The Vikings entered the Wash and captured the Isle of Ely but the royal forces closed in on the Fens creating a 'porous filter' allowing anti-social stragglers 'in' but not 'out'. Royal forces (small arrows) covered Cambridge and the Norfolk border (the rich Anglian shires), forming a defensive 'wall' until King William was ready to strike.

the location would act as a magnet for unwary brigands, so concentrating them in one 'killing zone'. Maybe that explains his absence up to now, a waiting game. Hereward would have been a fool to stay and fight. Anyway, King William was successful when he attacked and though Hereward saved his own skin by flight, others were not so fortunate. Some of those captured in Ely paid a heavy price of mutilation for their fraternisation, another application of Bede's concept of collective, associative, guilt.[24]

Rather than describing this as an act of barbarism and Hereward and his force as English patriots, we should perhaps accept that the men of Cambridge, Huntingdonshire and Suffolk welcomed it as properly stern and condign royal justice for many months of murder, rape, arson and destruction of livelihood. That William 'called-out the land force and the ship force' is attested by the Anglo-Saxon Chronicles.[25] These forces were not an inexhaustible Norman army but English fyrdmen and ship-sokes, making Hereward a treacherous brigand-renegade rather than a patriotic resistance fighter. Though the King must have hired numbers of mercenary miles, milites, and even crossbowmen he did not have thousands of Norman infantry; rich as England was, the pay chest was not bottomless. This had been the reason for his extending knight service to ecclesiastical estates. Where did his infantry come from?

Well it stands to reason that if the Norman 'supermen' had been alone, marching and fighting since 1066, there would probably have been very few of them left by now and those that had survived would be garrisoning northern castles and southern sea ports. There would have been no one to row the boats. Those battle casualties who were not killed outright could look to little or no medical assistance: sepsis, traumas and sickness would have carried off the serious and the walking wounded. Add to these problems exhaustion, lack of nourishment and exposure and it is likely that of the initial force of perhaps 10,000 fighting men, 90 per cent were by now dead or permanently disabled, leaving no more than 1,000 to march on Ely and the kingdom undefended.[26] One has to ask why any enemy should fear such a remnant? No, the answer was not mercenaries for they only serve you for as long as you can afford to pay them. Otherwise they join your enemies. The unavoidable solution to the infantry problem is that King William made use of English fyrdmen on a regular basis, including here in the Fens, and maybe some of them thereby aspired (in due course) to become miles? Once again we can say that without English help the Norman King could not have succeeded and there were, no doubt, many neighbours waiting to settle scores with the plunderers who had terrorised them for so long. They would have been only too pleased to see judicial amputees bleeding and starving to death. That is why they were not cleanly executed outright.

Next seizing the bull by the horns, in the summer of 1072, William decided to attack the source of these repeated attempts at de-stabilisation, Scotland.[27] Once again he marched north and having already laid waste much of the border lands (the area which still remained even into Elizabeth I's reign the province of the Moss-troopers and the Reivers and was equally infested with brigands in the eleventh century) and with no precedent for such a bold action since King Athelstan early in the previous century, he nevertheless took his polyglot force even further north. It was a bold move. Yet again we should consider carefully how he managed such a feat.

If we believe the pervasive popular presentations of history this northern borderland was now a wasteland over which Norman 'supermen' had to march and achieve the impossible, a frontal assault on an enemy with unlimited resources at his back. Kapelle, indeed, has chosen to represent this as a failed excursion which left William with his tail between his legs, but Kapelle's sources (such as Symeon of Durham) seem both unreliable and inflated.[28] Let us instead be realistic. To accomplish this feat he either had to have a sufficient force (if we suppose that he did not, once again, totally strip his southern ports and all 'castles' of garrisons) or a miracle, and there had to be either an incredibly efficient commissariat or a prospering peasantry in place by which to supply his army. I think that reality lay between these two options for provisioning: he prepared with his usual efficiency and also requisitioned on the way from vills and estates which had now recovered from 'the harrying of the North'. He also laid waste to the impoverished Scottish borderlands and this was probably little more than the foraging of a large expeditionary force. If reports are true, the Anglo-Norman army was also accompanied by a considerable fleet to blockade and, no doubt, ferry supplies.[29] Once again, such a force can only have included a large English naval contingent, maybe the one that had blockaded the Wash.

After the Anglo-Norman army had crossed the Forth King Malcolm quickly sued for peace and did fealty. Earl Waltheof replaced Gospatric in the North. William, now with a reputation as the most capable warrior in Europe (yet in a picturesque religious fiction chased south by St Cuthbert of Durham!), was able to turn his attention back to troubles over the waters, in France.[30] In his absence the new Archbishop of Canterbury, Lanfranc, took a high profile in both secular and religious affairs, asserting his authority. Lanfranc, however, had originally been unwilling to take this post and his letters detailing the situation in England early in 1073 certainly read like the disillusion of a man from a quiet life in an isolated, sheltered, religious community now entering the real and everyday world.[31] It was, no doubt, his position as Archbishop that placed his authority above that of Odo of Bayeux, a clever preparation for safe absence by King William. And again we are told that when William 'won the land of Maine' in 1073–4 he took with him English and French forces, which speaks for itself for his laws did not define Normans resident in England as 'English' but as 'French'.[32] Only the English were 'English'.

Nevertheless there were undercurrents of violence on the English side of the Channel once the King was safely out of the way. Earl Waltheof (safely in the north) settled a long-standing blood feud in the winter of 1073–4 by slaughtering two generations as they sat down to dinner, behaviour which the secular, let alone the religious, Norman authorities could not condone.[33] Tasked by royal authority, he compensated by agreeing to all the 'new' reforms of Christianity in his earldom, as now required by the new Norman Bishop of Durham, so that was alright.

There was undoubtedly a form of 'modus vivendi' when the joint interests of the powerful were to be served and (at least in King William's absence) one could turn a blind eye to feud-settling provided that Mother Church benefitted thereby. We need to judge all things and all people, even archbishops, by the standards of their Age. Yet in itself this act of murder betrayed the still untamed and dangerous, opportunistic attitudes of powerful magnates, whatever their origins. That Earl Waltheof was 'English' was hardly significant, like all his kind he sought autonomous powers and maybe he even had a secret desire to form his own northern kingdom? He was not alone in his secret ambitions.

Chapter 5

Keeping Faith

It is difficult to avoid the temptation to compare Lanfranc of Bec and William I, though, of course, they inhabited, and had always inhabited, separate spheres, the one religious and cloistered, the other political and military. Neither seems to have chosen a path in life, rather each pursued that which fate had ordained for them and yet did so with wholehearted devotion and unusual drive. They also had much in common in their reserve, determination and devotion to belief in the courses they followed. So, as opposites attract, it is probably just as well that they each operated within a framework which the other could not understand: the one religious, the other secular. The man who was instead troubled by the path fate had ordained for him and who seems vigorously to have striven to pursue an alternative, secular and worldly course was Odo of Bayeux and his very worldliness was the antithesis of the outlook of either of the other two. For William his kingdom was paramount, for Lanfranc it was the service of King and faithful, for Bishop Odo it was self. With William occupied in France it was as well that Lanfranc could balance out, by hierarchical superiority, the authority of William's determined half-brother, yet the fact that they now lived, nominally, side-by-side in Kent was itself bound to create disharmony.

Had it not been for treachery, made possible by the lack of any system to control what is generally applauded as 'feudalism', William's career would have ended when it really began, in 1047 at the battle of Val-és-Dunes. Here, allied by appeal to his (unavoidable) 'good lord' King Henry of France, he appears to have owed the day to the defection of Ralph Tesson of Fleury who changed at the last moment to the royal side. Of course, this ambiguity could also work against William. The trouble was that 'commendation' to a 'good lord' lacked specificity: the 'beneficium' was rarely if ever clearly understood and so 'fealty', the swearing of loyalty to a lord, need not be invariably binding. In William's case, in

1047, King Henry seems to have been his 'good lord' because as such he could enjoy William's revenues, William then being still a minor, and even after that as one of the King's '*vassi dominici*' (to use a Carolingian concept).[1] William clearly had no intention of offering such a wide-open gift in return, hence the subsequent rift between him and King Henry which led to the King attempting to assert his rights and William offering him successful resistance. This was hardly feudal systemisation or loyalty to one's overlord!

With the rank of miles as yet indeterminate, leaving a militus the status (as we would later define) of either knight <u>or</u> sergeant-at-arms, there was considerable fluidity in the definition of 'knighthood', from 'skilled horse soldier' to some sort of vavassour. Then again the evolution of specially trained bloodstock, or destriers, made the mounts used by such men especially expensive and different from ordinary mounts. A lord who required 'knights', milites, miles, would find it easier to acquire horsemen if he could supply the bloodstock; other horsed candidates would have their own mounts but look to receiving suitable remounts from their 'good lord' when the need arose. Not all of these equestrian contractual engagements would, by any means, have gifts of real estate as their beneficium, so not all miles had allodial ties and even then they were unlikely to be heritable unless the holder of this incipient 'knight's fee' had some especial hold over his lord. Lords were evaluated by the size of their hearth-troop or retinue of 'knights' and so such miles were required to be in constant attendance. The general breakdown, or evolution (choose which you will) into a Comital system (in France) by the eleventh century created a need for each count or duke to retain a massive bodyguard, a hearth-troop, in permanent attendance, for personal safety, so men who were little more than mercenaries and the mounted descendants of the ale-and-mead-bench companions of Heorot were their miles. Well, they differed in one respect from their Anglo-Saxon, now English, counterparts, they had (in France) no social ethic dictating that they should die with their lord and 'gold-giver'. In England, however, this was certainly the tradition if not always the practice.[2]

Such hearth-troops, basically mercenary associations, did differ slightly from the independent freelance mercenaries who worked for money alone for they were part of a great lord's permanent household.

In France the significance of these hearth-troops was that they had the status of free men, even though men in permanent attendance on their lord. Those vassals, we should now call them 'vavassours', who actually had grants of property had territorial responsibilities and also limits (gradually becoming defined) upon the time they should be required to serve in the field, with the household, or as guards for outlying properties (later called 'castleguard'). Hearth-troop members, however, were usually permanently in attendance on their lord. In France both status and *force majeur* dictated that a large hearth-troop was essential. And such milites, if faithful to their new oath of fealty (now the '*immixtio manuum*'), swore allegiance to their lord, above and against <u>all</u> others.[3]

What had once been, so Ganshof argued, an oath to do nothing <u>against</u> a benefactor ('good lord') now became (in France) an oath of allegiance to support him under all circumstances and so, we might say, moved down the social scale, rather like Collis' Hypothesis of the money economy.[4] In this England and France were poles apart for though households were required, in each dominion, to be loyal (in England to death) and to financially 'aid' their leader, in England there also arose a financial problem. England alone had a specie-taxation, not one redeemable in-kind; the 'geld' (or Danegeld, as it first was) which could only be paid in valid coin of the realm and since 991 this contribution to ransom had been equitably assessed on (that is against) landholdings.[5] Thus in England it was a case of knowing what a man could pay rather than of telling him he should pay. In a world which was dependant on 'freelances', mercenary miles, the advantage of (bullion) cash to a magnate-ruler was obvious: no need to market commodities, no need to value and hack-silver treasure, men could immediately be had for the bidding. What was more, England's specie coinage was of consistently high assay and not debased, unlike French and Norman issues, it therefore had greater purchasing power in the mercenary marketplace.

The English tax known as 'the geld' did, however mask certain disadvantages. For a start, being assessed on landholding, it was a tax which fell upon the rich, they alone had the means to market the produce of their tenants (that is to join the money economy) in order to obtain specie and English silver pennies, equivalent to modern high-value banknotes (one authority compared them to pre-war half sovereigns), were always beyond the aspirations of a subsistence peasantry.[6] It was the lord's, the landowner's, business to collect enough eggs from his peasantry to equal a penny or more at market for individual peasants could never produce a sufficient quantity to merit a penny. If the English peasantry had to cope with an unprecedented demand for produce at times their new Norman masters had to cope with the unfamiliar and to them novel geld, with its need to market in order to obtain cash.

In the end, of course, the Crown was paying for many military supplies, so now there was created an even larger ready market in which to sell. A second disadvantage, this time from the Crown's perspective, was that the geld could not take account of cash transactions, so it did not take the stewards of great lords long to work out that if in-kind and service payments <u>could</u> be commuted to cash, no geld was due: dominium was thereby retained without the burden of proprietas. Yet for this to work the vavassour sub-tenants had to be 'in' the cash economy, big enough to market their own produce or, most likely, concerned with some sort of industrial production. Of course, in time, the Crown caught up, when the law devised a distinction between 'realty' and 'interest', but in 1066 such niceties were not understood. There were other financial dodges as well and we will deal with them elsewhere. It all depended on the geld records going unchecked, without audit, for no such concept seems to have existed at the time of the Conquest or for many years afterwards.

Finally and most importantly, to the new Norman super-rich and aristocracy, by redistributing lands in their favour and by granting enormous estates, the Crown actually penalised its own coterie and supporters. Whereas the pre-1066 super-rich bracket had comprised about 4,000 individuals the 'new order' had only about 180 members and although we cannot precisely say how many dependant lordlings, vavassours or intermediate vassals (such as 'knights') might at this date have helped contribute from their own smaller (enfeoffed) estates, we do know that the much later (fully developed) feudal maximum was probably little more than 5,000 knights. However, post–1066, with forces concentrated in hearth-troops (within major households) there were certainly fewer landholding knights and sergeants than there were, say, a century later, maybe only 1,000 to 2,000, so the geld fell heavily on those magnates who kept large retinues of milites about them, which was just about all the tenants-in-chief. They could not lay off their obligations on sub-tenants if such tenants had no estates. Later we will return to this as well, it is critical to our understanding of what we might call the development of 'feudalism' and fealty in England.

Conflict does not occur in a vacuum, not in real life. Its effects are widely felt in the communities involved and even those marginally involved and not just through casualty lists but, in reality, through the whole structure of an economy. The demands of sustained, unremitting conflict on agriculture can be described as being both obvious and discreet, direct and indirect. Obviously soldiers require provisions to sustain them in the field and as a result emphasis is placed not only on food production but on certain food stuffs and preparations, subject to market forces. At this time food preservation consisted mainly of salted meat or fish in barrels, cheese (which was more expensive), or meat on the hoof, and cereals for bread or oat cakes.[7] In the 1070s the strain on agriculture from both demand and depredations must have assumed serious proportions, no doubt intensified by the creation of so many garrisons, yet these demands would also benefit the peasantry by providing fresh opportunities for production and new markets. It is unlikely that many would have anticipated the long-term effects that such intensifications as 'sod-busting' would have on yields, the consequences of over tillage would have appeared much later.

Of course there were other pressures at work, for example horse-breeding. The losses among the essential heavy horse, or trained destriers, was obviously constant, due to the constant campaigning, likely to be as wasteful as actual combat though spread over a longer period of time. If King William had been unable to make good these losses (to both loyal troops and to mercenaries alike) he would soon have lost both his essential strike forces and their loyalty. Specialist breeding must have commenced immediately and urgently at such places as Eastbourne-Pevensey and also within those Royal forests (as later records testify) which favoured the establishment of studs.[8] By 1068 remounts of some quality would be 'on-stream' yet the mobile nature of warfare would also require great numbers of ordinary riding horses and pack ponies and this leads us into another of the discreet effects of war on agriculture at this date.

For many centuries two, separate, systems of motive-power have been harnessed to the essential plough, ox-power and horse-power. The latter is deemed by most agricultural historians to be the more efficient and, therefore, the more advanced. Be this as it may ox-power was the universal (European) practice in 1066, for oxen are easy to raise and feed, have great stamina and, ultimately, can themselves provide food.[9] In England, in Domesday Book, we find the eight-ox plough employed as a standard unit, one equivalent to 120 acres (the 'carucate') and one understood (as a unit) moreover in Scandinavia and in France.[10] Yet on the Bayeux Tapestry, an English creation of *c.* 1070 or before, we see the use of horses <u>not</u> oxen for ploughing and harrowing, illustrations which <u>we do not</u> again encounter until *c.* 1500! These images, therefore, represent observations made *c.* 1066 for they cannot be anything else. Now there is no indication of such horse-powered agricultural work anywhere in Domesday Book (nor yet in Europe), that is in 1085–6, which is strange. What happened in England <u>in between</u> these dates to change the picture and the motive-power units, turning back the clock after 1066?

As a personal evaluation I would make a comparison with the English Civil War of 1642–8 when horses of all kinds were soon in short supply due to the attrition of stocks by continuous warfare. I therefore suspect that the demand for horses (of all kinds) by the military after 1066 caused a (similar) general reversion to traditional ox-traction in agriculture. There would, of course, have been a secondary benefit in the production of beef. William's immediate losses in 1066 might (by the spring of 1067) have been supplied by heavy horse shipments from France using the methods he had pioneered in 1066, and given the size of the treasury he had acquired. Maybe such purchasing was one purpose of his prolonged 'holiday' in Normandy in 1067.[11] Then, as money became tighter and a need for light horses, draft and pack horses more acute, he would need to requisition more widely and in England. It was common for miles to ride on hacks while leaving their destriers fresh for combat, and their 'squires' (servants) also required horses. Only by 1068, at the very earliest, could he really expect fresh English-reared heavy horses for his armoured strike forces and even then demand may have outpaced supply given the continuous and mobile nature of English campaigns. From the peasant's point of view oxen would also provide meat, saleable (either fresh or for barrelling in brine) to the Crown, once the horses had been sold. It seems that the military exigencies of the years 1066–86 (and beyond) actually set back an English agricultural revolution by several hundred years.

The importance of all these things is the relevance they have to our understanding of Bishop Odo's career and, ultimately, the influences it provided for the creation of a true 'feudal system'. The good bishop, one of the wealthiest men 'over the water' in France, clearly intended to become as much, or more, in his new sphere as the Earl of Kent. Under the indulgent rule of 'good old' King Edward there had been fewer outside threats to the realm (no doubt several foreign 'promisees' were carefully watching one another in the wings) so there was less demand for geld, and he was also known for his remission of the dues owed by his favourites. Turning a blind eye seems to have been one of his policies, consequently powerful families like the Godwines were able to act with some degree of impunity and (in return) probably ploughed their own resources into those military needs which served their own ends. Domesday Book tells us of many estates which avoided taxation under Godwine administration while 'acquisitions' of dubious legality also came into their possession. It seems that a significant number of these latter, in Kent and elsewhere, had concerned the archbishopric's temporalities and spiritualities and Bishop Odo, on inheriting former Godwine estates, was not particular about the legal niceties, past or present, neither did he scruple in acquiring archiepiscopal properties for himself. He seems to have had too much current business, such as acquiring even wider domains, to dwell upon winning the hearts and minds of his new tenants or even supporting the Crown.

Lanfranc, however, as a new type of archbishop, was deeply interested in the affairs of his see, especially those archiepiscopal holdings attested by charter. England, pre-1066, had been very good about legalities and charters defining real estate. The Archbishop had records available to him by which to compare, we might even say evaluate or 'audit', the bishop's claims. After all, as we shall see in another chapter, England led Europe as the cultural capital for administration, numeracy and literacy.[12] That was the underlying cause of the magnetism, manifested in the country's wealth, which drew so many invaders time and again. Only in England could a King so effectively raise a treasure.

While the new Archbishop wrestled with his muniments and glowered at Odo's worldliness and avarice other undercurrents began to stir. It is difficult to know whether Breton lords had been less well rewarded than Norman lords, but they had borne equal shares of the fighting and marching and now found themselves heavily taxed when they had hoped to enjoy their new possessions (as one might say) in peace. We should not forget that the original intention of the invaders had been to retire home with plenty of loot and, moreover, the Bretons were not William's subjects when in France. The Bretons now began to plot, for with King William so pre-occupied in France it seemed a good time to sound out surviving English lords. After all, they would need English support if they were to attempt a coup, they could not succeed alone for resources were limited. They needed English troops just as much as William did if they were to succeed in any English campaign. Ralph de Gael, Earl of Norfolk, the ringleader, was the son of a lord who had served the Breton King Edward before he subsequently joined with William of Normandy, so he knew the importance of involving English lords and he would also have known that King Edward had been very indulgent towards his favourites, which King William, in matters of national finance, never was. William never waived the geld and that must have rankled with Ralph.

As Earl of Norfolk he managed to interest the Earl of Hereford, Roger de Breteuil, son of William fitzOsbern. Waltheof, Earl of Huntingdon, son of Earl Siward of Northumbria, also allowed himself to be drawn into the alliance. He also knew how indulgent the last king had been to his favourites and, as Kapelle has observed, one of St Cuthbert's miracles tells us that the geld was the underlying motive for Waltheof's treason, though Kapelle (like the Church chroniclers) chooses to call such taxation 'unjust', representing it as King William's *cupiditas*.[13] Earl Ralph also sent secret emissaries to Denmark and to William's enemies in France: King Phillip, Count Robert of Flanders and Breton lords in Brittany were, it seems, all appraised and ready for diversionary actions over there. At a bridal, near Newmarket, the revolt was finalised: men whom William loved and had favoured were now ready to stab him in the back while his enemies had him pinned down in Normandy. It was a cunning plot and it had nothing at all to do with 'English resistance'. Where was Bishop Odo in all this, for a while conspicuous by his absence (as he had been when

Eustace of Boulogne attacked Dover) but, wisely, the kingdom had been left by the king in the hands of Odo's neighbour, Archbishop Lanfranc, and he was not going to be found wanting in the event.

Lanfranc may even have been privately appraised of this treacherous alliance well ahead of the event for he wrote to King William to say that it would be foul-shame if loyal vassals could not deal with such an internal uprising: not the words of a man taken off guard.[14] Wulfstan, Bishop of Worcester (a very different man from the homilist and defeatist Wulfstan of York who had died in 956), and Æthelwig, Abbot of Evesham, mobilised their troops and barred Earl Roger's progress. Odo of Bayeux, Geoffery de Coutances, Richard fitz Gilbert and William de Warenne next barred Earl Ralph's progress from Norwich. Ralph, outmanoeuvred, circumspectly left his castle at Norwich to his wife and fled abroad; the castle was besieged and taken and the Countess was allowed to depart to Brittany. Good riddance to the Bretons.

Cnut, son of Swein, arrived too late with his Danish army and a fleet of perhaps 200 ships, no doubt his warriors were now a little apprehensive, so instead he ravaged the coast around York (which we have been told to believe contained many of his supposed 'countrymen') and went home. York itself seems to have held out and formed some sort of refuge for the locals and the invaders now knew what to expect if they tarried too long. At Christmas 1075 King William returned to England to administer justice, bringing with him the surrendered and contrite English earl, and so the foolish Earl Waltheof was, like Earl Roger, thrown into prison only to be executed in May. He was an Englishman and this was the English way of doing justice, William was respecting 'local customs'. Besides, Waltheof of all people should have been prepared to pay the English tax. I think it neatly illustrates the innate arrogance of the super-rich at this time. It was certainly a lesson for residual English lords that however elevated they might be they would not be treated like Norman lords but as their own native custom had always dictated. However, treating Norman lords equally harshly would have rung alarm bells among King William's principal tenants and lords. He could not afford to do it, not yet.

Earl Waltheof had been shown every indulgence by his new King yet had been foolish enough to join in treachery by the Bretons. Once again this attempted coup does not make for a major 'English resistance' movement for two bellicose, senior, English clerics were willing and able to defeat Earl Roger. They were deciding factors, indubitably supported by English tenantry and so instrumental in defeating both Waltheof and Ralph de Gael. The fantasy world of 'English resistance' has only, in my opinion, been developed because historians could find no other simple explanation – and, of course, they generally believed 'the Normans' (Bretons and French) to be supermen as well as a unified (modern) French 'nation'. The explanation for this rebellion is, in my opinion, quite simple, the new super-rich had hoped for lavish rewards and so, though they had been made asset-rich, were cash-strapped by the English taxes necessary for defence and internal stabilisation. It was no more than greed and self-interest which drove their 'bridal of Newmarket'. The majority of Englishmen were loyal to their King, it was the soi–disant 'feudal' element in society that was not!

An immediate response to all this was the instruction, by William, to secure southern and south-eastern interests by building impregnable castles, stone castles, whatever the cost. The security of London was obviously paramount and involved transporting stone from far away. The second site, involving a monster stone keep twice the size of the 'White Tower' of London, was Colchester. The reasons for this second site seem to have been its location in East Anglia and the availability of reusable building materials, especially the massive foundations of a Roman temple and it was built with an annex (of earth and timber) big enough to accommodate a small army, an expeditionary force. Its purpose seems to have been to cover all essential routes to London from vulnerable East Anglia, the Wash and the Suffolk coast, including supporting the sea routes with shipping out of the Colne, to act as a base for flying columns on land and also as a protection for the vulnerable and very valuable East Anglian spinning and weaving industries located in north Essex and southern Suffolk in particular.[15] In the event neither behemoth was completed before King William's premature death, the falling revenues from the geld and a fresh emergency saw to that. Other magnates found alternative ways of cheating on their taxes and ultimately the King had to detect and correct these if he was to continue to find the resources with which to defend England, all of which is pertinent to our analysis and the establishment of fealty, but all of which lay in the future in 1076.

By the end of the 1070s the cash flow from the geld was not just expended, it was drying up, but on parchment the reasons for this were far from obvious: what had gone wrong with this 'perfect system', the envy of Europe? How could the yield from successive taxes diminish steadily? Surely the kingdom was not going to be lost 'for a horse', one flogged to death! One wonders if at first the King blamed his clerk-accountants, so that they were forced to voice their suspicions to him for their own preservation. The supreme military effort was yet to come and so was the political master stroke and one suspects that in the late 1070s there was possibly some sort of 'blame game'.

Well the recognition of subordinates who have ability is a gift in itself, one confined to the competent and confident and William fortunately also possessed this gift, which may have possibly encouraged his accounting camerarii to speak out. At some time around now he recognised in one of his 'chaplains', a camerarius, or clerk, who was part of the machinery we would now call 'chancery' and 'the exchequer', one of the talented members of his curia, an unique ability to comprehend both figures <u>and</u> the closed world of English agriculture with its arcane units. This senior clerk, who seems to have thoroughly understood the real problem, was to be encouraged to devise a solution to all the King's financial problems during the following decade. At this point in time he surely voiced his concerns, perhaps first to the Archbishop who then voiced them to the King. Anyway, this man transferred from Bishop Odo's household to the royal chaplaincy bringing with him not only rare skill sets but also 'inside' information.[16]

Then came a further blow, London, that centre of trade and financial milch-cow, suffered a disastrous fire in 1077. A dozen years after William had received the Crown fate was still conspiring against him. Well might he reflect on, yet perhaps feel justified by:

Those whom the Lord loveth, the Lord chasteneth ...
But if ye be without chastisement, whereof all are partakers,
then are ye bastards and not sons.

(Hebrews 12: 6 and 8)

Chapter 6

Husbanding Resources

Charged with the responsibility for building the King's new
fortresses the reluctantly worldly Archbishop Lanfranc now
seems to have had his mind concentrated, certainly acutely
focused, on finances. The King's burden had been partly transferred to
him. Money was the problem, cash with which to pay quarries, carriers,
ships, masons and the toiling mass of menials who mixed mortar, slaked
and burned lime, carried, hauled, felled timber, hewed wood and dug
on site. Yes, the Crown could offer food and it could requisition its own
timber and maybe stone from Crown estates but it needed wages as well
and in the King's absence the burden fell heavily on his locum tenens.
The actual castle architect is unknown, but it was the same man for each
site for the one was the plan-image of the other, except that Colchester
was a monster twice the ground plan of London.

What had happened to the river of silver that was the geld, why at each
geld was less received? Well, the archbishopric's own muniments would
reveal a local or subordinate problem in Lanfranc's own holdings and
sub-tenancies, perhaps leading him to a well-founded suspicion that the
problem was more widespread. The problem seems to have been two-
fold. Returns were diminishing, geld-on-geld, but (in addition) estates
which had once been there were no longer to be found and so could not
be taxed. Had the earth swallowed them up? Maybe it was at this point
(if not before) that the Archbishop discovered an able ally, a subordinate
in Bishop Odo's own household, an administrative genius who was
afterwards transferred to the royal curia? Anyway, it seems that someone
understood what was happening to taxes and so light began to dawn
around the geld, and this led on to other matters. Was it just a coincidence
that the Archbishop suddenly became aware of the deficiencies in his own
'empire', his own estates, as recorded in his (English) muniments?

An event which has long puzzled historians is the so-called 'trial on
Penenden Heath', near Maidstone, *c.* 1076. This was an inquiry, one

authorised by the King, into a dispute over estates between Bishop Odo and Archbishop Lanfranc and to which many important landholders came as witnesses. We know that they included an appearance in court by the acknowledged oldest authority on English law, Æthelric II, former Bishop of Selsey, a cleric so decayed with age that he had to be delivered to the court in a carriage. I think this not only tells us that we are dealing with property law but also that 'Norman' justice was not arbitrary but something that respected English practice. Clearly the court was seeking precedents. Though Bishop Odo constructed his own legal defence, he was certainly not without friends, for among the witnesses he called were sub-tenants and comrades of his, such as Richard de Tonbridge, Hamo Vicecomes (Sheriff of Kent) and Hugh de Montfort. Yet it seems that overall the English witnesses and records ultimately prevailed for, after three days of debate, a number of estates were restored to the archbishopric – in spite of this apparent attempt at intimidation and malversation by Odo. It is also significant, to my mind, that the ultimate authority in court rested with Lanfranc and no appeal was permitted, by order of the King. With Lanfranc as plaintiff and judge Odo's power seems to have been on the wane and so, just maybe, he had also (already) been detected defrauding the Crown and perhaps he had already been reported to King William.

If this was the case it probably concerned the organisation of his estates but it might just have thrown up other evidence in the minds of some of the senior Crown administrators? If so, they remained discrete and we have no immediately contemporary denunciation, but then who among the chroniclers would or could have known the secrets of the government? Maybe in the mind of the erring bishop his 'great work' of rebuilding Bayeux Cathedral justified all his actions and especially his financial ones – it was re-dedicated in 1077 – though it seems more likely that his personal dedication to this project proceeded from a personal conviction that he would thereby gain eternal salvation. Either the end justified the means, or such means would help alleviate his end. Maybe a grateful Lord would smile upon the bishop's endeavours?

Yet though the good bishop had had to relinquish some of his estates by the final secular judgement awarded on Penenden Heath, he was, to say the least, tardy in his compliance and he was also 'frying other fish', as was Richard de Tonbridge.[1] Odo and his friends were up to no good.

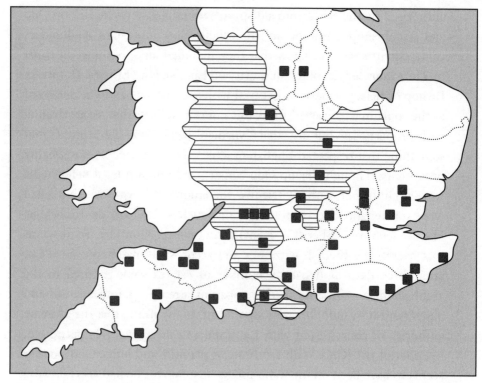

Map 6: 'Burghs' and 'castles'.

When such powerful magnates set about amassing money they usually had treacherous intentions and these men were certainly making money. To understand what they were doing, albeit in common with many others yet (in this case) with particular financial skill, we also need to understand something of the unique English skill in surveying and also the astonishing numeracy that this skill now discloses.

Alone in Europe the English had anciently devised a system of surveying, one which involved its own comprehensive units. They were alone in this, indeed unique, for such skill in surveying has not yet been found outside England. The key unit was the 'hide', an assessment of gross area most often applied to land (though it could be extended to terraqueous appurtenances as at Axholme and in the Fens) and by which the thirty-four shires comprising England had long ago been recorded in the Tribal Hidage, each former kingdom or folk-territory being at that time surveyed and then aggregated together.[2] This gave an initial total of

Map 6: 'Burghs' and 'Castles'
Map 6 shows the Burghal Hidage forts and some other later defences of pre-Conquest England superimposed on the (shaded) area covered by the 'County Hidage' of *c.* 1010. Defensive strongpoints were not unknown before 1066 and seem originally to have been commissioned to defend southern England (outside the Danelaw) from attacks by sea or river forces. The 'County Hidage' area fronting the Danelaw districts was therefore, formerly, only sparsely defended but (as we have seen) by *c.* 1080 had been given much better defences against northern incursions.

18.52 million acres for an area we would today measure at 18.75 million acres (all things being equal) or 98.773 per cent coincidence, then a final total for the whole of 24 million acres was obtained over an area which today is reckoned at 23.396 million acres or 97.483 per cent coincidence.[3] With such a statistical foundation it was then possible to put a numerical value on a man's status, so that a man who held 5 hides (1,200 acres) was locally important and, what is more, his liability for both military service and for supplies (food rent) could be assessed in hide–multiples (large acreages).[4] So in the Burghal Hidage, a document of a rather later date than the Tribal Hidage, we find assessments in hides related to the size and garrisoning of fortresses.[5] These enable us today to calculate the garrisons required and the nominal perimeters of individual burghs as well as the acres of nominal area encompassed by each defence work, some of which were large enough to be townships and others obviously no more than tiny 'castles'.

When Æthelred hit upon the idea of paying a (specie) ransom to the Viking raiders of 991 – which subsequently became known as 'danegeld' because it did not stop at one ransom – it was equitably levied on those in the money economy (viz. the rich) according to their status in landholdings, or (traditional expression) hides: raising so much on each hide in order to pay the raiders to go away. In areas where the hide had been supplanted by Danelaw units, or carucates, the unit of assessment was different but the principle remained the same. Of course, the Vikings then came back, again and again until the drain on specie finally made it impossible for the English to purchase mercenary allies to assist them in their defence. No other kingdom in Europe had such a specie-only land tax and so, as an apparently miraculous source of specie (silver), it accentuated the wealth of England in foreign eyes, encouraging the ambitions and avarice of foreign rulers and lords, even men such as Duke William of Normandy.

But, of course, these foreigners (and probably many Englishmen) had no idea how this system worked for it was a unique tax, and it was founded on a unique and traditional unit whose very noun was a mystery to those outside England, including generations of historians. All that outsiders knew was that England had a river of silver which a victor could tap on demand. The reality had by now, by 1076 (it seems), come home to William but it would have been foolish of him to reveal the secret to his magnates. His source of information must have been within the English administration he had inherited and, intelligence being power, it was best that no one else knew of his vulnerability except (perhaps) his loyal archbishop. And in the background was a royal chaplain or camerarius, a genius with a comprehensive grasp of all things concerned with the land.

From his English Coronation Oath onwards we see that King William had always had respect for English law and even English customs so a degree of co-operation between the 'invaders' and the English inhabitants is to be expected after 1066. This helps us to explain how, when no one outside England understood the 'hide', or even the name, the new (foreign) landholders still found stewards who could manipulate assessments of geld-liability – and so we can say that they simply retained these English officials. We have already discovered that some collaborators helped facilitate the invasion of 1066 so it is not unlikely that estate stewards (now with new masters and with no deep loyalties to obstruct their thinking through any as yet unknown concepts of nationality) would serve their new lords just as diligently as they had the old.[6] Even before the Conquest there had been a steady erosion of honest tax returns and the process simply continued afterwards. Why not, there was no mechanism for checking, no concept of audit. The County Hidage of *c.* 1010 tells us quite plainly that tax evasion had already progressed after only twenty years of the geld.[7] Now, after a further fifty years and a Danish monarchy, not to mention a Breton King and his court, it had become well advanced in many shires and on many estates for if these 'incomers' cheated, then why not the residents, the English, also? With no possibility of detection morality rapidly declined.

For the new 'Norman' landholders, who had no previous experience of such specific and efficient tax collection, the situation by the early 1070s must have been infuriating. Years of fighting had been their lot when they should have been enjoying the fruits of their labours and with little prospect of a cessation. Of course they were delighted when their English stewards suggested that there were ways of reducing this tax liability which had been credited to them along with the estates they had inherited.

From the tax payer's viewpoint there were five ways of reducing geld liability, if you knew them. Significantly the very rich and powerful were the worst offenders, by which (I think) we may gauge that they employed stewards or 'accountants' to manage their finances for we see no evidence of their own numeracy, much less any grasp of the English language, or units, or of agriculture. First of all one could simply massage the hidage assessment downwards, incrementally, so as (hopefully) not to be noticed, for no one was auditing the figures (there seems to have been no concept of auditing as yet) and, of course, estates do fluctuate over the years due to many factors. More imaginatively, though it really required some collective or group action over a broad area, one could alter the assessment unit from the English 'hide' to the Danish (Breton, or Norman) 'carucate', to halve the liability, for when Alfred and Guthrum had divided the nation into England (Wessex) and the Danelaw the new Danish settlers (who had no notion of the hide, nor records of areal surveys) had used the carucate (a unit of annual ploughing and one equivalent to half the value of the hide) as the measure of the land which they actually tilled. This conveniently ignored the untilled land, so carucages were invariably smaller than hidages and this would have impacted on geld collection from its outset.

Then again, any landholder actually divided his tilled (arable) land into what his tenants ploughed and tilled for him (demesne, 'in dominio') and what they (his tenants)[8] had for their own sustenance, that is into what he lived on directly and what he let out in order to receive such services. This made it but a short step to declaring as the carucage only the amount in dominio, for the rest 'belonged' one could argue (though not actually relinquishing dominium or proprietas of course!) to the peasants, so why should a lord pay for that? From the Crown's point of view this was not acceptable, for subsistence peasants were not in the money economy and had no specie, but as no one was checking the figures anyway, how could the Crown know? Observance of the law invariably rests on the ability to detect its disregard and so enforce it.

Of course, if one was fortunate enough to discover minerals, or to have industries, on one's estate, the commutation to cash payments immediately removed that 'diversification' (in modern terms) from tillage and also removed land use to the money economy, and the geld was not designed to assess added value, what we would call legal 'interest', only the legal 'realty', the physical asset. Treasure has always belonged to the Crown, if it hears about it, and that could be another bonus. All of this was, of course, dangerous. To refuse a royal command was 'lese-majeste' (as later defined), so equal to treason; one obligation on any vavassour was to support their lord in need: tax evasion was (at this time) therefore treason. Sometimes, when particularly sensitive to the wish to evade taxes or maybe when particularly greedy and dishonest on their lord's behalf, estate stewards resorted to admixtures of English and Danelaw units to disguise blatant shrinkage of geld returns, presumably confident that there was no way of checking their presented figures (of realty) against any reality? Perhaps newly appointed Norman stewards also became confused by the unfamiliar units and they (of course) lacked ability? We cannot exclude the honest mistake. Within a few years they were all to be sadly disabused by the Domesday Surveys for what I have christened 'scribal apothegms' were the means of secretly reporting detections of these clever evasions in a sort of code. This will be dealt with later. For the present I am merely illustrating contemporary tax evasions, we can examine their futility in the face of 'exchequer' methodology in due course. Here I am dealing with the pre-1086 situation when all men thought themselves secure in the knowledge that no one was checking the realty or the realities.

It is impossible to speak of the Exchequer, at this date, for we have no certain reference to it as a distinct government department and the English equivalent seems to have been the 'hordere' or 'gerefa' located at Winchester. [9] Indeed Winchester seems to have been the location of that repository of older documentation which we would now call 'records', or the 'national archive', thus the nub and hub of the geld administration.[10] This was the administrative branch of the executive known as the Curia Regis, the King's Council of noble advisors, the real workers behind the Royal Council of nobles. King William made significant alterations to the Old Palace here building his new '*palacium cum aula sua*' early in his reign either on the site of the 'officine' of the New Minster , which had been destroyed by fire in 1065, or on its cemetery.[11] This seems to have effectively doubled the area of the palace at Winchester so that in the opinion of Gerald of Wales it was equal to the Palace of Westminster in both size and in quality.[12] Here at Winchester we later learn of the treasury being relocated in the castle, which may have saved Domesday Book in the following century when the Old Palace was burned down and, one suspects, many older records were tragically lost.[13]

Nevertheless, we can see in the two separate records made in Domesday Book, that is the state of tax returns in 1066 and their newly deponed (witnessed) equivalents in 1086, that whatever the tax losses to the Crown had been before the Conquest, they increased considerably afterwards, either through the ignorance of landholding lords or through their deliberate treachery in altering their liabilities and disguising their assets. Not at all a 'band of brothers' or a united coterie! For Lanfranc, now charged with the Lord King's building programme, the situation was infuriating for the royal demands for money, with which to conduct campaigns in France, would have simultaneously continued to proceed from the King. With the detection of some of Bishop Odo's peccadilloes *c.* 1076 I suspect, therefore, that there came a wider insight and further suspicions grew in Lanfranc's mind and so, from there, percolated into the administrative machine even if, as yet, the loyal Lanfranc had not dared advance his misgivings to King William. There was also someone, as I have said, close to Odo who had now joined the King's servants, maybe at Lanfranc's invitation, someone (it seems) who knew more about tax and administration than anyone else in the kingdom.

After all this discussion of the wealth of England and its temptations for the ambitious it is perhaps time to make a comprehensive review of the sources of such wealth. Although historians have readily accepted both the existence (and maintenance) of a high–purity English coinage and the value of the geld/danegeld tax, they have consistently failed to explain the mechanisms by which such standards could be created. Many seem to assume that in 1066 (and before) money grew on trees. Sadly it never has, so I have tried to make a realistic appraisal of the development and generation of national wealth during the period that separated Britannia from Anglia, from the Migration period to the eve of the Norman Conquest of England. It is time we understood just how England became fiscally pre-eminent in Europe and why this became so important in the country's future development, especially in the evolution of a single-minded and enforceable command structure by which to secure polity. The evidence has long been overlooked as well as misinterpreted yet we cannot really comprehend her wealth or her ability to sustain so many attacks, let alone the King's freedom to campaign simultaneously at home and in defence of his French territories, unless we have a firm grasp of the economic picture, that grasp which King William seems to have acquired by the late 1070s. This analysis can be found in the supplementary chapter at the end of this book if the reader wishes to consult it now or later.

As for the physical events of the reign of King William, King Malcolm of Scotland attacked Northumbria once again, ravaging up to the Tyne, killing, burning and slaving, while King William was engaged in Normandy fighting an alliance made by his son Robert with Count Robert of Flanders in 1079. The 1080s were about to usher in the crisis of his reign and he now had to contend with that further curse of the early Medieval king, the impatient and ambitious offspring. Of course, Robert on his own was merely a nuisance, but as the puppet of more powerful enemies who could make alliance with other kingdoms as well as funding attacks on Normandy (and possible invasions of England) he was a significant pawn. Chivalry and even true fealty were not to be found among the French and Norman magnates just as sons could not be loyal to their fathers and the Church looked to its own local and hierarchical interests. The concern of the Papacy was to increase its power and wealth, the concern of each abbot or bishop was to increase the wealth of their convents and estates. Fortunately the stability of William's reign and kingdom fell among the former group of Archbishop Lanfranc's interests for his fealty to the King was his guarantee of power and he seems to have become the King's right hand after the thwarted 'bridal' at Newmarket. He was now to play an important part in stabilising the kingdom.

Now Bishop Walcher of Durham was allowed to purchase the troublesome earldom of Northumbria and, presumably, he thought he could establish relationships with local magnates of the house of Bamburgh for he took one of them named Ligulf as his close advisor. Obviously in making this purchase he intended to recover his outlay, so he must have thought that in raising the King's geld he could provide simultaneously for his own needs. This simplistic and ignorant fantasy is one we have seen played out so often in Robin Hood dramas and it obviously enjoys some antiquity. It seems that Bishop Walcher was both ignorant of the nature of this tax and greedy, for such an imposition was hardly possible. According to the chronicler Symeon of Durham, who greatly admired his Bishop (which was circumspect), there was also a problem in controlling the Bishop's milites and perhaps in this wild frontier region these soldiers also believed that they could do as they pleased, or even subdue the brigand elements infesting this landscape through a harsh repression of local populations. Meanwhile over the border in Scotland King Malcolm Canmore had eliminated his own chief (internal) rival and so could now take stock of the situation. William was abroad and fighting his son in France and in his place, on the borders, there was a weak bishop who could not (or would not) control his troops. This was an opportunity too good to miss, for who knew whether King William would ever return to England. He decided to 'test the waters'. In the event he was right, Bishop Walcher provided no resistance as the Scots swept south into England.

Chapter 7

Growing Suspicions

Of the late 1070s and the opening of the 1080s we really know very little and have to piece the evidence together. The chroniclers who sought to flatter King William and enlarge his achievements, even those religious who wished to deplore the (aspecific) wickedness of the Age and the King's *cupiditas*, have left us little meat by which to make a meal. What are we to make of this lacuna? Historians are circumspectly quiet, maybe (they suggest) all the records of 'nationalist resistance' have been lost? If so, why are records before and after apparently so replete with information? Could it be that their own ignorance of grand strategy has left them guessing, searching instead for some long lost fantasy? The 1080s actually became a decade of the utmost importance in English (our modern) history so this silence possibly represents the calm before the storm, or is this the catastasis of our drama? What was happening?

Could it be that this apparent quietude represents not English quiescence and acquiescence to cruel fate so much as the leavening of a society that was learning to live with itself, a new self, settled to a 'new order'? After all, changes of lords, local apprehensions and tragedies, were nothing new to the general peasantry: national events and even taxes only really concern nationally important figures, the rest of the population just have to endure whatever happens from year to year. 'The wheel turns and is forever still', as Elliott put it. The pattern of rural life, generally and for most, continued, but behind the scenes, under the existing polity, displacements were occurring, shocks and murmurs at which we can only guess, but which were soon to have seismic effect. Historians have perhaps noticed the ripples on the surface but they have never realised their significance because they were obsessed with 'nationalism'. Let us rather think of a kingdom attempting to survive, attempting to break free from this endless cycle of invasion and plundering. We need to take stock before we can refer to Bishop Walcher and the Scottish invasion.

The accepted interpretation of this period revolves around the supposed superhuman abilities of the conquerors and their agreed, unified approach to the 'English resistance' movement. The Norman nobility, it is argued, acted in concert out of collective interest, though of course we have no record of such alliance and purpose, only speculations by historians. There was no such harmony and fraternity in France or in Normandy and we can hardly believe that men such as William's son Robert behaved in one way in England and another when in France! Well, English administrative functions, we have been told, were now deliberately modified in order to pre-empt and disadvantage any residual hostility to the 'new order', though there is no evidence to support these proposals, none has ever been produced. All that we can see are a number of logical and useful administrative changes, developments fit for purpose.

It is true that the occurrence of 'earls' diminished and instead shrieval powers were enlarged while the Witan was replaced with a Royal Curia of cronies. Why should this be sinister? Even English (Old English), we are told, was 'forbidden' in documents and replaced with (good Norman) Latin. If this was nationalism then why use Latin? David Douglas set it all out years ago with wonderful clarity, except that it was all constructed without evidence and, in fact, in total ignorance of the one catalytic source which would, which could, have put such events into a proper perspective.[1] We can concede that all these postulations contained factual kernels but, with historians blissfully unaware of the witness eventually to be provided by Domesday Book, these kernels were elaborated by them to represent a paradigm-fruit which would suit the acknowledged doctrine of brutal conquest, military and moral superiority and so (in fact) the justification of the English class system which had by the nineteenth century survived down the centuries: the descendants of this 'master race' were still the best people to run a modern state, even in the twentieth century!

As indeed Douglas remarked, the Curia Regis of magnates was superficially very similar to the traditional English Witan.[2] Neither resembled a modern parliament, so at first the Norman ducal assembly was assimilated into the English tradition, but after *c.* 1070 English names disappear and it becomes a strictly royal summoning of non-English nobility. Not enough thought has been given as to why this should have happened, it was quite logical when we consider that the principal landholders either were or had become Norman-French. By 1085 we do learn that the King was consulting three 'courts': his court (Curia Regis), the synodial court (Synod) and his Witan. So the ancient Witan had not actually disappeared, it is just that its records are rare. Moreover in private he had his bureaucracy in a minor curia, we might say an administrative curia regis, and it seems certain that these clerks and 'chaplains' included English administrators who understood the historic records. Looking at the outcome of this joint consultation in the light of our new discoveries in Domesday Book now makes us suspicious of any earlier changes. Is it not possible that during the 1070s the King, and any who were truly loyal servants of his, were looking to separate dissident political interests not among the English but among the new French and Norman lords, even perhaps encouraging their insularity and arrogance and so playing the various interests and secret factions against one another? It was one way of assessing the loyalty of the rich and powerful.

Why should Norman magnates care, for the first time in French history, what their conquered vassals thought, or even their weaker social equals, why should the widely separated secular and religious spheres care what each other thought? These spheres were not a united 'Norman' or 'French' nation-state. If there was any group identity it was the separation of secular and religious spheres and interests, sometimes of temporary factions, but mostly each lord was out for himself. Maybe instead of promoting Norman-French 'interests', in the interests of governance and polity, it was the King himself who cared about stability as well as personal safety? How else was he to separate and clarify so many conflicting interests and personal ambitions among his new lords, men who had brought their 'French' attitudes, ambitions and disregard for fealty with them to England?

The former proliferation of English-style earls and ealdormen, often reflecting revenue rather than territorial entities, began to diminish (in fact) as earldoms (now officially seen as French-style Comital units) were concentrated to form special frontier (that is territorial) jurisdictions – in the troublesome north and over against alien Wales.[3] It would have been dangerous to also encourage such Comital units in the heartlands of England, as Kent was soon to prove and, again, as a civil war was to emphasise in the next century. That is why these new landholders were not to be allowed to become counts with co-terminal estates. Instead the Franco-Norman model was adapted to reflect English practice and requirements. On the other hand sheriffs (now officially addressed as 'vicecomes', presumably for the benefit of 'Frenchmen' ignorant of the English language or even the English official) increased their powers: after all, the machinery of geld collection had to be maintained, so now it devolved onto these officials. So we see in 1076 or 1077 a Commission enquiring into the conduct of sheriffs which involved Lanfranc, Robert Count d'Eu and Richard fitz Gilbert.[4] The King was quite sensibly also making sure of their loyalties and probity. None of these measures need be represented as repressive, they were instead a strengthening of English administrative and defensive functions which could otherwise have become confused in yet another ethnic and linguistic palimpsest, a mess which could then be exploited by malignant magnates.

As the decade following the Conquest drew on, so we see the English administrative machinery, at first adopted by the new King in its entirety, gradually altered, adapted to accommodate new administrators in the new regime. Thus, after *c.* 1070, writs in the vernacular (Old English), otherwise unintelligible (of course) to the newcomers, were replaced not by Norman-French (as might be expected of 'nationalists') but by the Latin intelligible to all parties. Such a change no doubt also facilitated the movement of Norman servants into the royal household? If the old and the new servants were to work together they needed a common language for Norman officials were not competent to run the sophisticated English administration. King William had enough problems without prejudicing his finances and machinery of government. He needed to improve, not to destroy, the existing machinery of government if he was to survive.

This was itself most important for, 'the King's household officials (or curia) directed the royal administration in all its aspects'.[5] One could hardly expect a new dynasty to rely absolutely on the comprehension and diligence of an older, linguistically separate, administration which was no doubt set in its ways by familiarity with a previous social structure and court protocols. Incoming political parties still like to replace civil servants of the 'old order' if they can, in order to facilitate 'change', if only for its own sake. The royal household's clerks were <u>the</u> 'administration' serving that 'executive' now represented by the Curia Regis, so in both we should expect an influx of new men. The knowledge-base, however, remained essentially English: the distinctive English use of writs, as opposed to charters, and (most important of all) the records of landholdings and geld liabilities, together with the accounting machinery required by specie taxation, these all remained and were all English. This last, the accounting machinery, was not yet identified as the Exchequer, but some sort of exchequer (or 'hordere') had to exist within the royal household. Both the Exchequer and the Chancery, and then the courts of law, emerged from the Curia and its royal household (clerical) servants after 1087, before that they were within it, but the emerging process had, it seems, begun within a decade of 1066 as the old and new orders fused together in matters of administration.

Now that we understand the nature of King William's administrative machine, its English and linguistic shift (it had already coped remarkably well with Cnut's reign), we are, I think, in a better position to understand an event which triggered that seismic shift in administration which marks the final years of King William's reign. That event, never adequately explained in the past, was the arrest of Bishop Odo of Bayeux, Earl of Kent by the King himself, followed by the Bishop's incarceration which his brother, the King, said was to be without remission! Such an astonishing change in political structure and fortunes, with its repercussions for polity, did not come, could not have come, from nowhere and out of thin air. Whatever occasioned the King's fury must have been discovered some time before and have taken time to uncover, taken someone the utmost care and circumspection in preparation of the evidence in order to place it before the King. Whoever it was denounced Odo, he had to be certain of his facts. I believe that the new melange of English administration and Norman administrators disclosed material which led this innermost cadre of the Curia's servants to delve deeper into ancient English records at Winchester. Who was behind it, well that is impossible to say but the moral force to drive an established conviction does suggest the implacable will of Archbishop Lanfranc. My guess is that the evidence was first passed to him and that he then actively encouraged investigations. I also think that it probably all began on, or just after, the Penenden Heath 'trial'.

The remains of the giant Keep of Colchester Castle which was completed after the Conqueror had died. Originally it was surrounded by an extensive earth-and-timber bailey. (*Courtesy of David Merrett*)

The East face of Colchester Keep showing the battlements of the half-built walls in 1084, a unique survival. (*Author's Collection*)

Greensted-juxta-Ongar Church showing the split-oak stave walls dendro-dated to circa 1060. This claims to be the oldest timber building in Europe. (*Public Domain*)

Ely Cathedral from the south. Even in 1070 this landmark, perched on a prominent island, could be seen for miles across the Fens. (*Public Domain*)

The magnificent rebuild of Peterborough Cathedral which followed its sacking by Hereward in 1070. (*Courtesy of Michael D. Beckwith*)

Peveril Castle today, perched on High Peak and dominating the country all around. King William's castle here guarded the lead-mining area of North Derbyshire which was probably the richest source of mined silver for his currency and revenues. (*Courtesy of Steven Newton*)

Chepstow Castle from the River Wye: just right of centre is the massive "Great Tower", an audience or presence-chamber built for King William c.1081 in order to impress the Welsh princes. (*Courtesy of Stewart Black*)

The White-Tower, the Keep at the heart of the Tower of London. Once again this was commenced by King William I and completed by his son "Rufus". (*Courtesy of Wei-Te Wong*)

Clifford's Tower at York, a later keep sitting on an impressive Norman motte. (*Courtesy of Michael Kooiman*)

King Edward in his Palace at Winchester, the opening scene of the Bayeux Tapestry. (*Public Domain*)

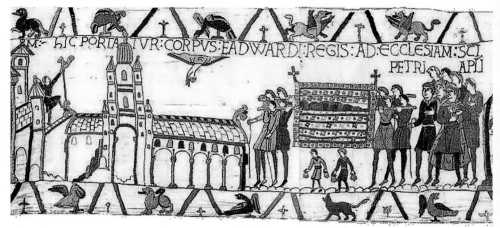

The funeral of King Edward at his newly built Westminster Abbey, January 1066. (*Public Domain*)

The modern town of Battle showing the Abbey and the traditional battle-site in the foreground. To the north rises the higher and steeper Caldbec Hill and Mountjoy where the actual battle was probably fought. (*Historic Military Press*)

The modern town of Battle from the opposite direction. Though later developments have obscured much of the landscape it is still evident that the Weald began just beyond Caldbec Hill. (*Historic Military Press*)

In the lower margin of this scene from the Bayeux Tapestry we can see the use of horse power in agriculture prior to the Norman Conquest, another apparently unique English development. This Tapestry was made in England and that is how we know it is an English scene. (*Public Domain*)

A William I penny. (*John Grehan Collection*)

A reconstruction of an earth-and-timber, motte–castle. Many of the early Norman castles were of this type which can be seen on the Bayeux Tapestry. (*Author's Collection*)

'*Radix maleorum est cupiditas*'* and not even his admirers would deny that Bishop Odo was excessively greedy for wealth.[6] With any medieval magnate such accumulation of money and power always indicated treachery, it was the accumulation of a 'war chest'. In 1080 King William finally made his peace with his ungrateful child Robert, granting him Normandy (after his death) and then he returned to England. Here he discovered that the Scottish King Malcolm had grown bold and raided Northumbria and that (perhaps) two months before his return the Bishop of Durham had been murdered when he sought to intervene and mediate in a deadly blood feud between two of his English chaplains and his local advisor Ligulf. Though Bishop Walcher of Durham had next shut himself up in his castle, he then made the mistake of agreeing to meet the late Ligulf's relatives, provided he was allowed to take a strong escort. It was to no avail, the escort were all butchered and summary justice wreaked on the Bishop and his chaplains.

The resulting chaos quickly assumed the appearance of a rebellion and so William now despatched brother Odo to pacify Northumbria in the summer of 1080. This the Bishop did by giving open rein to his lust for loot and bloodshed, showing (it seems) no regard for justice: in the event he seems to have virtually annihilated the Northumbrian nobility. It may even be that some of the damage traditionally attributed to 1068–70 (using the entries in Domesday Book) was actually perpetrated in 1080. Meanwhile King William was occupied in south Wales creating a show of force in order to overawe and pacify two feuding Welsh kings in the borderlands. This was far from a pointless parade or mere show, it had to impress and overawe. He now knew from experience that a campaign on one border only encouraged another border to erupt, so he dealt with both borders simultaneously. 'Uneasy lies the head ...'. Perhaps it was while on this progress that he ordered the great stone 'presence chamber' at Chepstow, as insurance for the future? Perhaps it implied some concessions as well as demonstrating Anglo-Norman power and majesty? Meanwhile William seems to have made a point to King Malcolm by sending his son Robert north of the border with another expedition, apparently little more than a

---

* 'The root of (all) evil is the love of money'.

show of force as no battle seems to have been fought. Perhaps, just perhaps, the King was testing his suspected dissidents by providing opportunities for treachery while holding another army in reserve, under his own command. Yet all these expeditions together required a vast expenditure of both men and money, greater manpower than the Normans alone ever possessed. After all, the campaign of 1068–70 must have resulted in losses of 30–40 per cent, though the Vikings must have lost more men than this. Such losses are not easily replaced.

From Chepstow the King next made progress to Winchester where he 'wore his crown' at Whitsun. Here, beside a cathedral so large it rivalled anything outside Rome, he remodelled the accommodation for those nascent offices destined to eventually become the Exchequer and the Chancery in due time, and he also created a new palace second to no other in England. We know little else of this year, 1081, but we can perhaps surmise that it was while these new building plans were being realised that, somehow, serious seeds of doubt and mistrust concerning brother Odo were growing. Perhaps his brother's excesses in the North gave the King cause to rebuke him for such wanton destruction of assets and reduction of the tax base? We can say that by now the effects of 1068–70 must have become all too apparent without Odo's contribution, even though no chronicler gives us any hint. After all, the running of the machinery of state was a mystery to all outside the royal curia and would remain so until civil war in the next century had made it necessary to set down a private memorandum for another monarch. Even then it was only for his royal eyes and not for scrutiny by others.[7] I refer, of course, to the 'Dialogus de Scaccario' one-hundred years into the future. King William's chroniclers really had no idea what he was doing, or why he did it, and no one was going to explain such matters to them, least of all the King.

The English peasantry did not breed like rabbits or like swine and so the repeated massacres and eliminations of whole districts enthusiastically proposed by some historians would have left whole swathes of countryside devoid of tillers of the soil and of food, therefore unable to provide food or fuel for manors, or money (or men) to support milites, which means there would have been no revenues or markets, no taxes, no horses, no new weapons or armours and no soldiers, and this even before we come to the vastly ambitious programme of 'castles' with supporting castellries and their necessary building and delving work. Yet King William now embarked on an ambitious castle-building programme all along the Northumbrian coast and, in the west, from Carlisle to Sheffield and the Peak, all established as fees and castellries under lords with formidable delegated powers. Some of these defences may have been commenced in the 1070s but most seem to have been begun circa 1080 so that by the crisis (to come) of 1084–5 all the passes leading south (down to a line between the Mersey and the Humber) were impeded by garrisons, 'dragon's teeth' to any invader from the north.[8] And remember, each of these garrisons required local produce from an active and local peasantry, for these Anglo-Norman garrisons had no 'service corps' on which to call for regular supplies.

We now have sufficient evidence to say that William was a clever strategist who believed in careful preparation and step-by-step planning, keeping his cards close to his chest, so his absence from England in early 1082 may have been deliberate. Bishop Odo's northern expedition may also have been part of his plan for it gave Odo the opportunity to contact other lords, especially in the northern Marches of Wales where one could expect treachery. Again it is speculation, but if the King already had suspicions he would, no doubt, have had secret reports made on his brother's activities in 1080–1. So in 1082 we find a large gathering of 'knights' and nobles, including Earl Hugh ('the Fat') of Chester, on the Isle of Wight, the traditional rendezvous for expeditions to France, with Bishop Odo at their head.

Some historians have claimed that he next intended to march across Europe and depose the Pope, a present incumbent of that office who was not particularly favoured by either William or Lanfranc, or perhaps Odo was going on Crusade?[9] Neither enterprise sounds likely to have been Earl Hugh's preference and so, and in the light of what followed, I favour the theory that Odo intended to make a play for the throne of England and was gathering an army of his own on Wight in order to take advantage of the favourable winds and currents, which would take him round to the Thames (and even perhaps beyond) in the King's absence. Anyway, in 1082 King William returned to England to 'discover' this interesting foregathering for war, made in his absence and certainly without his authorisation. Had Lanfranc developed an intelligence network and so sent King William a timely warning? There do seem to be grounds for such a suspicion.

Perhaps Odo had acted prematurely for there seems to have been a now familiar plan of conspiracy developing, one involving Norman magnates and also foreign powers. As far as we can tell William returned late in 1082 and then ordered the arrest of his brother. No one (we are told) dared to attempt this so William personally (so we are told) restrained him. Odo then pleaded benefit of clergy, only the Pope could arrest a bishop, to which the King retorted that he did not arrest the bishop, but an earl![10] And this seems a convincing anecdote if, as some sources say, William then actually charged him with offences against his secular and English subjects. Anyway, Odo was bundled off to the impregnable Tower of Rouen together with orders that he should never be released. Earl Hugh seems to have laid low but King Cnut (IV) of Denmark was plotting with Count Robert of Flanders and also assembling an enormous fleet (does this now sound familiar?) and probably in 1083 William's son Robert 'Curthose' was again planning insurrection, against his father, being now safely over the water. Just where and when (we can now ask) had Odo planned to move with his expeditionary force during 1083? If it was onto London and East Anglia he might have hoped to join up with Cnut landing from the Wash? Of course, no one tells us this because no one knew, they did not even know why the King had imprisoned his brother.

Now I will once again depart from anything speculated in the accepted history books and discuss my own conclusions, which are based on my own research derived from the hard evidence contained within Domesday Book, so presenting an holistic picture of military success not unlike more modern strategic solutions.[11] As a result of analysing this source I have concluded that the Earl of Kent (Bishop) Odo's arrest was the covering movement (in tactical terms) for the King's most able and committed administrators to close in on the Earldom of Kent's finances and properties. The first folio and survey in Domesday Book (as we now call it and conceive it to be) was Kent and its survey's structure is remarkably different from all those that followed, ostensibly in 1086. I therefore surmise that in 1082 what we might call the exchequer clerks and their 'mandarin' had presented a plausible theory to the King and that in 1083 they were consequently given free rein to implement a working model (or paradigm) on this escheat, for fiscal summaries of escheats to the Crown were nothing new. What betrays this as the first of the 'Domesday' folios (apart from its position at the head of the final collation of folios) is the inchoate nature of the audit paradigm employed. The clerks involved 'on the ground' were obviously directed to follow a broadly conceived model, which they dutifully did, but what it then divulged in its lacunae allowed a more specific and closely directed paradigm of enquiry to evolve, one to be followed in 1086: in fact what is certainly the very first evidence we have of a government audit. Indeed in both the first and second folios of Domesday Book, in Kent and in Sussex, we see many more gaps and evasions than in subsequent surveys; after them the questioning is tighter and stricter, less open to evasions and there are safeguards to prevent intimidation of witnesses.

It is probable that the new Norman under tenants of Odo (and Odo himself) were only following established practice when they altered their geld assessments, but the pressure which Earl Odo put on everyone for money certainly seems to have been formidable and an encouragement to dishonesty. In 1066 general valuations of estates seem to have been low, yet they had usually increased dramatically by 1086 (or, as we might venture, by 1083) and often, it seems, valuations were now being demanded as cash from estates 'at ferme', that is at rent. Emphasis was certainly placed on arable land, on tillage and not on overall area, but even then the established (or old) arable values recorded bore no relation to the ploughs now (in Kent in 1083) actually at work while in many places no total was entered, that is no total was admitted at all for the established 'plough lands', so that it was impossible to check the old and the new against one another for tax purposes. The areal unit used in Kent was (uniquely) the 'sulung' or 'solin', not the 'hide' but it was identical with the hide at 240 acres and had obviously once been employed in the same way to encompass all land uses. Many of the actual returns of 1083 simply ignored the traditional (areal) sulungation and proffered ploughs, or plough lands (arable), instead! There were also at least seven different formulae for woodlands, just to fudge the statistics, as well as unquantified 'denes' (Wealden clearings) of no apparent value.

Well, unless the denes in the Weald were producing amazing amounts of sausages, ham and firewood, how could their tenants be in the money economy rather than subsistence, for the peasants in these enclosures were paying rents in cash! The answer is that these Wealden denes were industrial enterprises concerned with ferrous metallurgy, but Odo was careful to disguise them as wastelands.[12] Despite their alleged 'villein' status these were not ordinary 'peasants' but ironmasters. There was 'gold in them there denes'!

In (as we surmise) 1083 this 'pilot audit' used local juries, as became the standard instruction in 1086, but it seems that (as yet) there was no precaution to remove local landowners when evidence was called forward. This left the husbandmen (peasants) so empanelled in a fix, they durst not make outright and obvious testimony against their lord or lordling's stated figures, but neither did they dare to openly lie to the King's agents. Their solution to the predicament was often to testify that they did not know the name of their vill! The recording clerks settled for listing the several juries they had empanelled in such cases, as with Hugh de Montefort's holdings in Romney Marsh which were altogether attested by <u>four</u> juries <u>and</u> other men. What else could the clerks do to shake the evidence of terrified and suborned testators? The same plea suited some of the landholders as well. Hamo Vicecomes (Sheriff of Kent) had $10^5/_8$ plough lands in Wye Hundred, but he could not remember the name of the place! No doubt he knew its revenues well enough. The 'facts', we can say the truths, which now came tumbling out were sometimes fantastic and preposterous to our modern eyes, used as we are to statistics, but to the clerks collecting them they must have been a revelation. No doubt their 'mandarin', who was directing their working paradigm, was also genuinely pleased with their results. Now he also had evidence of suborned witnesses and hidden assets.

The pressure for money was unmistakeable and the Earl-Bishop's demands had a knock-on effect down to the grass roots in Kent. 'For this it defends itself' is a recurring formula meaning 'this is all the holder thinks he will pay': the clerks recording the evidence had the measure of their men, suave though their enrolled records were, all they had to do was record everything and then hand it in to their 'mandarin'. Of course, who was to know how much you ploughed and, remember, the Normans only knew the carucate, the plough land, and not the hide (areal unit), much less the sulung (areal unit), and these Norman landholders must have felt quite safe in their treachery.[13] The Anglo-Norman clerks knew it all however. So Hugh claimed that at Blackburn he only paid on 120 acres though his tenants were actually ploughing 1,080 acres! Questioned by the survey team about the veracity of his statement, he declared that most of his estate was 'outside the division of (his) lands', in other words his rents were all commuted, he received no services from the actual tenantry on his estates. This division or separation of dominium from proprietas, of interest from realty, was generally appealing because it was quite legitimate – the geld lay on the land. No doubt when hard-pressed by the Earl-Bishop for cash any estate-holding sub-tenant would be grateful for 'a word in the ear' of this type by their reeve or steward for who can serve two masters? Paying the bishop's rack rent was bad enough without the land tax on top and which was (to the tenants) the more immediate danger, the distant King or their 'good lord' the Bishop?

Richard de Tonbridge deponed liability for 2,880 acres of tillage though he had 4,860 acres tilled and owned at least 5,525 acres overall. Just to make doubly certain of the impression made he dropped his own annual valuation from £70 15s. 0d. to £60 15s. 0d. Finally he had to admit to another £45 12s. 5d. in specie rents and, oh yes, he remembered another 220 acres of woods and an unquantified dene of woodland 'somewhere' in the Weald. Nor did he stop here for in Surrey he halved some of the former geld returns on his holdings: Tonbridge itself fell from 40 to 10 hides, Chelsham from 20 to 4 and Tooting Bec from 11 to 1 hides of geld payment. Other estates, he claimed, had 'never paid geld' – so, perhaps he wondered, why should I be the first?

Hugh de Pont held of Odo at Hawley and 'answered' for 120 acres but he had 720 under the plough and another 22 acres at least. At Swanscombe he 'answered' for 2,400 acres but only listed 1,966 acres, which sounds a little more honest; at Hartley he 'answered' for 240 and had at least 620 acres. The rot was developing, but it was not yet comprehensive. William d'Arques held Folkestone of the Earl-Bishop as 9,600 acres ('now' only 9,360 , he claimed) but somehow with established tillage of 14,400 acres ('now' only ploughing 10,440 acres) and the post-invasion valuation of £40 (which might then have been accurate) had risen to £145 10s. 0d.! Perhaps he hoped in this statistical confusion to mislead the clerks? Well he did not, they set it all down, inchoate or not, it was a record which their 'mandarin' could sift. Why did he not declare its value prior to the Invasion, because that would have given the game away!

The Earl-Bishop himself held Wickhambreux for 960 acres but the clerks listed 1,320 acres of tillage, perhaps 554 acres of woodland, a 'park' (a large tract of land used for hunting), another 120 acres, salt houses and fisheries (as well as three houses in Canterbury), so something well in excess of the 1,994 acres actually listed and with an even higher cash value and very much more than the geld assessment of 960 acres. To cap it all he gave the valuation as £3 0s. 0d., 'then and now'! At Elham he presented 1,440 acres for the geld which were actually 2,880 acres of established tillage and at least another 28 acres, while the valuation had risen from £30 to £40 and it actually paid £50, presumably to Odo. At Bekesbourne he declared 480 acres tilled, with another 13 acres, a mill, a salt house and 44d. as well. It was valued 'then as now' at £12 but it actually paid £18. At Hoo the Earl-Bishop had 12,000 acres which he had reduced to a tax declaration of 7,920 acres: there were 6,000 acres of established arable or tillage and yet 6,060 acres were actually tilled, there was also a mill and fisheries. It had all been valued 'then as now' at £60 but 'whoever holds it' now paid £113! Nor are we surprised to learn of similar sleight of hand in other shires, or that he had 'attempted to usurp' the revenues of Southwark (in Surrey), that is cispontine London.

Of course for the putative 'exchequer' clerks this detective work was by no means cut and dried. No one, as far as we know, had attempted an audit of any kind before and even the scale of one shire (as yet only Kent) was formidable. These clerks of the Lord King's own chamber, his *camerarii* as I shall call them (after Tout's seminal study), had been ordered to find facts and undoubtedly they compared the witness of the many juries they had empanelled with the existing geld records, that is with the hidages (sulungations) they already had on record at Winchester.[14] They seem to have become a special department here, one competent to deal with all sorts of units. The great weakness of this first, or Kent, model however was the fact that juries had to testify/depone in the presence of their immediate overlords, which did nothing to negate intimidation.

After collecting and collating all this evidence, this 'scene of crimes' detail, the clerks had to make sense of it, though even this working (or exploratory) model which they had used in Kent, this incondite paradigm, was itself a stroke of genius. I have argued elsewhere, basing my identification on Professor Southern's work, that the mind behind it probably belonged to a man who had begun his career in Bishop Odo's service before transferring to become camerarius and chaplain to King William, one Ranulph Flambard.[15] Others have pointed to Archbishop Lanfranc as the initiating genius and I have no doubt he was involved, but the breadth of knowledge contained, even in this first crude, paradigm of an audit, betrays specialised, detailed 'inside knowledge' of ancient English records and methodology and so I rather place Flambard as the protégé discovered by Lanfranc.

This 'senior clerical officer', though really only a humble 'chaplain' cleric, was now to sit down in 1084 and 1085 to flesh out and construct his 'master plan', for such the final and perfected model became. This was a man who had made it his business to understand every English unit and he also seems to have comprehended a wide range of agricultural and social practises for his final audit model even allows us today to distinguish regional patterns among these fixed English units. He was certainly exceptional in this Age, maybe in any Age. Yet by 1085 he had also to draw very clear parameters for his subordinate clerks to follow for there were no such things as glossaries of terms, lexicons, enchiridions or dictionaries, not even a body of case law to assist legal precedent. His parameters had to be clear, yet also flexible enough to accommodate the nuances of everyday, unstructured usage of common nouns if the information to be gathered elsewhere was to be of any real use and capable of mathematical analysis and comparative methodology, one shire (or one hundred) with another. The logic had to be perfectly understood yet able to encompass such degrees of meaning as the several titles given to degrees of men: for example, there was no fixed definition of villeinage, we have nothing surviving in law and no such aid even today.

What was important was not a rigid classification but what men called themselves and what their masters understood by their social (often local social) degree. Without even a contemporary definition of freedom that could be rigidly applied the identification of fixed legal status was not only unimportant but impossible. The best description of a villein was not the universal application of a rigid contractual arrangement with given legal rights, duties and obligations, not even a property qualification, no, in truth he was a tenant farmer, for that was as far as any definition could stretch and be universally applicable, yet even then it might merge into the term 'socman'.[16] Finally this 'mandarin's' subordinates had to be fluent in three languages, writing Latin, speaking Norman-French to superiors and listening (intently) to deponents speaking in Old English (as well as reading Old English). The advantage here was that none of their supervising superiors (legati) were likely to understand Old English and very few of them Latin! Winchester does seem to strike a parallel with Bletchley Park in both the quality and the secrecy of its staff.

Meanwhile with the errant, treacherous Earl-Bishop safely 'banged up' in impregnable Rouen and William's humble servant wrestling with his own secret work (as closeted, no doubt, as later Bletchley Park, for no hint of the forward planning must be allowed to leak out to warn chief lords and tax payers), King William was free to mourn the passing of his Queen and lifelong companion and to prosecute his affairs and pacts along the borders of his French territories. However, in 1084 while (at least ostensibly) besieging the castle of St Suzanne he was called back to Normandy by very urgent intelligences. England was potentially facing her most serious military threat since 1066 and the King now desperately needed money, lots of it. This was the crisis of his reign, one it is impossible to overstate. The consequence of this crisis was to be the formation of a true systemisation of society through the enforcement of fealty and it was England that made this realisable through the stimulus of the unprecedented geld now called for by the King. Now we are approaching the climax of our story and (strange as it may seem) it has all to do with the Domesday Surveys, known to us now collectively as 'Domesday Book'. England's unique yet still misunderstood muniment was King William's great military resource and then became a bequest which provided the bedrock on which subsequent polity was securely founded, providing security in centuries to come.

Chapter 8

Crisis and Resolution

All historians agree that the danger facing King William in 1084–5 was extreme and that it came from King Cnut IV of Denmark, in alliance with King Olaf of Norway and Count Robert of Flanders, for Cnut was assembling an enormous invasion fleet. Now, as we know from William's own performance in 1066, such preparations took much more than a year and could not be kept secret, the demand for materials, ships and chandlery would have travelled all along the northern seaboard together with the inducements to mercenaries.[1] Nothing else in King William's reign so far had approached the gravity of this emergency, not even the Danish invasion of 1069–70, even though he had now succeeded in eliminating his half-brother Odo from this poisonous confederation. What historians have not had, up to now, is the full picture provided by the evidence of Domesday Book for they have been unable to read its statistics and so have been unable to context the events of 1084–6. They have been unable to explain just what happened or why. We will now do this for the first time to see what the real evidence discloses.

In the first place King William would have been urgently demanding funds from all his dominions (though Normandy was to be left to its own devices) and ordering (as the chroniclers tell us) the strengthening of English 'castles' and defences. The standing evidence tells us that the incomplete Colchester Castle was hurriedly embattled as it stood, the traces of merlons and embrasures are still there to see, absorbed in the final heightening of the walls a decade later. Although not now evident, I think we can assume that the incomplete 'White Tower' of London was put into a similar defensive state. What else were the urgent finances for? Well, simultaneously, the King would have been attempting to sequester the assets available to his enemies by purchasing both the naval supplies and the mercenaries they required. I suggest that this was his immediate, though clandestine, task in Normandy in 1084 (especially if Lanfranc had been able to give him early warning in 1083) and the result was that he arrived in England in 1085 with an unprecedented contingent of miles and (probably) of crossbowmen, both of which had served him so well in 1066 and both of which, thanks to his silver, he was well-placed to acquire.[2] His clear intention was to lock up significant reserves on his island, along with any Norman lords harbouring lingering sympathies for Odo or the northern confederation.

On his arrival in England with this fleet-full of mercenaries he ordered a 'mickle geld'.[3] In addition he farmed out these newcomers among the households and hearth-troops of his (tax-paying) landholders. Indeed everywhere was 'o' sib' with the breed and the larger towns complained that there was no longer room for their inhabitants. It became the responsibility of landholders large and small to billet these men and they were distributed (note the words of the Peterborough Chronicle) 'to each (landholder) according to the amount of his land'. The historic (the geld) records were useful not only for equitable tax assessments but for other purposes but, of course, this was a double blow to landholders who now had to billet, pamper, flatter and attempt some sort of discipline among these detachments, a sure recipe for resentment and secret dissent even among a landholder's own loyal men. But what else could the King do, he had to keep these 'military assets' locked up in England until the emergency had passed and he had to keep them happy. He was pushing everything and everyone to the utter limits and it was a desperate but brilliant strategy, as long as it did not backfire.

It seems that for some people these requisitions presented fresh opportunities. In the Babergh Hundred of Suffolk (styled in 1086 the 'Two Hundreds of Babergh') we see historic evidence of extensive 'sod-busting' (probably the origin of the 'Two Hundred' classification as the tillage had doubled by 1086).[4] Also a subsequent change in secondary emphasis, with pork/bacon then giving way to sheep, and with such animals on demesnes rather than peasant holdings, so these were commercial enterprises and not just the 'peasant's pigs'.[5] Leaving aside the infrastructure of the established craft industry in the economically valuable spinning and weaving district covering the Essex–Suffolk border, the obvious customers for surplus cereals and pork/bacon would now be the military while the sheep carcasses could be barrelled for garrison (or other) supplies.[6] Colchester Castle was close by, and had obviously been heavily garrisoned, and this shift to sheep in Babergh had apparently only recently happened in 1086, so I think we can safely predict the change was made in 1084. Garrisons were invariably supplied with salted meat and the Essex and Suffolk coastal regions produced a good deal of salt. It was also possible to produce good keeping cheeses for 'five sheep to the cow will double the dairy' during their lactation period.[7] I suspect that if we make similar detailed analyses of other places we will also find similar increases in foodstuffs production.

To appreciate the burden on landholders, especially those holding 'incapite' (in chief, of the Crown) we need to examine their special financial position. These were the men ultimately responsible for paying the geld, on their landholdings, 'according to the amount of (their) land', so they had also to convert the in-kind payments they received from their subsistence under tenants into specie in order to pay the land tax (geld). They were the human interface with the money economy and so they depended on markets and trade (as we have seen) in order to raise money on commodities, while also living directly on the produce of their estates and distributing such resources to their households. Finding markets was irksome but the alternative, letting the peasantry go to market was even more undesirable as the landholder needed the specie and so, quite apart from quantities, it was essential to keep the peasantry in their traditional (subsistence) economic role. Allowing them into the money economy would encourage their independence. Moreover, a large hearth-troop conferred (and confirmed) status, ensured personal defence and local order, and also discharged the obligation to provide 'knights' for the King's service (on campaign, on escort, or for castle guard), and these men lived under their lord's roof (unless detached on royal duties) and they expected to live well.

However, those miles who had been granted sub-infeudations (sub-tenancies) by their lord, and so had received a minor detachment of his overall estates as free (alias 'French') men, could afterwards manage their own affairs and (most important) they could now pay tax on their moiety of a larger estate, for they became liable for geld once they held any land as free men. In this way the overall tax burden of a major landholder could be laid-off by granting sub-enfeofments or minor lordships and while such an arrangement did proportionally diminish the overall produce of a magnate's estate, also the immediate defence response at times, it did, when taxation was high, reduce its fiscal impact on him without diminishing the 'show' of status. The peasantry, however, had to have incentives other than money and they needed to be incentivised as never before to reap, sow, plough and mow 'for victory'.

At this date it seems that many of the great lords still retained large retinues under their direct control, which was fine under a reasonable tax regime but not under a 'mickle geld' for in 1085 such a lord had to pay it <u>and</u> provide for his hearth-troop and, most annoying of all, the tax paid had now brought in new mouths to feed and house. At this point many magnates must have realised the desirability of creating sub-infeudations if only because, with the King in situ and all the borders closed, they dared not plot to join his enemies. They may also have gained some financial respite by selling commodities to the Crown, if close to a garrison or to a town, thus receiving some of their taxes back, ready to pay all over again! Economies on a war footing have always benefitted the rich and employed the poor.

By extending 'knights' service to the Church, whose lords-spiritual kept hearth-troops anyway, the Crown had already increased its reserves yet this fresh influx of mercenaries, distributed among lords both temporal and spiritual, made the burden even greater. Existing household troops of any great lord would expect to be treated, rewarded, at least as much as the newcomers, so on top of having to pay to bring in mercenaries these landholders would then see their guests eat them out of house and home and disaffect loyal servants! This was not such a clever expedient as to be foolproof and it therefore could not be maintained for long, but King William was desperate. Yet by importing so many French, Bretons and Manceaux he had secured many of the best mercenary horsemen otherwise available to his enemies. If heavy cavalry was a speciality of this northern region of France at this date, then Count Robert would now have had to look to his own resources in Flanders alone. Moreover, he would have to ship the horses (destriers) he needed for invasion across the Channel as William himself had done in 1066, no easy task, especially if opposed by English ship-sokes and massive land forces.[8] Maybe William also purchased ships, or was he cunning enough to just buy up all the available, essential chandlery?

Mesne or minor lords (of course), local enfeofments of whatever size, owed their feudal obligation (just like the hearth-troops proper) to their immediate overlord and only then to the Crown through their lord, for he had received his estates from the King (viz. 'in chief'). Meanwhile the true mercenaries owed allegiance only to the best paymaster and, of course, to themselves, so at the heart of every household in England lay a nest of vipers: collectively they represented a snake pit of potential trouble for the Crown. To keep them 'banged up' on an island required the best of provisions and steady pay, with no access to shipping. We can surmise that the ports were held by the most dependable forces and as the shipping had to be English, we may therefore conclude that the most loyal of William's forces were English. The subsistence peasantry was now burdened with constant demands for food and drink and no doubt subjected to a licentious soldiery not amenable to discipline. This expedient, designed to prevent the worst excesses of living off the land, became increasingly dangerous the longer it was employed as a means of sequestering the international supply of mercenaries. It could not be safely maintained for long without degenerating into robber bands as separate companies established contact with one another.

Yet this was also a war of attrition and it was a question of who would waver first. The Danish Fleet in Limfjord, having predictably run short of provisions and pay due to delayed recruitement, now dispersed while King Cnut was away and his subsequent attempt to impose disciplinary penalties resulted in a mutiny and then in his own murder. Most satisfactory, from the English point of view. Cnut had not planned so well as William had done. By the end of 1085 King William had obviously weathered the crisis and so numbers of his mercenaries were then paid off and escorted from the kingdom.[9] The speed of their dismissal might suggest that William was running out of specie, but then he still managed to pay them off; rather, I suggest, it indicates that he was apprehensive for the continued loyalty of his landholders. You can push anyone too far. There was also a further problem, one which surfaces in the Anglo-Saxon Chronicles for 1087, that first horseman of the Apocalypse which is always the concomitant of armies and garrisons, disease.

Remember how I said that there are always unforeseen consequences of war? Well, by 1087 there was 'a very great famine' early in the year;

in other words the sowing of 1086 had been inadequate, which sounds as though some of the seed corn had also been consumed in 1085–6 and maybe many of the essential plough beasts or oxen, leaving the ploughs deficient, so that in the lean spring season of 1087 (before crops ripen) resources were running out. Now even more of the livestock would be slaughtered in order to avoid starvation. At the same time came 'pestilence' with 'fever', a problem that classically moves from epidemic to endemic among the undernourished and vulnerable. For the monks at Peterborough and Ely the military presence must have been particularly heavy in 1085, in order to guard the Wash and Fens, so they would have been writing their observations from bitter experience and, in a never too–healthy environment prone to marsh agues and fevers, they were now suffering more than ever. Well, in the event the co–conspirators Robert and Olaf also abandoned their intentions so we can say that the desperate measures had worked to ensure a bloodless victory. Success not bloodshed is the object of war, as William's next move was to demonstrate to posterity for he had an even more astute move 'up his sleeve'. He was not a man to rest on his laurels, forgetting to plan for the next emergency.

At Christmas 1085 King William decided to 'wear his crown' at Gloucester, in the heart of one of his finest hunting preserves, yet the place also served as a nodal point and there was method in its choice. By Christmas 1085 the King's 'mandarin' was ready with his final paradigm. He had that <u>and</u> he had the final solution to the problem of falling gelds. Undoubtedly he briefed his lord and master in advance of the formal activities for in addition to the normal business there was (this Christmas) another assembly.[10] First, as custom now required, the King held his Court, his Curia Regis, where he consulted his lords temporal. Next came a Synod where the lords spiritual could settle ecclesiastical matters under his jurisdiction and control. Then, and it seems exceptionally, he called together his Witan, the Old English council of 'wisest' English advisors and it was this body, under the guidance of his 'mandarin', he particularly wished to question. I have detailed elsewhere the reasons I adduce to this.[11] Curia and Synod were matters of persuasion and deception to the main business in hand, the Witan was instead consultative, they would know the answers to those final proofs King William required from his 'mandarin' before committing unprecedented resources to an unprecedented survey.

One-fifth of the land in England 'belonged to' (that is it remained with) the Crown and the Crown does not tax itself, though it can receive rents and services (tallages) from its tenants. What the King now wanted to know, throughout his realm, was an accurate statistical picture: not only a count and double-check (audit) of the total of physical area(s) involved (and mainly recorded in the past) but also an accurate count of those degrees of men who paid tax or were assets to that end; he wanted a verbal picture of woods, pastures, meadows, mills, fisheries and their valuations and he wanted to know the changes in such totals made during his reign. In particular he asked about socmen and freemen, those taxpayers he had not created (who often seem to have been in the money economy), and he wanted to know 'if more can be had' all round.[12] He was treating the whole landscape as his personal estate and all men who could pay as 'tenants' of the Crown. There were to be no opportunities for the development of independent magnates, no Comital entities, in England. Yet the 'if more can be had' sounds as though his 'mandarin' was already thinking beyond the limitations of a land tax when drawing up a fresh and more efficient paradigm for the royal clerks to follow. It seems significant that among all the fixed and objective statistics to be gathered were subjective opinions in the form of 'valuations'. These valuations would then disclose otherwise occluded or hidden revenues enjoyed by the landholder.

The King's 'mandarin' certainly needed to satisfy him as to the simple statistics involved (both historic and prospective), and to demonstrate the importance of plough totals, and of regional and local patterns of logic, those things which would influence commercial practice.[13] These statistics are the fundamental economics upon which taxation and warfare (including defence) depend. What this 'chaplain' had devised, or what his scholarship had revealed to him, was the ancient CAPITATIO or, more accurately, the Roman POLYPTYCHUM or combined CAPITATIO TERRENA, HUMANA ET ANIMALIUM.[14] By comparing the older (English) territorial 'extents' and the geld records with up-to-date statistics an audit might finally (and uniquely) be achieved of the property holdings of each chief lord in each shire where he held land,

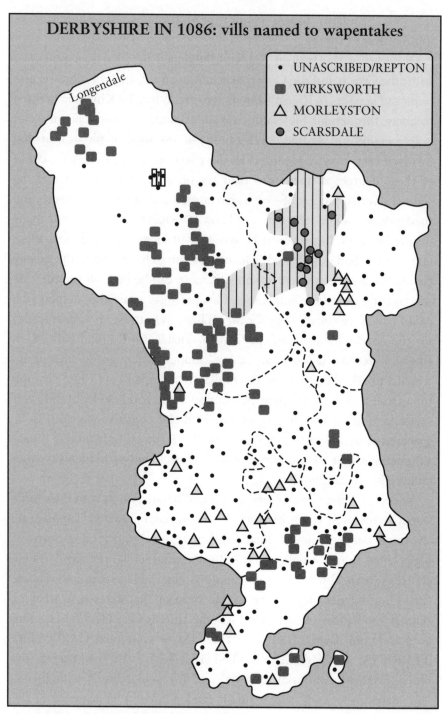

Map 7: Vills and berewicks named to wapentakes.

Map 7: Vills and Berewicks Named to Wapentakes
We can see from Map 7 that here in Derbyshire (which can be compared with Map 3) there was considerable competition for shares in various land uses, in both fertile lowlands and in uplands (including the lead-mining district by Longendale). Though the millstone grit was here, as in Staffordshire, less attractive the other uplands of Derbyshire have always possessed unusually fertile soils. We can see from this that the picture 'on the ground', even when restricted only to agriculture, was far from simple. In more fecund shires the patchwork of berewicks and local arrangements was even more complicated and so verbal depositions had to be taken at face value while the clerks attempted simultaneously to maintain some unitary consistency.

a further check on his regional power base or bases.[15] This would then disclose any potential strategic risk attending his holdings. I surmise that this 'mandarin' had already proposed a collation, collocation and conflation of the hidations, sulugations, geld returns and 'extents' (viz. all relevant records) held in the royal archives at Winchester and that now he was proposing a series of regional inquests which would empanel juries, in order to swear to the present (up-to-date) statistical picture. Half the work was therefore already done. Nevertheless this was still a staggeringly ambitious proposal, one never attempted in England before, or anywhere in Europe afterwards for centuries to come, and the Lord King needed to be persuaded that it could work.[16] Only a Witan, an English Curia Regis as one might say, possessed the requisite knowledge base to confirm the methodology. That is why this type of comprehensive series of surveys was never repeated in England or copied abroad, the statistical base and consultative expertise did not exist elsewhere and it was not afterwards maintained in England under later Franco-Norman administrations.

In fact this process was double-check auditing and more, for though the geld only concerned landholdings this comprehensive stroke of administrative genius was to reveal (maybe accidentally, maybe intentionally) the extent of the 'black economy', the cash economy which was not (as yet) taxable because it was unquantified, unknown and without legal concept. We have no record before this date of the separation of legal 'realty' (in this case real estate) from 'interest' (in this case both cash valuations and commuted payments) yet it subsequently makes an appearance. The precisely detailed brief which was proclaimed in 1085 has survived in both the 'Inquisitio Eliensis' and the 'Anglo Saxon Chronicle' (Peterbrough 'E' Chronicle), though each have minor variations, and the resulting surveys closely mirror all these instructions – though with the addition (in places) of extraneous and presumably accidental material, which is in itself invaluable evidence of social organisation, commerce and polity.[17] When in doubt it is best to err on the safe side, too much rather than too little. This vast undertaking, when finally collected and conflated, was to become a single entity known as 'The Lord King's Own Book' or 'The Book of Winchester', now known to us through an English religious irony colloquially applied as 'Domesday Book', though it naturally falls into two parts, the 'greater' and the 'lesser' Domesday.[18] Its reworked paradigm was indeed far more sophisticated than the pilot study previously made in Kent, far more effective in delivering the truth and the full picture.

Satan finds work for idle hands to do and so, with the immediate danger of invasion past (though not entirely removed), it became the King's intention to employ his magnates gainfully for a while and then to return to France and settle with King Phillip, now a grown man and doubtless angry that his sometime nominal vassal had refused to hand over the kingdom he had taken. In the meantime William needed to disguise this great scheme of surveys and so, in order to ensure that his magnates endorsed it and complied, they must not know its real purpose, even if they could have comprehended such a thing as an audit. To openly doubt their honesty would, of course, be to doubt their loyalty, their honour, in itself a deadly insult, so it was doubtless put to them (in Curia Regis) at Christmas 1085 that the King wished to ensure that each man 'had his own', and then the natural jealousy and greed of human nature did the rest. Lords temporal and spiritual accepted positions as legati, commissioners, Crown agents, to ensure that this time the jurymen empanelled at each place were in fear of the King more than their own immediate lord. These Legati were then sent into areas 'where they were not known' (that is, where they personally had no or few estates) and they seem to have set about their work with relish, disadvantaging their social equals. In the six months that it took to complete these surveys there was no opportunity for plotting against the King, at home or abroad, everyone was 'on the road' and busy, often (one suspects) settling old scores in the process.

Of course the real work was done by specially briefed royal clerks, men who (like their 'mandarin') were lowly characters created by the King, protected by him and hated by every blue-blooded nobleman as upstarts. They had everything to lose by even the slightest breach of security and they were also clever 'civil servants' who certainly received 'task specific training' before they set out. Few of the chief lords could read and even bishops were poor mathematicians, it was not in their (aristocratic) training, so for the Legati it was an 'expenses paid jolly' to listen to agricultural matters they could not comprehend narrated and deponed by despised peasantries and local officials, the real work being left to the clerks.[19] They all went out as perhaps seven separate circuits, generally lords travelling over lands 'where they were not known' and so the deponents could at least reassure themselves that they would not be victimised. Perhaps there were a few 'undeclared interests', favours for friends on another circuit, but the willingness of so many nervous deponents to tumble out superfluous details to these noble lords is only matched by the diligence with which the royal clerks entered everything told to them. They were not judges, merely clerks who reported what they were told to their master, so that he could tell the King. That, after all, was the training of a clerk, to copy everything, we see it time and again in copied manuscripts. It was all set down for their master to edit as he thought fit. He alone, it seems, engrossed the epitome once all was gathered in. The clerks were not the executive, merely the recording machines.

Not that these camerarii were without wit or even deceit in their secret pursuit of the truth, as 'secret agents' they were quite capable of formulating secret messages within their statistical records, plain texts which could even fool any commissioner who <u>could</u> read, say a bishop, just as they have fooled generations of historians. The complexities of tax evasion we have already observed and some 'tell-tales' were obvious. If a man had more plough capacity than the tillage he deponed he had obviously been sod-busting and so he not only had more land than he let on but greater agricultural output and reward. Then again by adding together all the land-use statistics deponed by local jurors for a given estate or holding deceit became obvious when the result was a greater area than that claimed as taxable. It is eloquent that great lords, whether laymen or clergy, clearly knew so little about agriculture that they even missed such obvious tell-tales when written down under their very noses by these clerks! These were <u>not</u> eigtheenth-century gentlemen farmers, they were fighters and prayers who lived off the sweat of other men and occupied separate worlds to the mass of the peasantry.

So there were 'secret messages', entered when a more obvious comparison would have been dangerous to clerk and/or project. So in Leicestershire at Bruntingthorpe the tenant deponed 'two parts of a hide' but the clerk discovered 12 carucates, so he wrote down 'two parts of a hide are twelve carucates'. An innocent record. The 'two parts' could be taken as two moieties of a 240-acre unit or two times 240 acres but the reality is then recorded in the folio by the clerk as 12 x 120 acres, or 1,440 acres, a massive evasion. His secret message to his master was, 'two parts of a hide is a lie, I have found 1,440 acres'. At Saltby (Framland Wapentake) there were 28 carucates of land and 26 ploughs at work but only a declaration of 'two hides and three carucates' for the geld. Well now, 840 acres of geld did not cover the 3,360 acres discovered! At Melton Mowbray Geoffrey de la Guerche deponed 7 hides, 1 carucate and 1 bovate (1,830 acres); suavely the clerk noted 'in each hide are fourteen and a half carucates'! The record then lists nine other places as part of his Melton Mowbray estate and if we add them all together and include his stated meadows and woodlands we come to about 12,300 acres; when we multiply his declared geld hidation by the clerk's 14½ we come to 12,330 acres. This is 19 square miles and when we consult the map we discover a block of contiguous place names with a berewick to the north which, according to recent surveys, today still adds up to 19 square miles.[20]

I have called such coded entries 'scribal apothegms' because of their clever and succinct arithmetic. At a casual glance it is only another record but to our 'mandarin' back in Winchester, pouring over the statistical details of such returns, familiar with their standardisation, they would instantly stand out as anomalous. In the West Derby Hundred of Lancashire, a wild place on the borders of the kingdom, Roger of Poitou's tenants deponed a mere 8 hides and 3½ carucates (owed by Roger as geld) though the area was detailed as 28 ploughs among 111 sub-tenants and 7,980 acres of 'woodlands' (here mostly moorland and crags with falcons' eyries). Suavely the clerk again reconciled the geld with reality by noting that, 'in each hide are six carucates of land'. So his record was actually 6,180 acres of land of which 3,360 acres were tilled by the 111 sub-tenants. The total estate, in the end, came out at 14,160 acres with its woods and moors.[21] Whether Roger should pay taxes on tillage alone or on total area really did not matter, what did matter was that his blatant tax evasion was no accident, it was intentional, and at this date tax evasion was lese-majesty, it was treason. The Crown was being undermined on all sides by seigneurial anarchy, the kingdom thereby betrayed and left open to invaders. The King had more to fear from his magnates than from his indifferent peasantry or the minority of surviving English landholders. This is what he had suspected, this was the reason for these surveys.

Naturally one cannot claim that every landholder was overtly a traitor but Domesday Book makes it clear that tax evasion was very common and that the very rich were especially reluctant to support their King, though they knew best (through regular Curiae Regis) the reasons for his repeated demands. They also, clearly, knew (evidenced by their actions) that they should <u>not</u> be evading taxes and so it is difficult not to suspect that they were, some of them, inclined to throw in their lot with another invader, anyone who would demand less. This novel taxation was not what they had expected when they came to England, where was the promised 'loot'?

Meanwhile hundreds of minor landholders were following the lead of the super-rich in ignorance of the real need for specie. Probably many of them were being 'hammered' by their 'good lords' as well as by the Crown, for they were 'freemen' as well as under-tenants. Worst of all, allegiance was sworn by a vassal to his lord, so the hearth-troops and even the infantry of great lords constituted private armies. If they were called to do so, they would support their own 'good lord' against the Crown. Adding mercenaries to such households only increased the danger, especially if a magnate could promise better remuneration than the Crown on top of generous provisions. If men like Odo, with Comital estates, could hold back geld payments, then (in time) they could hope to out bid the Crown. If they then acted in concert the Crown could change hands, to everyone's advantage, 'comes' and 'knight' alike. We can see the proof of this in later reigns when new monarchs unwisely gave tax concessions (all be they brief) to their supporters.

There were also included, though so rarely mentioned in our ordinary and everyday (school) histories of the Conquest, English lordlings, men loyal to King William alone, men holding of him 'in capite', in chief. Their titles vary from 'King's Freemen' to 'servants of the King', 'Almsmen', even 'King's Sergeants' but a compact group of shires titled them 'King's Thegns' directly, in Nottinghamshire, Lincolnshire, Huntingdonshire, Berkshire, Hampshire, Gloucestershire, Wiltshire and also Yorkshire. It is pure mythology to claim their 'widespread dispossession' or that they were 'reduced to pitiful circumstances' (as some have said); and whether they stood alone, or whether there were others like them but unrecorded because they were in the hearth-troops of magnates, we cannot know but Domesday Book records that there were numbers of them holding <u>directly</u> from the King, holding anything from 60 acres to 1,280 acres and they had serfs, villeins and socmen as under-tenants. Alsige, son of Beorhtsige, held at least 966 acres in Hampshire including 840 acres of arable, yet sadly only declared 480 acres to the geld even though his antecessor, Tosti, had offered 720 acres. Ælfsige of Farringdon, holding Windrush in Barrington Hundred (Oxfordshire), declared an honest 840 acres, which was more than his 720 acres of arable, while Godda (and Wulfric his son) held Woolley in Hampshire, declaring 720 acres all of which was tilled, though their 20-acre wood seems to have escaped taxation before 1086. They had fourteen villeins as tenants. In Lincolnshire Svartbrandr declared 660 acres on his 300 acres of arable, but he was tilling 600 acres and also had 100 acres of 'meadow' and 8 of 'scrubland'. The King's Domesday 'mandarin' (Ranulph Flambard) also held several manors in different shires, as one would expect, and he did not cheat on them at all, wherever they were.[22]

Looking back to his first battle in 1047 King William would remember the defection of Ralph Tesson of Fleury, in the middle of the battle, it had been the deciding factor that gave William (then the Duke) the victory. Yet defection could work either way. Such unattached, unrestrained, lords were the curse of early medieval armies unless they were working for you. Worse still, William had discovered (in Odo and in Robert) that the ties of blood were no guarantee of loyalty, or gratitude, so how was he to ensure that his military tenants-in-chief (including a carping Church) would respect their master's voice? Domesday Book was his answer for it had the means to enforce compliance with honesty, that was its purpose. Think of the shock to any landholder when he discovered that the King knew everything! Was it magic? It was William's strategic acumen that put so many elements together to work for a dynastic end, to finally enforce fealty. Now we will see just how he did it. This was the instrument of 'feudalism' compelling service and loyalty (fealty) to the Crown and he owed it to English ability and English education, so do we.

Chapter 9

The Legacy

W hat was England worth in 1086? That is a question we should ask because it tells us of the 'War Budget' available to the Crown. What should the Crown have received from a geld? That, of course, depends on the principle involved and on the rate levied, and the formula was 'so much on the hide' which raises another question: how harsh was William's taxation? The established, formulaic, answer is to take all contemporary commentators at face value and they said it was terrible, that the country groaned under his avarice.[1] What we need to remember is that these complainants were from the very rich (and recorded by their 'literary instruments' who obviously had no idea what the money was for), most of whom thought they should not have to pay taxes at all. Being in the main innumerate they had no idea of the cost of conflict, even if they knew the purpose of the tax. Let us, therefore, attempt a measure of common sense together with a shot at calculation for finances govern wars.

We are told of a geld of sixpence on the hide and that can be reduced to 40 acres per $1d$., one of $8d$. would be 30 acres per $1d$. A tabulation of acres per $1d$. geld made in Norfolk and Suffolk discloses more comparators in the 20–40 acres range (median 30 acres) than in 40 alone.[2] A $12d$.-on-the-hide geld is also a possibility. At Dorchester and Shaftesbury we are specifically told of $16d$. on each urban hide (where profitability would encompass more than agricultural output alone, so it was a guess); the 'mickle geld' of $6s$. would give us $72d$. on each hide! Maitland, indeed, proposed indicators which valued the hide at £1 per annum making $1d$. per acre so that an $8d$. geld would be $1/30$ and a $12d$. geld $1/20$ taxation in terms of the much later Lay Subsidy taxes, which ultimately superseded the gelds.[3] The 'mickle geld' therefore represented a $1/3$, or well beyond even a tithe!

The 24 million acres of the thirty-four shires (entered under the Tribal Hidage) – today reckoned at 23.396 acres – would therefore (in theory) render a total of £2,500 from a 6*d*. geld by 1086 while a 6*s*. geld would deliver (in theory) £30,000![4] Of course these figures are theoretical. The Crown does not tax itself, so if ⅕ of the kingdom was TERRA REGIS the geld return would be proportionally less, though we may assume that the Crown would be letting and tallaging within its estates in order to add to its revenues by other means. This would be in addition to the normal service contracts and 'fermes'. This was a staggering amount of money.

The 'mickle geld' of 1083–4, 72*d*. on each hide, was obviously a desperate measure, consequent on a desperate situation, yet it probably raised no more than half its potential and maybe much less, given the numbers of evasions. For the tax payers a geld of 1*d*. on every 3.33 acres would have seemed disastrous, especially if we think of each silver penny to be the equivalent of a half sovereign in the mid-twentieth century.[5] If a yield was 10 bushels the acre and therefore 8 bushels consumed (viz. one quarter), then the tax would be 1*d*. on three-quarters (heaped measure, 'quantagium'). For many it must have represented a call upon accrued rather than annual profits and all too often it appears, from our Domesday Book records, that it was the larger landholders who escaped most lightly under any geld: the larger the falsification the greater the 'profit' and little men feared detection much more than rich magnates. So a need for verifiable assets (and liability) saw the Domesday Surveys of 1086 focus on statistical solidarities rather than such mutable insubstantialities as historic payments, though by comparing the historic evidence, the geld declarations, the range of statistical assets deponed by local witnesses <u>and</u> the local valuations, it was possible to produce an audit. The CAPITATIO TERRENA comparisons, of past and present arable acreages, were usually clear indicators of themselves.

Of course if this collection of local jury verifications was conducted over only six months there was no way in which the detailed state of overall honesty could then have been revealed to the King before he left for France. However, a general report made to him by mid-summer by a 'mandarin', by now with a grasp of the fuller picture, would have verified the generally anticipated picture for him as well as those suspicions which had caused him to authorise these surveys in the first place. Individual examination could come later but then, due to his premature death in 1087, this did not ultimately rest in William the Conqueror's hands. When it was said by chroniclers that 'all that was written down was brought to him afterwards' it simply meant that his loyal servants, his 'mandarin' no doubt in person, confirmed what they had jointly set out to prove was possible before, at Christmas 1085.[6] Now, in mid-1086, the King had to make use of it, to somehow turn it into law for law was (as we shall see) mystic and Divine wisdom revealed to kings.[7] The quality of the law confirmed the divinity of kingship.

To this end, we are told, he summoned to him all the landholders of England, which I think we can take to mean all those with military obligations, whether magnates or merely 'knights', to meet him at a place on Salisbury Plain. His ostensible purpose was to assemble a large expeditionary force on the Isle of Wight, ready to embark for Normandy and France, though not all who gathered on his order would go with him. The landholders would have been predominantly, but not exclusively, 'French' for there would also have been 'English' tenants among this concourse. Of course all who had received lands had received them over the course of the last twenty years, often with no mechanism by which to verify honesty of acquisition or the exact boundaries, so there was confusion and even dishonesty in many cases, the strong preying on the weak and former practices confusing the present picture of real estate and of jurisdictions, to the concern of all recipients.

No doubt at Christmas King William had promised his major lords, temporal and spiritual, that their participation in his scheme would resolve everything and yet, of course, at this gathering on the Plain he could hardly have resolved every individual case. Maybe he never intended to, so I think that he <u>now</u> promised that on his return from France his clerks would review every case presented to him using the surveys just conducted 'so that each man should know his own right and not usurp another's' (as we are later told by the 'Dialogus de Scaccario'). In return he now clearly required something from all these individual landholders, both high and low, chief tenants and sub-tenants alike, he now required their sworn fealty, that is fealty sworn to himself and directly: 'whosoever's vassals they were, they all bowed to him and were his vassals and swore him oaths of loyalty that they would, against all other men, be loyal to him' (Anglo-Saxon Chronicle). These were the legal chains to bind them, we might even say 'the one ring' such was and is the magnitude of this 'spell'. Was this entirely honest and honourable? Well, this was politics and the end would justify the means.

The English process (and William always showed great respect for English law) had traditionally been to issue charters to individual landholders, charters recording their grants, though more recently (before 1066) these had been replaced by English 'writs', curt royal instructions to enfeof, a process which the Norman-French chancery clerks readily adopted after 1066. Yet even to issue writs to perhaps 180 magnates, tenants-in-chief, let alone to perhaps 2,000 (maybe more) military sub-tenancies and perhaps also hearth-troops was quite unrealistic. The direct hearth-troops, the landless knights and sergeants, were obviously of no (real estate) concern in this respect but they had also to be controlled in some way, so the assurances given to and by the magnates would surely have required them (at the least) to be not only personally loyal to the Crown but also to stand surety for their subordinates and to make such men understand that there would be no excuses accepted by the Crown in the future. The very minor landholders, sundry socmen and freemen often with business interests rather than military service obligations, could be ignored in this oath-taking.[8] Nevertheless this gathering on Salisbury Plain must have been a vast concourse for it was, in truth, an army.

What the King now required was a direct oath of allegiance and fealty, or at least a collective understanding that each <u>individual</u> landholder, high or low, publicly gave such because he now held as of the Crown and <u>not</u> as of his immediate overlord. The King was supreme in the land. From now on fealty sworn by a vassal was also sworn by proxy and pre-eminently to the Crown, while the fealty promised by magnates was not that of France or Normandy, semi-autonomous, but (as was said of villein tenure) 'at the will of the lord' (in this case the King)! In England estates had always been granted by the King and the custom would continue, with loyalty to him the authorisation to retain one's English status, viz. tenure. The establishment of a land tax doubly reinforced this status for failure to pay it was treason, yet it was assessed on the estate held which meant that the Crown had to keep its bargain. Loyalty, now and in England, was quantifiable and no longer an abstract concept. No doubt the Norman-French magnates who had co-operated in 1066 had expected to receive territorial rights comparable to their Continental holdings, even Comital rights comparable to Duke William's or Count Eustace's own, but instead England was now to be the undisputed and personal property of the King of England. The coinage had been his exclusive right (unlike Continental practice), the geld had been his and demisiant power had been his, *ipso facto* the kingdom was his alone to dispose (without dispute) as he chose. William's respect for English customs and laws had enabled him to create a unique polity.

Was this supremacy instantly recognisable, even universally acknowledged, on Salisbury Plain at Lammas in 1086? I think not, though it exhibits some of the attitude of a sophisticated Viking chieftain as well as an English King and a French Count. No doubt most of his magnates went away secure in the belief that on his (and for most their) return from France their vast estates would be confirmed, ratified and legally theirs 'in tail male', heritably. This was indeed a departure from English 'in laen' practice, to now hold 'in feudum' and not just by virtue of force as a grant only for life. So they would be, but unwittingly, tenants as well as vassals 'at the will of the (lord) King' but their posterity could inherit. Of course, had the kingdom not been settled as a co-operative union of Englishmen and Frenchmen, this could not have happened. It was the security that such a settlement gave to all that finally secured the acquiescence to heritability.

Although so much had been accomplished in six months by the proto-'exchequer' (of King's camerarii) the real work was still to be done in secret and rather than granting exclusive charters these clerks were really to be occupied, during William's absence, with the task of calculating tax liabilities, maybe even the defaults, of the magnates. On his return the King would know who to trust, how much he had 'in money and in orfe' and 'if more could be had'.[9] This was not a King in mortal fear of a 'nationalist' uprising but rather one secure in the knowledge that however duplicitous his coterie might be he could now secure his kingship and inheritance against any dissent and according to English law, with English assent and French compliance. He must have been quite sure that he could rely on English military support.

In the autumn the King crossed to France with his army, no doubt having heard by now of the assassination of King Cnut IV at Odensee.

There is just a possibility that early in 1087 he returned briefly to England but if he did it was probably only to ensure that necessary finance would follow him, for he must surely have heard of King Phillip of France's plans to attack Normandy?[10] This, surely, was the reason for such an Anglo–Norman expedition late in 1086, a preparatory move, for William seems to have entertained ambitions of his own and may even have had designs on Paris?[11] If so he got no closer than 30 miles: during a ferocious and ruthless attack on Mantes he was thrown against the high cantle of his saddle and sustained injuries which were to prove fatal. He died in agony deserted by his children, discarded by his soldiers and despoiled by his servants, yet he left behind that which would bind his Kingdom of England to his posterity and, one might say, to the continuation of his will. From the grave, as in life, he proved himself the supreme planner and executive.

Not that contemporaries recognised such achievements and attributes any more than many historians have done. How could they, this was not an Age of Reason but of Divine Intervention. The latter have accepted what the former said, basically without question, emphasising avarice, brutality and 'control' rather than seeking out ability, determination and statecraft, yet those who later copied out and repeated such a false template made no such lasting impression on history as William himself had done. In fact it seems that contemporaries are often the least reliable analysts of outstanding historical characters, they are too close to the events and people concerned, a lesson historians need to take to heart. To quote Kipling, 'we know what Heaven or Hell may bring, but which man knoweth the mind of a King?'. As the poem illustrates, only a fool is so presumptive.

Who, for example, among all those who complained so loudly of the King's avarice had any idea where the money went? No one says he dined off solid gold or kept a harem of mistresses, quite the opposite. Corpulent he may have become in later years but no one accused him (even after he was dead) of greedy self-indulgence. That corpulence could well have been a medical condition which, through an accident of fate, became prematurely fatal. Contemporary churchmen were only concerned to record that he took money from them and so they instructed their subservient clerks to write such things and to say that these were sinful things to do, so that future kings should 'eschew all the evil and go on the way that takes us to the kingdom of Heaven' (Anglo–Saxon Chronicle). The knowledge of how defence was conducted was a closed book to them. In their spiritual world God ordained victories, castles built themselves, soldiers (like peasants) got on with their roles in life because God had made them such (or the devil), what need had Kings of money but to spend it on themselves? Instead kings should allow the Church to glorify (i.e. build for) God. The emerging Cluniac movement was firmly focused on the *opus Dei* and believed that God's Kingdom on earth required physical substance and continual enlargement. Give to God (Mother Church) and He would reward you, even reward you with victory. Many evangelical churches today advocate such 'planting of seed' in expectation of Divine Intervention.

This distorted and selfish contemporary view of the King's motives (and all subsequent re-iterations) was certainly applied to William the Conqueror's successor, William 'Rufus'. So it was that the 'E' chronicler of the 'Anglo-Saxon Chronicles' wrote an epitaph for the Conqueror himself which was filled with the selfish complaints of Peterborough and the Church at large, claiming that 'he had castles built and poor men hard oppressed', though no doubt the 'poor men' were not poor at all, certainly not peasants, for he 'deprived his subjects of many a mark of gold and, more, hundreds of pounds of silver that he took by weight and with little justice from his people with little need … into avarice did he fall and loved greediness above all'. Peasants do not have gold or pounds of silver! Yet the Chronicler had the grace to add that 'no one, however powerful, dared do anything against his will' and 'any honest man could travel over his Kingdom without injury with his bosom full of gold'. Well, any 'honest' and <u>very</u> rich man! No one had praised such good governance in Edward 'the Confessor's' reign, it echoes Alfred the Great, yet the ploughman with a basket full of eggs and a 'bosom full of gold' continues to be the pitiable object presented by historians. Moreover, no one asks how any man could have securely travelled the kingdom with his treasures in the absence of castles and their security patrols.

Let us consider this King who, all agreed, had given internal security and justice to this realm yet who had spent his twenty-one years of reign in almost continuous campaigning. What does such resolution and perseverance say for a man who could, at any time, have taken the ready money, accepted the highest bid on top, and 'run', gone back to Normandy secure in the wealth of Croesus? For all the accusations that he was greedy and loved wealth we have here a King who spent enormous sums on defence and more on the regal foundations of his new kingship.[12] He thereby secured his Kingdom and its peoples, creating that confident aura of kingship and ceremony so important to a kingly profile and leaving a legacy of peace, security, administration and buildings to his posterity. The mean, selfish and greedy prelates who dictated to documents like the Peterborough Chronicles could see no need for a network of castles which impeded any invader, secured districts and ensured the secure passage of the geld, nor any need for themselves or other lords to contribute to 'fighting funds': in their minds God decided outcomes, especially battles and who cared about the peasantry? The poor and the toilers are always with us, they supposed. They also seriously objected to the curtailing of their own hunting activities and supply of choice (game) viands such as harts, boars and hares; in the centuries to come prelates were often before the Forest Courts for breaches of 'vert and venison'. So with William now safely dead, they denounced his conservation policy and farming of the wilds.

He gave them all generous endowments but, just like the secular lords, they had not expected to also share in restrictions and privations, in any burdens of state, yet this was a King noted for personal frugality, temperance and faithfulness.[13] Those detractors who dictated the texts of the medieval chroniclers were prepared to accept as a great monarch even the corrupt and venal, provided he did the same for them: quid pro quo. 'He loved the tall stags as though he were their father' complained the hunting prelates, forgetting that the royal court actually farmed such game for the royal table. Historians have been seduced by aristocratic cadets who used chronicles to create false 'histories' (though the term 'histoire' only meant 'a story' in French, not an accurate and true record) which 'histoires', they hoped, would sway influential opinions in their favour while serving as warnings to future kings to do as Mother Church directed. Objective history was a concept even further removed from their comprehension than it is from ours.

In the future men like William of Malmesbury were to bewail the lack of 'English' lords temporal and spiritual and, of course, they bewailed taxation, but we must not be misled by recent nationalism into thinking that he spoke on behalf of the 99 out 100 who were ordinary medieval men, the peasantry, or that he spoke the truth.[14] We have seen that English lords and 'knights' existed as well as Normans and that the English lords of the late King Edward's day had not suffered such harsh taxations. Taxation, as opposed to 'gifts', was still an alien concept. His view of the world, like that of Henry of Huntingdon, was a Spode-like aristocratic division of power in favour of the status quo ante, especially an English kingship that made concessions to the rich and to the Church.[15] In fact King William's respect for English law and process (he even tried to learn the language) was to show fruit on his death, except that he divided his domains among his sons and rather than preventing dispute, as he no doubt intended, this created it, for his death also saw the release of brother Odo. Henry received money, William received England and Robert Normandy and it did not take the scheming Odo long to go to work on the latter.

Historians sometimes excuse the Odo–Robert alliance by suggesting that many nobles had lands in both England and in Normandy and wished to 'stabilise their position' by re-creating the 'joint domain'. No doubt there is some truth in this if it meant that they would have supported any claimant who would place England under the same chaotic polity as Normandy! Given Odo's track record I am more inclined to see him as the evil uncle at Robert's ear. If he had had designs on the English throne in 1067–8, as an analysis of the Bayeux Tapestry suggests and then continued to scheme up to his arrest in 1082 as Domesday Book testifies, he probably needed no encouragement from others to immerse himself in another such intrigue after his brother's death and I believe he would have promised anything in order to acquire support.[16] William 'Rufus' found himself in possession of a kingdom rich in assets but drained of cash by both his father and by the bequest to younger brother Henry and within a year he was challenged by the Normandy faction. And note, this faction was headed in England not by brother Robert but actually by Uncle Odo who, presumably attempting to rework the former successful paradigm of 1066, had seized the key fortress of Pevensey.[17]

The concept introduced by the Salisbury Oath-taking was very new and novel and no doubt poorly understood, so the military tenants and chief vassals of the Crown now showed themselves equally divided between the new 'feudal' (English) concept of kingship and the older, more convenient (Norman), opportunistic vassalage. For the magnates in particular promises of Comital power would be attractive if they were at all possible. Not so the English, for once 'Rufus' had been crowned and had taken the ancient Oath he was their King and so the fyrd turned out en masse in support of King William II. This tells us three things. First, that the English had not been deprived of weapons (which we already know) and, second, that the professional soldier-cadre (select fyrd) was still intact, though probably depleted by endless campaigning on behalf of William I. Thirdly it tells us that William I's respect for English law and custom was advantageous for him. From these indicators we may confirm our former suspicions that King William I had had more to fear from 'Frenchmen' than from 'Englishmen' and that he had been aware of this; thus his deliberate accommodations with his new subjects now paid dividends to his heir. Even those magnates who had English (now quote, 'French') milites among their retinues must have felt unsafe, unsure of the loyalties of such men and aware that they were ultimately outnumbered by loyal English supporters of the Crown. Now that ordinary 'knights' probably knew that they owed a higher loyalty to the Crown no magnate could be quite sure of the absolute loyalty of his men if he personally encouraged rebellion.

It was this English alliance of English and Norman interests, this 'coming together' (collusion if you like), that drove out the rebel Norman invaders from Pevensey and next from Rochester, and then from the kingdom. That accomplished the new King had to replenish his coffers and now he had at his disposal a tool of unprecedented power and worth, he had the completed folios which were, collectively, to become known as 'Domesday Book'. It was only now that the information contained in these surveys could have been and was deployed by the Crown and as a result the 'pips' certainly began to squeak.

Bound by their oath of fealty to the Crown the King's vassals and magnates, and some of their lower vavassours, were largely 'in mercy' of the new King for their fiscal treachery, their defalcations, whether wittingly or unwittingly committed against his father. They could hardly refuse to give generously to the man who now owned the absolute rights to the kingdom and, what was worse, magnates who sought to indiscriminately lay off their debts on their enfeoffed vavassours could not do so with impunity. These vassal sub-tenants being both legally and militarily attached to the Crown now, now additionally had the right to appeal to a higher 'good lord' if aggrieved, to the King himself. Great men had acquired, they now discovered, only partial allodial rights, all tenures were still at 'the Will of the lord'. In the next century the 'Dialogus de Scaccario' tell us just how well this protection of the lower vavassours worked when magnates attempted to offload their own larger liabilities on sub-enfeofments.[18]

For a short time King William II, 'Rufus', had the guidance of his father's old mentor and friend Lanfranc but when Lanfranc died the vacancy remained open for some time. While William waged a successful punitive campaign on his brother Robert in Normandy the royal 'exchequer' appears to have been busy with the revenues of this vacant See of Canterbury. They discovered that even Archbishop Lanfranc had been seriously evading the geld, possibly a 'sin of omission', so for three years the See's revenues were now paid directly into the royal treasury. When 'Rufus' did finally relent, it is said after a serious sickness, he attempted to replicate Lanfranc by appointing another Italian-academic, Anselm, in 1093. He could not have made a more disastrous choice. He should have looked at the man and not at his qualifications.

The ensuing feud between See and Crown was well, if inadvertently, documented by the monk Eadmer, panegyrist to Archbishop Anselm.[19] Cunningly the King observed the shortfall in revenue over the years and after some hesitation the Archbishop offered a one-off 'goodwill gift' of £500 to the Crown 'to secure for good the King's favour', which 'Rufus' at first accepted with good grace. After all, he had already pocketed three year's worth of revenues. As the revenues of the See appear to have been running at around £1,500 per annum it is not surprising to read that the King then had second thoughts, no doubt on accountant's advice from his clerks, protesting that this was not enough.[20] Indeed, given the penurious state of the Exchequer after it had paid off brother Henry and the expenses of fighting brother Robert, together with the need to finish Colchester Castle and London's 'White Tower', not to mention other castles and garrisons plus the inadvisability of bearing down too heavily on loyal vavassours, money was desperately needed. The best prospects were the known, proven defaulters, among whom abbacies and bishoprics (all of whom had extensive estates) were not uncommon culprits. Of course the Crown could not plead such cases in open court without revealing the methodology employed, the secret methodology of Domesday Book, but the sheer shock of realising that the Crown knew the hidden facts was enough to make people think that such knowledge was diabolical!

Well aware of the wider dispute taking place in Europe, known to us as the 'Investiture Controversy', Archbishop Anselm dug in his heels over the payment of geld on his own and other ecclesiastical estates, insisting that all revenues belonged to God, through the 'persona ficta' of Church immunity and privilege.[21] It was a position which was to remain a point of major dispute and not only for Thomas Becket in the twelfth century but until abolished by the Reformation. To punish the King Anselm preached against long hair and effete manners at court, which were probably no more than English fashions (and so suggest integration with English subjects) but which, as such an attack, would gratify the pro-French faction. In a homophobic age he was commencing that vicious reputation by slander that has followed 'Rufus' ever since. Though it could hardly have been openly and fully directed I think, from such comments, there can be little doubt as to the source of these stories or those linking the King with devil worship. After all, his insight was diabolical and the invention of diabolical phenomena was a religious stock-in-trade by which to rally the faithful!

Next the Archbishop went on to claim that Christianity in England was virtually dead![22] Following this unbalanced outburst he applied to hold a Synod while Rufus and most of his lords temporal were in France. He knew full well that as Metropolitan over all the lords spiritual he would then be able to force through whatever measures he chose. 'Rufus' was not taken in and refused permission, so Anselm resorted to threatening him with eternal damnation! Finally, in a fury, 'Rufus' told him, 'very well, you do as you like with your manors and shall I not do as I like with my Abbeys?' Here we have the root of the Archbishop's venom, once again it was taxation. This was a clever riposte by 'Rufus' for all the English abbeys had been despoiled and destroyed by Vikings and all had then been re-founded by King Edgar, they owed everything to the Crown. The presentations, therefore, belonged to the founder, so Rufus could legally delay appointments for as long as he wished. Sure enough, as abbacies fell vacant so Rufus sent in his 'exchequer' clerks under Ranulph Flambard to make thorough inspection and audit of their accounts while simultaneously refusing to use his 'presentation to the living' to nominate or ratify an abbatial successor: royal consent was always required to any ecclesiastical nomination anyway. As long as an abbacy remained unfilled all its revenues came to the Crown.

The demands on the royal revenues were largely occasioned, as in the Conqueror's reign, by the exigencies of state and these kept 'Rufus' (just like his father before him) largely in the field. In this respect he was his father's son, though now the chroniclers were quick to record how he lavished money on mercenaries, though they had never dared say as much before when it had been equally true for his father. In 1091 he was called upon to repulse an invasion in the north in which Durham seems to have been besieged by King Malcolm of Scotland. His army had been pillaging Northumbria throughout the summer and so although King William drove them back into Lothian, when the English supply fleet was lost and with little food left in the landscape behind him, 'Rufus' was forced to negotiate a peace and retire southwards in the face of winter.[23] As a consequence, in 1092, King William II built a castle at Carlisle, after he had conquered Cumberland. Here he established a military colony with settlers from the south, thus a self-supporting unit able to resist Galwegian threats and able to protect Yorkshire and Lancashire. King Malcolm's quiescence now would seem to support Kapelle's opinion that Cumberland had already gained its independence from Scotland in about 1070.[24] 'The enemy of my enemy is my friend', as one might say.

Malcolm seems to have become incensed when he finally realised that William was intending to hold on to this territory and then (in his choler) he made the mistake of marching his Scottish army southwards in November. Earl Robert de Mowbray (Earl of Northumbria) was, however, waiting for him with an Anglo–Norman army, having anticipated such a response. Malcolm, his son Edward and most of the Scottish army were killed or drowned. There then began an inheritance dispute in Scotland which was settled in favour of Edgar mac Mail Choluim (assisted by Edgar Æthling): King William also assisted this claim as Edgar had already had the good sense to acknowledge William's overlordship. Thereafter the two kings seem to have remained on good terms even though the internal fighting was not concluded until 1097. In the process, on the English side of the border, King William found it necessary to depose Robert de Mowbray, Earl of Northumbria, who, in the fashion of Norman lords, had taken this opportunity to rebel.

True to form his revolt in Northumbria was supposed to be in alliance with nobles on the Welsh border, in order to force William to divide his forces. The plot seems to have been betrayed and the Earl was captured and incarcerated. What is notable is that a revolt was deemed possible, no doubt thanks to security engendered by the destruction of the Scottish threat, though the removal of this Earl and this Earldom by 'Rufus' now also (and finally) put Northumbria directly in the hands of the Crown. There was now no danger of future Comital ambitions creating an independent territory. Thus English power was ultimately extended over Northumbria at the same time as a friendly ruler was installed over the border in Scotland. I think that we can credit King William II with the cunning and the ability of his father. He needed them for he was still dealing with the same aristocratic Norman mentality.

In 1096 'Rufus' was in Normandy, fighting brother Robert (when he complained bitterly about the inferior quality of the 'knights' supplied by Archbishop Anselm) and then the brothers reached a concord when Robert decided to 'go on Crusade'. To this end Robert offered William 'Rufus' the whole of Normandy (in pledge) in return for 10,000 marks ($£6,666$ 13s. 4d.). This was an attractive offer, Robert might never return and even if he did, where would he find the pledge? It meant another crippling geld in England, but the imaginative Flambard was going through the land 'like a flame' applying the information revealed by the Domesday Surveys, those surveys he had devised and directed for Rufus' father.[25] Bound by their legal oath of fealty, given at Salisbury in 1086, the lords temporal and spiritual had no choice but to comply, if they wished to keep their estates. Earl Robert de Mowbray's fate had proved to be a useful example to his class. Once again, 'Rufus' had proved himself to be his father's son.

The good news in 1097 was that Archbishop Anselm took himself (without royal permission) into exile abroad. Now the revenues of the See, about £1,500 p.a., could all be added to the war chest. At home 'Rufus' decided to take the Welsh Marches in hand by setting up castles in Wales just as his father had done in Northumbria, not the last English King to apply such a remedy. Though this only moved the border westwards it gave some welcome relief to the neighbouring English shires. From 1097 to 1099 King William 'Rufus' was largely in Normandy, campaigning against opportunists who thought that Robert's absence on Crusade was an opportunity they could not ignore. It is no surprise to find that the chroniclers, or panegyrists, complained as bitterly about 'Rufus'' 'avarice' as they had once done about the Conqueror's. In 1099 Ranulph Flambard was made Bishop of Durham for his 'services to the Crown'. Now he was acting as both justiciar (lord temporal for the Crown) and as a lord spiritual (with the King's especial ear) in synods which were now devoid of any religious figurehead to oppose the Crown's will.[26] The Church was now under control.

The reign came to an abrupt end in 1100 for King William 'Rufus' was shot fair and square in the chest with a crossbow bolt in the New Forest. Later this 'accident' was blamed on one Walter Tyrrel, an apparently excellent shot whose bungled discharge was said by some to have ricocheted off a tree! He was never apprehended. Brother Henry, who was one of the hunting party, left his brother and King to die and rode hell-for-leather for Winchester where both the royal treasury and the 'King's own book' (Domesday Book) were housed together. He was, after all, the prospective heir, so he wasted no time in having himself proclaimed. If 'Rufus' had inherited his father's martial character, Henry had inherited some of his political and executive talents so, thanks to the paradigmatic shift in polity which his father had bequeathed to his posterity, Henry was now able to avoid civil war by citing fealty to the Crown. The courtiers in the hunting party followed Henry and his promises, those at Winchester endorsed his manifesto; 'Rufus'' body was brought in by a peasant on his cart.

The cornerstone of Henry's manifesto was lower taxation, 'for there is no new thing under the sun', as Ecclesiastes says, especially for the Church. Instead of now imposing large gelds he subtly introduced a new series of feudal reliefs, what we would today call 'stealth taxes'. Who it was suggested this approach we do not know but Ranulph Flambard, by now the most hated man in England (to the Church and to the rich and powerful) was slammed up in the White Tower of London – for protective custody, and given a very generous allowance by the Crown. So, no complaints there. Having deflected any criticism of his actions in this way Henry settled back to enjoy the fruits of kingship, pending the day (a little way off) when he could re-impose heavy gelds under the direction of the one man who knew Domesday Book inside out and who was presently safe and happy. As for Flambard, he sat tight while the heat (lust for his blood) abated and then, to make sure, noting the return of Robert to Normandy, quietly and safely 'escaped' across the Channel. He did not return until 1102 when the Crown welcomed back this 'escaped prisoner' and restored to him his suspended bishopric. Maybe in the meantime he even improved on his portfolio by spying on (brother) Robert for King Henry, who can say?

Of course the accession and early years of Henry's reign were not without problems. Henry and his brothers had never enjoyed total amity and certainly not trust. Let us take stock. In 1088, for example, Henry had purchased the Cotentin from Robert (who, you remember, had been left Normandy by his father) but then Robert, goaded by Odo and assisted by William, treacherously dispossessed Henry in 1090, so the then penniless Henry had allied himself with William though (again) he failed to receive (as a reward) his mother's estates in Buckinghamshire and Gloucestershire. In effect his brothers beggared him! Still, Henry proved himself a capable warrior, apparently better than Robert, and when Conan Pilatus turned traitor on him he captured him and had him thrown from the Tower of Rouen. I think we can say that Henry was not a forgiving man, which may perhaps help explain the fates of both of his brothers? His treatment of his lords and barons was equally autocratic and it was heartily reviled.

Anyway, in 1094 when Henry took Domfront by force he gained great power in Normandy, which may well have influenced brother Robert's decision to join the First Crusade? Fortune (of course) also smiled on Henry when William died so unexpectedly and so, having seized Winchester on William's death and having had himself crowned in short order, Henry found that brother Robert had now returned from the Crusade and wished to dispute the succession. No doubt with his father's strategy in mind, Henry gathered his forces at Pevensey to oppose any invasion only to find that many of his barons wished to support Robert. Their initial enthusiasm for the 'right order' had worn off and no doubt Comital dreams now beckoned again.[27]

Well, the astute Henry immediately invited Archbishop Anselm to return, promising him significant 'tax breaks' for the Church and so (in response) the English bishops obligingly despatched their knights to him at Pevensey. It seems that a combination of Church support, English support and this superb and impregnable strategic position (which would allow Henry to sit tight against any attack until his treasure had brought in mercenaries) made the baronial opposition waver and Robert to hesitate and so a treaty was agreed at Alton. I wonder just how much influence the many ex–hearth–troop mesne lordlings also wielded. Would their immediate baronial overlords have now felt entirely confident in asking them to forswear their fealty to the Crown, asking them consequently to risk losing the sub-enfeofments so hard earned in years of bitter campaigning? Land encourages proprietorial ambitions and we may guess that these shire 'knights' were happy in their new possessions and wished to keep them in the family.

Once order had been restored and Robert had been bought off, Henry (now feeling safe) set about disgracing and punishing his principal baronial opponents. He was not a forgiving man. He also fell out with Anselm, now that the danger had passed. Then, presumably after gathering financial resources and with Flambard safely returned to his service in England, in 1105 Henry invaded Normandy (determined to settle with Robert) and in 1106 at Tinchebray he defeated and captured brother Robert. Robert was now destined to die landless and in captivity, just as he had once wished for brother Henry in 1090. That was both of them accounted for!

In the long perspective, although William the Conqueror's immediate succession by 'Rufus' would seem to have been the decisive political and dynastic victory, I wonder if Henry's successful coup (if it was such) was not the real test of the new polity? Everyone was apparently fearful of the consequences of initiating a Continental-style scramble for power (especially with Normandy so evidently in chaos), fearful now of the power of the English Crown under the law, English law endorsed by the English nation, but also fearful of losing that which was now theirs not by force alone but now also 'in law'. Now we see 'each man', as was said, 'content with his own'. For almost forty years the new super-rich had experienced one invasion threat or crisis after another and for every one they and their fathers had paid in blood, sweat and silver. Now they had 'their own' and some prospect of stability, security and fulfilment. Lower down the scale many mesne lordships, shire 'knights', had been created and a significant body of these shire 'knights' seem to have felt secure in their little worlds. As for the commonality, they now had what no one could remember after half a century of turmoil, they had peace and security. Here was a system which unified all aspects of the contemporary political spectrum, a polity for all seasons: carpe diem! Equitable application of the geld made all things possible for ultimately, as we have repeatedly seen and as Thucydides had once said, money was the power, at least when allied with good management of resources. So, as Thucydides observed at Melos, might, by its superiority, becomes right.

And so we leave the final establishment of 'feudalism' and fealty, its flowering in England, English 'feudalism', the paradigm for Europe. Here was unity. Not of all classes, for the vast majority, the peasantry, had no interest in politics, only in peace and security; all the same, finally and quite unlike the Continent, there prevailed unity of a sort among the influential and the empowered affluent class of England, a combination of both circumspect fear and of self-interest. And, I think, there was one more thing. The 'Frenchmen' (who were sometimes assimilated Englishmen) of *c.* 1100 often had ancestors who had come as invaders looking for loot, some already had lands in Normandy, Brittany or France while some sought to retain their social position. The largest of these 'newcomers' were keen to increase their estates in both places and to increase their wealth and power. But the many smaller sub-infeudations (made in response to taxation) were often located only in England, created as mesne lords in truth by the influence of the geld on their great lords, and these 'knights' certainly wished to retain their modest estates. As Normandy disintegrated into chaos with the opening of the twelfth century even the great landholders could see that English stability had advantages over continual internecine warfare and (of course) the 'smallmen' were now joint stockholders in a viable promotion. Under a strong king they had no doubt (at last) where their primary loyalty must lie.

True, there was a recrudescence of anarchy following King Henry's death, but then a 'feudal system' could only function under a strong king, one who both enjoyed and who exercised more power than any 'good lord'. However we seem to be presented with a realisation, by the later chroniclers, men looking back on the civil war of Stephen and Matilda in Henry II's reign, that there had been a time before this twelfth-century civil war which had been infinitely better, together with indications that the magnates had eventually come to realise, by the mid-century, the futility of continual, reciprocal, rapine, wreck and penury. What we do see, with the reinstatement of a strong king in Henry II is a period of exceptional progress, progress in legal development, administrative methodology and fiscal subtlety.[28] There is a sudden flowering of structured and accepted 'feudalism' (polity) which united and focused all degrees and languages of Englishmen and which, despite the ultimate disintegration of a massive French 'empire', still united Franco-English resources. It was this solidarity which created an identity destined to become increasingly assured and confident in the centuries to come.

Ultimately, as I said when I began, this systemisation of loyalty through fealty to the Crown created a class system synonymous with a 'feudal' (fealty) system but the polity so created did not fade with the social changes of succeeding centuries. Through a long process of evolution there came about a Constitutional Monarchy which we still have today in state and Crown. Yet in one undiluted respect King William's master stroke for stability remains. Today each and every individual member of the forces of the state swears personal fealty to the Crown. The rich and powerful may still be able to buy some temporary loyalty somewhere but, under English law, they cannot seize the Crown from the fealty of its loyal vavassours.

Chapter 10

Overview: A Comprehensive Structure for the Norman Conquest

Let us now summarise all we have discovered or can deduce concerning the realpolitik and grand strategy of this period, a period always so conveniently christened 'The Norman Conquest'. Let us review the Anglo–Norman achievement and its several stages of progression towards Anglo–Norman kingship. Here we unfold a battle for survival.

Late in 1066 Duke William of Normandy and Count Eustace of Boulogne land on the south coast of England with an expedition composed of Normans, Bretons, Boulonnais, other Frenchmen and mercenaries. The high command is top heavy with William's relatives and their intention is to extort a massive ransom, just as Cnut had done some half century before. We have no reason to suppose otherwise. Of course they are aware (as is King Harold of England) that a massive Norwegian and mercenary force has also gathered for the kill: no one could miss the demand for ships and chandlery created by the forward planning required by these two amphibious forces. Such preparations commenced in 1064 if not before. King Harold has now to watch and wait, who will land where and when will they land?

The Norwegian army lands in the north of England just after harvest time – a wise precaution. King Harold strips all his southern garrisons, except perhaps London and Dover, and marches north with his select fyrd in support of the local fyrds. With winds and tides supposedly changing in their favour (at this time of year), William and Eustace wait anxiously for the right wind and for a calmer sea on which to float a novel and precarious arm, heavy horse. They apparently know from sympathisers at Pevensey that this fortress and harbour now has few defenders so when the weather finally changes in their favour, that is where they make land. It is one of the few places equipped to handle their precious cargo.

Quickly they set about securing and provisioning such a key strategic position, while simultaneously preparing their forces for battle. They have been lucky, they have arrived while Harold is busy in the North, but their mounts in particular require time to recover from the crossing. Maybe the need to fight Harold will not arise but, maybe, they will have to fight the Norwegians, who can tell?

By a miracle of English infantry Harold trounces the Norwegians and secures the North, only to force-march his exhausted fyrdmen south to meet the other invaders. They are sitting tight, watching and waiting his deployment, so he orders a rendezvous for both his select and the (local) general fyrd at 'The Hoar Apple tree', a local landmark just south of England's most important arms-manufacturing area, the Weald. Here he knows that a certain local topography will grant him an almost impregnable position. He knows his land so he has selected his ground.

The Norman-French host cannot afford to delay, lest another English army join the first, so they advance confident in their 'secret weapon', their heavy horse. What is their shock and horror to discover that Harold's choice of battlefield has conferred on his host a perfect, natural, infantry stronghold, yet they cannot now retreat. Yes, William and Eustace always have the option to escape back to Pevensey, but if the wind was then against them would they escape the vengeance of their fellow stockholders in this joint-venture scheme? Battle is inevitable and during a long day, four times longer than it should take, they hurl themselves forlornly against superb English infantry. But William wisely reserves his cavalry and, by an accident of fate, at the end of this desperate day, his remaining forces finally discover the key to victory and they prevail.

In the falling night the flower of English nobility and power die around their king, just as English morality decrees, leaving England devoid of leaders and now incapable of organising any administration. England, those few nobles who remain, is too stunned to act; William in desperate need of recuperation for men and horses pauses to bring up remounts from the Eastbourne stud and to replenish his firepower. No further opposition appears, so instead of falling back onto Pevensey he marches on Romney in Kent and burns it out. This ensures that Rye and Pevensey become the only (lagoon) harbours, both of them apparently loyal to the invaders, but he dare not strike at the Wealden industries for the topography there is too difficult for his infantry to negotiate, let alone for his cavalry to traverse. Instead he now moves on Dover with its 'castle' at the old Pharos and it capitulates to an attack from the land. He has thus skirted and isolated the Weald.

Should he wait for reinforcements now that he has secured the south-coast crossings? Instead Duke William decides to strike at Canterbury, seat of the archbishopric, presumably as a threat to the English Church hierarchy. With the examples of Romney and Dover before them the citizens of Canterbury quickly send out an embassy and submit. Still there is no sign of either opposition or tribute, so he now sends a strong flying column to seize Winchester, ancient capital of England and the centre of her administration, seat of the Dowager Queen Edith. Immediately she and the city fathers capitulate: now William has another pawn, Edith, under his control. Now the deaths from battle, permanent disability and wounds are being joined by increasing numbers of deaths from disease, always a more serious 'harvester' than actual conflict. Perhaps 20 per cent of his 10,000-strong army have been eliminated, maybe another 5 per cent will soon succumb to sickness, he has to force the issue with the English.

Leaving the sick and dying behind and also garrisons, the invading army now marches for London but they find that the bridge is down and so all they can do is set Southwark on fire and then march along the Thames seeking a crossing point. Duke William is considering his options, he does not want to see London itself sacked and destroyed, it is too valuable. Cutting a swathe of terror westwards he secures the massive, ancient fortress of Wallingford and then circles eastwards. Archbishop Stigand now surrenders to him, apparently with an embassy, so he seizes the 'castle' of Berkhamsted and here a 'field Witan' offers him the Crown of England. England desperately needs defenders, not only against further coastal attacks but from her traditional enemies to the north and west, as well as the already depressed peasantry of the far south-west, all of whom have now heard the news of King Harold's death and are stirring.

Duke William, nominal general of this composite force, vacillates and then agrees. He accepts the Crown, marches into London and at Christmas is crowned King at Westminster. The English administrative machine can now function and so the tribute is paid. God has created a new English King and dynasty.

King William now rewards his survivors, both with money and with, for the nobles, massive estates as well, then he departs in triumph with captives, an escort and a mort of treasure in order to tour his duchy, leaving his trusted lieutenants (with perhaps half of the invasion force or less) to guard the coasts and his new kingdom. Count Eustace retires with his contingent to his Comital empire, reducing the army even further, and licks his injured pride: his claim to the English throne had been greater than William's. Now (it seems) he secretly contacts Bishop Odo and together they plan a coup; this appears to be recorded on the Bayeux Tapestry. In spite of the heavy casualties they have sustained the Bretons remain and with them the Basque crossbowmen who are William's other 'secret weapon'. This is just as well.

Late in the year, when wind and tide are in his favour, Count Eustace returns with an expedition of his own and descends on Dover, Pevensey being beyond his means and Dover being Odo's caput. Odo, however, is diplomatically absent and the garrison, not being appraised in advance, unites with the townsfolk, who have bad memories of Count Eustace, to defeat and hunt down the Boulonnais. Eustace escapes.

Simultaneously the collaborator who has been appointed to the Earldom of the North is ambushed and killed and Northumbria relapses into chaos. In Herefordshire an alliance of Welsh princes with an English brigand ravages the borders. Clearly many of the mercenaries have gone home and so, by now, the vestigial invasion force is far too thin to defend the kingdom. In the far south-west Gytha Godwine appears with an Irish mercenary expedition, determined to seize and enlarge her hold on Cornwall and Devon. She takes Exeter but not having English support then sends envoys to the Danes for reinforcement. They have not yet recovered, whatever their family ties to Gytha.

Over the water King William awakens to the danger and despite the dangerous winter season he returns to London for Christmas. Calling out the English fyrd and mustering his remaining Norman-Breton forces, King William marches on Exeter and is welcomed by its citizens. However, Gytha is waiting and appears to have raised the subjugated Damnonians with promises for the gates are then closed on the Anglo-

Norman army and a bitter siege ensues. It ends when the Godwines flee and the terrified citizens are relieved to be reasonably treated by their King, who then goes on to Winchester for Easter. Gytha's estates are forfeited for treason and Northumbria is sold to another bidder, enabling King William to pay off his mercenaries yet again.

But his troubles are not over. Elements in the North conspire with the Welsh in the west (including two disgruntled English earls on that border) and once again King William is obliged to raise an Anglo-Norman army. Marching north he methodically establishes 'castles' with garrisons at key points as he goes, thus tying up even more of his forces, but he still arrives with an army large enough to compel the King of Scotland to make peace. Taking advantage of this vacuum the Godwine faction makes a raid on Somerset but is obliged to return to Ireland when it meets strong English resistance. It appears that, finally, the King and his magnates can relax and so the Anglo-Norman forces wind down and disperse, leaving the troublesome North in the hands of yet another new earl. Predictably this man's mercenaries do nothing to reassure the ever belligerent locals.

Once again William is forced to turn around, call out the fyrd and the house-troops of his magnates and march north. The 'castle' at York holds out until William arrives so the revolt fizzles out and he then builds a second 'castle'. Returning to Winchester he now leaves a trusted lieutenant in charge of York. From Easter to midsummer 1069 there is peace, then the Godwine faction return with their Irish pirates, perhaps 2,000-strong, only to be seen off by local forces. Are the borders now secure? Not in the view of King Swein of Denmark for he has been preparing, even perhaps since William landed, an invasion of his own, claiming to be (like William) the rightful heir to the English throne, as nominated by King Edward!

Late in 1069 his 300 ships arrive in the Channel, they are forced to turn north (presumably by an English fleet), so they enter the Humber and with perhaps 12,000 men sack York and set about ravaging the lands on either side of the river. Once again King William raises an army knowing that it has to be at least as large as theirs by the time it reaches York, and he marches northwards. The Danes have taken over a large area of fens called the Isle of Axholme to act as their winter camp and strand;

it is possible that their largest warships will not penetrate quite so far inland but careening and maintenance during the winter months will be essential for those that can travel up-river to Axholme.

Somehow, probably because he has already had experience of fenlands at Pevensey, King William surprises these Danish pirates driving them clean out of Axholme and over the Humber to York. By now his forces are more 'English' than 'French', in order to take on such an enemy host in such a place. Still the pirates have their fleet, one largely intact, as a floating camp on the Humber estuary where, without an equal fleet, William cannot touch them. Simultaneously there is also trouble in the West Country and on the Welsh borders; an Anglo-Norman column dispatched to the Welsh borders finds their enemies dispersed and so they move on south-westwards to assist the West Country. As they depart, so the Welsh and brigands emerge again behind them and flood from Shropshire into Staffordshire, jubilant at their cunning. But King William now has the measure of this guerrilla warfare and is waiting in the wings in south Yorkshire. In yet another astute strategic move his column catches them at Stafford and destroys them. William then returns to Lindsey and Lincolnshire and, in winter weather, drives the Danes back to York. In order to escape they take to their ships and now King William has them where he wants them.

Pinned inside the Humber estuary by winter gales, with Anglo-Norman forces patrolling on either bank and the King himself in burnt-out York, the pirates cannot now come ashore. They must remain on their ships to starve, freeze and die of disease and exposure, many of them being non-seafaring mercenaries anyway. William will not leave them, he has them in a vice and by the spring his army will be the largest and the fittest of the two, he is determined to win this battle of attrition. Meanwhile the King's army ravages the already stripped environs of York in order to find food, fuel and drink for themselves and their mounts, so the surrounding peasantry see all soldiers as enemies. Yet with the spring, King William hopes to destroy Danish ambitions once and for all.

Shrewsbury, on the Welsh borders, finds itself under siege but William marches to their relief and raises the siege. As a result brigands disperse across the winter Midland landscape. Now the King determines he will add to the chain of 'castles' and garrisons beginning to cover routes southwards from the North. With spring comes King Swein with more ships only to find his supposedly victorious army decimated and confined. Offered a 'ransom' Swein's local commander accepts and sails out of the Humber to raid the Lincolnshire coast. Unable or unwilling to dispute the matter at sea in such unpredictable weather William marches his army in parallel to the coast, building defences as he passes and obliging the Danes to keep to the sea until they come to the Wash. Here they descend on the Isle of Ely in order to recover and to service their ships for the journey home. Not everyone is aware of their desperate plight, however, for a brigand named Hereward who is being pursued southwards by the King's forces takes his band to join the pirates. On the way southwards he sacks Peterborough then escapes to Ely. The royal forces now watch and wait.

Meanwhile Holy Mother Church is seeking her reward for sanctioning the invasion. The newly arrived Papal legates insist on generous concessions and William, desperate to pay off mercenaries yet also desperate for 'knights', counters with a clever political device. Then to seal the bargain he and his magnates expiate their sins by giving generous grants of real estate to various monastic houses and orders. Now he can campaign while garrisoning those 'bones of the kingdom' he is simultaneously building. While his lieutenants hold his Danish prey in view, safely locked up inside the Wash, King William is negotiating both the means to continue prosecuting his actions and the religious sanction he needs in order to implement this defence. The legates go home to make happy report to the Pope leaving new abbots to make grateful donations of men and money to a generous monarch.

Once again free to concentrate on the pirates William offers them terms to leave England and they, feeling as ready as they will ever be, sail off in their mainly unseaworthy ships with their slaves and loot. On the way home a great storm sinks many of them. Fortunately, or so it seems, for Hereward and his brigands there was no room for them on the ships, so they take over Ely. It is a comfortable billet but the royal estates to the east and south proffer solid defences and the royal army now covers the west and south. All sorts of outlaws and brigands now seem drawn to this 'thieves' kitchen' and the 'porous filter' lets them through. King William can afford to wait, so leaving enough men to imprison them he departs for Normandy to deal with the opportunists there. Two treacherous English earls slip away from William's court but one of them is foolish enough to be drawn to Ely.

Once again experience of wetlands and amphibious operations stands the King in good stead: he returns and makes a decisive attack on the Isle. Hereward escapes but his assembled brigands are not so fortunate. Now William has actually secured the north, south, east and west of his kingdom from attacks but he has also tied down and committed many soldiers to garrison and port duties. The losses from exposure and disease have far outstripped the dead and wounded in battles. It is always so, yet the major source of so much trouble to England still remains a potential threat, Scotland.

In a move unparalleled since the great warrior King Athelstan, William marches into Scotland, devastating the borders as he goes to ensure that they cannot be used to provision an enemy for many years to come. With both a massive English contingent and a considerable fleet at his command he forces King Malcolm to do fealty and submit. Appointing yet another new earl to these northern marches, King William returns to his troubles in France, taking with him to Maine a considerable English contingent.

In England there is now a new Archbishop of Canterbury, Lanfranc, a man struggling with his introduction into the wicked world of politics. With the King safely out of the way the new earl in the north decides to treacherously slaughter his blood feud enemies, so emphasising that royal authority still does not run in the absence of the monarch. The horrified Lanfranc provides a diplomatic penance. Nevertheless, he is to prove a faithful lieutenant, one whom the King can trust in a world of secular and religious self-seekers, not a man to compromise his principles yet a man with similar vision to William. This man is a worthy Justiciar and when it comes to his ears that the Breton lords are now hatching a plot he knows how to behave. With William pinned down in Normandy these Bretons send emissaries to Denmark and to France while attempting to recruit English support. Everyone needs English fyrdmen if they are to succeed. Lanfranc writes to King William to tell him not to worry, his loyal friends can handle this and then he mobilises senior English clerics as well as Norman magnates to throw their hearth-troops into the attack on the Breton lords, who are attempting to secure Anglia. The Breton faction is destroyed, the Crown is victorious.

William now orders his loyal Archbishop to arrange for the construction of impregnable castles with which to protect London and East Anglia. These structures are tremendously expensive, as is the King's campaigning overseas, yet the unique and essential English tax, the geld, is drying up! How to pay for constructions, garrisons, levies, mercenaries, the fleet, munitions, that is the problem. In the shadows, it seems, Lanfranc now discovers a lowly clerk with special 'inside' knowledge of such affairs and also of the affairs of the worldly Bishop Odo, a man Lanfranc especially distrusts. Then to add to the King's troubles, London catches fire.

The mystery of the falling revenues has now been recognised as work commences on these two amazing castle-monuments, neither of which will be completed in King William's lifetime. Nevertheless, there is light at the end of this fiscal tunnel for we now come to the Trial on Penenden Heath. We may, I think, suspect that 'inside' information has already been voiced for King William authorises Archbishop Lanfranc to act simultaneously as plaintiff, judge and jury in a major property dispute with Bishop Odo, the King's uterine brother and apparently the most powerful magnate in the land. Odo presents his own defence, calling not only on his own sub-tenants but also on powerful friends, while technicalities are put to the acknowledged (and very venerable) senior expert on English law. Lanfranc finds for the plaintiff (himself) and by the King's command no appeal is permitted. In retaliation, Odo is decidedly tardy in his compliance: it seems he had never been questioned, let alone crossed, before. And for all that this seems a one-sided trial it is under-pinned by superb English surveying and records. Such science is beyond Norman comprehension and that is to the Crown's advantage.

Now we are entering that complex world of English administration which makes such endless taxation possible. What is more, the taxation is equitable. The richest men are supposed to pay the most and Odo is undoubtedly rich, as are his friends. Though the Church also falls into this super-rich bracket Archbishop Lanfranc is attempting to balance his duty to his King with his duty to God. The Bishop of Durham has a more practical application for this dilemma: he purchases the earldom of Northumbria and then sets about recovering his outlay. Neither are his mercenary 'knights' subjected to any strong discipline for the King is still in France fighting both French enemies and his own son. Over the border the Scottish king eliminates his rivals and then reflects on the opportunities now available in England. When he sweeps southwards the Bishop is no match and, being equally foolish in his actions, the Bishop is now butchered by his own side.

Granting his son that possession of Normandy which he desires, but only after William's death, is William's compromise in order to secure peace. This leaves him free to return to England and to despatch Odo to Northumbria, where the Bishop gives full reign to his lust for blood and loot. With Odo safely employed and remembering how his enemies had allied themselves in the past, King William himself leads a massive show of force into south Wales in order to overawe any opportunistic Welsh princes. With his other problem in mind he then dispatches his errant son to Scotland and King Malcolm, faced with two field forces in the north, withdraws. So, at vast expense and by employing far more men than the Normans could possibly have numbered even in the invasion of 1066 King William has pacified his internal unrest. All over the North he continues to build and garrison 'castles', one can say 'dragon's teeth', in order to impede any attacking forces, but he has also given brother Odo the opportunity to make contact with the northern Welsh Marches. What is his intention? Well, once again he slips away to France.

Low and behold, in 1082 Earl Hugh of Chester, on the northern Welsh Marches, is one of the magnates who elects to join Odo on the Isle of Wight, where an army is being formed in King William's absence. It is impossible to say just how closely and secretly Odo had been watched while in the North, but the faithful Lanfranc seems to have apprised his King of this dangerous development for William now returns to England and 'discovers' these preparations. If there is an alliance afoot, Odo's army is well placed either for overland travel, or, by sea, to London and East Anglia. Striking swiftly and surely King William personally arrests his brother, charges him with secular offences (as Earl of Kent) and despatches him as a high-priority prisoner to the impregnable Tower of Rouen. He then orders that Odo is <u>never</u> to be released.

Deep in the machinery of state, in the heart of the administrative system at Winchester, there has formed a clear impression of widespread corruption. The King orders a comprehensive audit of Odo's earldom of Kent and consequently discovers just how he has been able to finance a potential insurrection. As a result secret orders are issued to the putative 'exchequer'. No hint of the royal plans must be allowed to leak out.

Though the King is forced to return to France in 1083 he is probably doing as much secret recruiting as fighting; Odo apparently 'jumped the gun' for the intelligences from Denmark clearly indicate that another invasion is in preparation. A massive fleet is being assembled with the help of Norway. In 1084 urgent dispatches call William back to Normandy and thence to England. There is every indication that the most serious threat yet made on England is about to unfold. Can King William meet it or can he prevent it? He is the man for such an occasion.

The massive Danish fleet now forming is to be joined by the forces of the King of Norway and aided by the Count of Flanders, and the King of France will certainly be preparing to make a simultaneous descent on Normandy once the coast is clear. This is like nothing experienced before. In England all 'castles' and defences are immediately strengthened against this potential invasion but the real invasion comes back with King William for he returns with a fleet carrying unprecedented numbers of 'knights' and soldiers. It is his intention to turn his kingdom into an armed camp while simultaneously locking up all the mercenaries he can find on his island. If an invasion is attempted he can field more than one army, if it is not then it becomes a war of attrition. Who will waver first?

In addition to a 'mickle geld' the King billets his mercenaries on everyone who can feed them. It is a dangerous expedient for should an enemy land with more treasure than England possesses (a most unlikely eventuality) they could change sides. While they are isolated in England they must feed on the best and this can cause growing disillusion among the whole population. Then again, they might become free agents, brigands, or a magnate (like Odo) might have the financial resources to bribe some of them, who knows? Certainly the ports and shipping have to be under the control of loyal English forces and the food resources, including seed corn and plough beasts, are being severely diminished.

It is a high-risk strategy but it works. Short of provisions and pay the Danish-Norwegian army mutinies and then murders the Danish King. With this the threat is over and so King William rapidly returns his mercenaries to the shores of France. However the shortages they have caused mean that they leave behind them both famine and pestilence.

There is still the underlying problem to solve, how to ensure the loyalty of magnates (even those who are family) to the Crown. Now William's secret administrative orders are brought into effect. After extensive consultation he orders a never before attempted, national, audit: the Domesday Surveys. His intention is to embark for France in 1086 and there teach the French King a lesson he will not forget, but, in the meantime, he intends to keep all 'idle hands' gainfully employed with the overall object of then securing their absolute loyalty once and for all. The magnates (chief tenants) believe that he is ratifying their accumulated real-estate as a preliminary to granting them full heritability but the royal clerks, who are actually doing the work, have a separate and secret brief. They are quietly working to an information-gathering (statistical) model which is capable of detecting a very wide range of frauds and deceptions. In order to threaten a man effectively one requires sound intelligences.

The question that the King is succinctly asking is not 'what is the geld-tax paying me', that he knows already, no, his actual instructions include 'if more can be had'. His question is 'what <u>should</u> everyone be paying' and in the process of revealing this the model (paradigm) devised also identifies potential <u>new</u> areas of taxation along with the frauds. It is all actually accomplished in six months by adding local jury testimonies to older, pre-existing records, which are then compared with one another, and the King is informed by the humble genius who devised the paradigm that it 'works a treat'. Obviously there is not enough time for the King to be given an extensive brief, but he has the reassurance.

Now King William puts his final scheme into place. He calls all men (who hold land by military tenure, large and small) to meet him on Salisbury Plain and there they swear fealty to him above all other men, over and above their own chief lords (magnates), in return for the right (on request) for their nominee to inherit when they die. This is the creation of the English class system, what we now term 'feudal' in structure and in inheritance. Henceforth there will be no excuse for disloyalty (that is treason to the Crown) and this measure also provides a standing army of Norman-French and English tenants who are sworn to the Crown. It is the extension of the old Anglo-Saxon ethic of loyalty to one's lord, to the death, applied to all men who bear arms and hold lands. They are bound to the Crown, that is to the kingdom, now we might begin to speak of 'the nation'.

King William now leads his retributive army to France and there, by an accident of fate, dies prematurely. His son, William 'Rufus', inherits the kingdom, the unique tax base, the absolute fealty and the opprobrium. After all, he is the first monarch to apply the findings of the Domesday Surveys.

Chapter 11

What Had Made It Possible?

hat was it that made this kingdom so desirable in 1066–86, apart from wealth? Put it this way, what made it unique and then also so capable of sustained defence? Of course it was the ability and determination of King William that defended it and wealth, especially a high-value specie currency, that attracted brigands and opportunists but where did that wealth come from and how could England have become so different from the rest of Europe? The first of these questions we will answer in the next chapter, it is the second question, what made her different, which holds the key to her wealth generation. Something rather more than accident was involved in this creation of the national wealth which continued to attract predators.

It was not money alone that made it possible to both sustain a stream of military activities <u>and</u> create a stable society just as wealth alone, today, does not of itself create technological or organisational superiority in the military sphere. Rather it was education, yes, the English ability to survey, calculate and record that had made the underlying structure of taxation possible and this fully evolved taxation was then the cornerstone, all four cornerstones, of defence. This was something the Norman adventurers only discovered after they had taken and received the kingdom. This, if you like, was in itself a secret conquest of the invaders and one so far unremarked by historians, the triumph of education over ruthless brutality. Far from the Norman-French exercising a civilising influence over the English, a parody (to my mind) devised with the dawn of the Edwardian era, in order to please that monarch and to diminish German claims of superiority, it was the English who established for the Norman-French invaders the might of the pen, certainly of the pen when combined with the sword. The other element of defence was the united determination to resist, though on its own this could not have succeeded, just as the Normans could not have succeeded without English co-operation. So

England might have been beggared yet again had it not been for King William's strategic vision and his tenacity.

Duke William, a 'French' adventurer who stumbled into and then accepted this kingdom, had the intelligence to absorb and deploy not only the martial prowess of his new subjects but also their successful administrative and economic systems. He was no blinkered pirate or brigand, though generations of historians have often done him this disservice. He had the vision to create from a complicated (and to some degree ad hoc) legal structure not an entirely new and unproven imposition of alien ideas but, instead, a unified concept of the totality of those things which shape the course of conflict and which especially encourage victory, in his search for elusive peace and stability. In a turbulent age and among the promise of chaos he fashioned the means to retain that which he had acquired, but he also re-formed it into a novel polity. This was 'collusion' in the positive sense of an agreement to combine and co-operate for the common good, truly a 'coming together'.

By absorbing both the knowledge and officials left by his English antecessors, the English kings, he seems to have created a new social model and this not by force (except when defending his kingdom) but by determination and energy, added to his personal appreciation of the value of past practices. We should not represent his reign as one of brutal repression and exploitation of 'the masses', as it is so commonly portrayed for dramatic effect, but as working towards social cohesion and security through the control of powerful and potentially dissident social elements, elements largely exampled among his own coterie and across the Channel. King William had no need to suppress or repress the vast numbers of Englishmen for they were culturally loyal to their elected King. The English had always proved themselves loyal to such rightfully appointed kings. And this king appears to have been loyal, in his turn, to his (English) Coronation Oath. Nor should we forget that security (which includes justice) for the majority of the population is the bedrock on which any society is built. If they enjoy this, then the silent majority are largely acquiescent to political change.

So, what of eleventh-century education, how do we explore this English phenomenon? Well it is usually assumed that for lack of any formal education the English peasantry of 1066 were, mentally, little better equipped than the oxen which pulled their ploughs. We have arrogantly forgotten that most of human progress was achieved before formal education had ever been invented and that peasant agriculture has often been more successful at making the best of a given environment than the intensive and mechanised agriculture of more recent decades.[1] We are now having to rediscover the truth of this, having progressively destroyed even the value of our basic soils since mechanisation and urbanisation took over *c.* 1850. Turning elsewhere, the legacy of Old English literature and language handed down to us through fortunate survivals has been appreciated for some time, though it is only very recently that the evidence of a pictorial 'language' contained on the Bayeux Tapestry has become a further gateway into the vernacular, the common and everyday state of knowledge, in 1066.[2] Equally recent is the proof that Domesday Book was an English and not a Franco-Norman creation, an achievement moreover based on the ancient English facility for surveying and calculating, an expertise not apparently possessed by any other European kingdom.[3] So the English were not just literate but also numerate and we have evidence that they were capable of some degree of arithmetic even at the basic level of the local peasantry. We have no evidence for saying as much of any other kingdom even though we cannot say how the English came by such knowledge in the first place.

Nor in the Franco-Norman sphere do we have anything to compare with the pictorial 'language' in the margins of the Bayeux Tapestry, nor do we have any comparable evidence from Scandinavia, although attempts have been made to undermine this tapestry's importance by claiming it as part of a 'Scandinavian tradition', on no sound evidence.[4] As an English creation the Bayeux Tapestry can be seen to involve completely different techniques and traditions and it has a unique design concept. The Oseberg, Overhoydal and Rolvsoy (Scandinavian) tapestries involve a Byzantine-Caucasian soumak (or snare) weave, not at all like the embroidery on the Bayeux Tapestry, and they also have purely decorative and not didactic margins.[5] It seems that only in England could each 'everyman' viewer personally command sufficient knowledge of so many images of the creatures found in Isidorus of Seville's *Etymologiae* (bestiary) or from some familiar Aesop's fables and then comprehend their significance, thereby enabling a coherent narrative to be created in pictures. These 'captions' then form a commentary which enlarges on the images shown on the main frieze or schema of the Bayeux Tapestry. The importance of this discovery is that it takes us into the minds and psychology of everyday people, not of 'scholars' but the minds of 'the peasantry', for we too can now see what they were thinking when they saw such images. We are actually reading <u>their</u> language and for the first time, the language of people we would call illiterates.

If we look at Domesday Book it further tells us of 'peasant' education, as we shall see.[6] In Suffolk and Norfolk we encounter pre-geld (that is pre-991) local surveys called 'extents' which surveys precisely measured individual locations at some earlier period than 991 and we have also seen even older general surveys preserved in the Tribal and Burghal Hidages. Then we also have the 'scribal apothegms' designed to send coded mathematical messages between 'civil servants'.[7] The royal clerks (or scribes, camerarii) were given task-specific instructions as to the land uses important to the Crown, which were 'pasture', 'meadow', 'woodland' and, in the case of arable, the records of past assessments, but these are also there so that they (our clerks) might further record details of the present and actual area under tillage. This in itself was no mean achievement. These landscape classifications also seem to have originated in Isidorus of Seville's *Etymologiae* (Book XV) where landscapes were similarly divided into 'Arvus' (arable land for sowing), 'Consistus' (trees of all kinds, fruit, nuts, timber, wood) and 'Pascuus' (land for grass and grazings) and finally 'Florus' (the floral garden for bees and their wax and honey). The English land uses are, we should note, more accurate, specific and practically useful! Columella, probably the most comprehensive of the classical writers on agronomy, went even further for he defined two different types of meadow.[8] I do not know how well his works were known in the eleventh century but men on the ground in 1066 and in 1086 certainly defined two types of meadow.

Look carefully, therefore, at the Domesday records and you will observe that these 1086 records are, consistently, even more precise, homely and accurate than any of the formally 'educated' Isidorian classifications <u>and</u> that they were, nevertheless, understood and locally used by the peasant juries required by the survey: English peasants in 1066 and 1086 were, therefore, more precise and knowledgeable than Isidorus! This certainly proves that such things were not informed by 'book-learning' and by Church-trained scholars, no, these jurymen instead deponed as they actually practised and recorded, organically, in their own and local communities, for there are also detectable local and regional variations to be seen enshrined in their logic. Isidorus, in his turn, had certainly improved on Virgil (author of the *Aeneid*) who had been so impractical as to classify all uncultured fields as 'forests' and all open country (*rus*) as pasture land: he was definitely no agronomist! He was an academic theorist without practical information or experience.

Surely, you might ask, could we not then expect Church-trained clerks to quote Virgil's 'authority', at least at times? Well, I think that in Domesday Book we can at times detect this Virgilian influence, what we might call a scholarly corruption of native common sense, presumably because the local etymology actually varied with the logic of each record or local jury. It was reflecting purely local, practical influences on otherwise unrecorded and informal educational matrices. When a Domesday record seems to imply that all open country was 'pasture', then we can say that we might have just such a scholastic (Virgilian) influence at work, if only because other deponents in other districts had much more precise terminology and terminology which better fitted land usage, and also better fitted the royal paradigm when applied to land use. Incoming 'foreign' tenants could and did bring their own units and logic with them which, thanks to scribal training, were then anomalously entered in the Domesday records.

Thus at Shalbourne, Marten and Burbage we find meadows actually measured in 'arpents' (a French unit otherwise and correctly reserved for vineyards) by Frenchmen who were 'King's servants'. The rest of Wiltshire consistently used English units when measuring meadows![9] The poor old camerarii just had to do the best they could with local and regional variations, they had no judicial or executive powers, they (being so schooled) simply set it down as it came from each set of deponents. Clerks were trained to be careful copyists and not to alter what was read or said, that is why (at times) they even copied earlier mistakes when reproducing a text or maybe they reproduced the distinctive alphabet of their exemplar instead of maintaining a consistent scribal hand. We regularly encounter this last weakness on the pages of Domesday Book.

Have a look, this weakness actually betrays the incorporation of earlier written records in the final text, and that is how we know that such records existed and were consulted.

On the margins of the Bayeux Tapestry we encounter birds and animals which are not yet supposed to have been known, instead of seeing only the commonly known fabulous beasts and birds. These were strange and (to scholars of course) unknown creatures only found far away, creatures <u>not</u> listed in Isidorus. We can only conclude that some of the embroiderers had personal experience. We also see unfolded fables that were, supposedly, discovered much later.[10] Peasant viewers and 'readers' of these margins (just like the peasants calculating the acreages of their fields) could therefore comprehend and define such things to a degree we have <u>never</u> before suspected. England, unique in Europe, even had its own survey unit of land, as we have seen, the 'hide'. How it came to be found <u>only</u> in England I cannot say but the source, as far as I can see, was a fable in Virgil's *Aeneid*.[11] Moreover in England alone in *c*. 1066 we have evidence of the use of horse-power in agriculture, though the traditional vocabulary, in common with France and Scandinavia, instead expressed units of ox power.[12] We have to wait for the fifteenth century before we see such illustrations again. All these things add up to a unique (in Europe) common educational foundation.

In the Burghal Hidage of *c*. 900 (or before) we encounter mathematical formulae enabling us to calculate both the garrisons and the areas and defended perimeters of camps and 'castles'.[13] I know of no European parallels. Turning to language, some researchers claim that the literary epic *Beowulf* was not a purely Anglo-Saxon creation, yet it occurs in Old English long before the Scandinavian Sagas or the French *Chanson de Roland* (this latter the foundation of French literature) were ever recorded. Between them Andrew Bridgeford and Professor D.D.R. Owen have argued a strong case for the similarity of the *Chanson de Roland* and the *Carmen de Hastingae Proelio*, a case which focuses on the person and depiction of the Bayeux Tapestry figure of Turold, 'jongleur' to Count Eustace II of Boulogne, so linking a pre-1075 date for the Bayeux Tapestry to the genesis of the aforesaid *Chanson*.[14] There would seem to be in this a strong connection between the foundation of French literature and a purely English and vernacular work of decorative art of *c*.1070, in fact our Bayeux Tapestry, both of these creations emerging long after *Beowulf* was set down. We can say that even if *Beowulf* was borrowed from some Scandinavian source its insular expression predated by far the conception of the *Chanson du Roland*.

Now, we will make bold to ask, what of the decorative and applied arts in England? By 1066 England was famous throughout Europe for Opus Anglicanum embroidery in silks and bullion, seen as one of the *opus Dei* (works in Praise of God).[15] The *Liber Eliensis* also tells us that such works were secular as well as religious for Ælderman Brytnoð left rich embroideries from his clothing at Ely as nuncupative evidence when on his way to Maldon in 991. The *Lindisfarne Gospels* and the *Book of Kells* are well known as early illustrated books but there are also a number of later, English, artworks which show that native draughtsmen were equal to anything produced on the Continent. The place of the Bayeux Tapestry in this artistic milieu is as an immediate and vernacular (decorative) production by a professional workshop, not *opus Dei* but rather a work of contemporary, as we might say of 'modern', art.[16] Its images and messages are demonstrably <u>not</u> scholastic borrowings from esoteric and earlier sources (as so often claimed in the past) but direct and everyday visions of the world around its embroiderers, which further secures its value as evidence of education.[17] Yet the big surprise is not really this vernacular, visual or cartoon language in the margins but the 'Tituli', the sporadic Latin superscripts which intrude in places, for these were designed for those with a formal education to read, whatever their spoken tongue. These were for the 'educated' viewer to follow and no doubt they also gave educated Church scholars the opportunity to show off in translation but their 'message' to non-English Latin speakers was very restricted in scope when compared with the pictorial 'language' in the margins! Why are they set out in Latin (and with English spellings)? Because both English and French clerics understood this common language – and because the cleric who provided them was himself English.

I think we can dismiss post-Conquest (French) claims that the English clergy had forgotten Latin as no more than flimflam French clerical propaganda. Both the English court and the English clergy could write equally well in English or in Latin, and we have plenty of pre-Conquest evidence to hand to evidence this. After the Conquest, as French clerks were undoubtedly intruded into the King's personal Curia (for Chancery and Exchequer purposes), so it became necessary to change the language of charters and writs to something they could also understand, to the lingua franca of Latin, a language that both English and French speakers could understand, but note that the English practice of issuing writs was nevertheless retained. 'Alone in Western Europe and in the Early Middle Ages, the Celtic countries seem to have had professional learned men ... in England at least (Kings) may have employed officials ... the task would eventually have devolved upon the King's chaplain–clerk', concluded David Dumville.[18] Casting around for some scholastic tradition superior to that of Europe he therefore suggested Celtic missionaries in England, but I maintain that classical (insular) 'Celtic' continuity is more likely to have been the real influence on the professionalism of the Anglo-Saxon Church scholars. There is no evidence for Britain's 'barbarian' isolation as England, her isolation might well have preserved and promoted insular civilisation when Europe was overrun by barbarians.

Wormald questioned why Latin was the chosen language of most Germanic legislators on the Continent when in England the vernacular was generally adequate prior to 1066.[19] He concluded that in England there was such an imperfect understanding of Latin that the vernacular had to be employed, as if these laws were created spontaneously instead of being copied from existing Latin texts! His suggestion does not explain the nuances necessary when making accurate translations of technical matters from Latin in the, universally employed, originals into Old English vernacular, where any inadequacy on either part would lead to certain legal disaster. He then went on to actually example Continental Latin 'howlers' which, if they prove anything, undoubtedly indicate that Continental scholarship was so imperfect that it <u>required</u> the employment of the original Latin in order to avoid textual mistakes. We do not find such evidence in England. He had the telescope by the wrong end! The English (vernacular) phenomenon can rather be attributed to a much greater fluency in <u>both</u> languages, resulting in an easy interchange between them and so ensuring safe employment of the vernacular tongue in and at court. It also promoted the myth of Divine kingship and reinforced the universal application of the value of law in governance. Such wisdom must surely come from God.

The great encouragement in law came from kingship for, as Wormald put it, it was not so much a matter of what kings did for legislation as what legislation did for kings.[20] A competent and impressive exercise of judicial functions gave kings an enviable authority, it gave them otherwise inexplicable insight and wisdom 'on tap'; in England there was (as yet) no lex scripta of precedent by which to seek guidance, so practical applications would need to be clearly expressed but also to be seen to rely on scholarly and ancient research, despite being delivered under despotic authority. In this way kingly judgements and wisdom appeared to be Divinely inspired, clear evidence to all men that such a king was Divinely ordained to rule. The secret, of course, was that such wisdom actually came from ancient Latin exemplars but outside the 'circle of power', who was to know that?

The most obvious source of information (let us say 'education') for the mass of the population came from the Church, but it was not the esoteric knowledge of scholars, rather it was the homely deliveries of preaching clergy. The Vulgate (Bible) was in Latin, so it needed to be translated and presented in a way that ordinary folk could comprehend. The wide vocabulary of bestiary and Aesopian fables we see on the Bayeux Tapestry also tells us that these priests had absorbed some further scholarship which they then included in their sermons, apparently thereby rivalling the oral attraction of pagan beliefs and popular superstitions.[21] These English sermons were certainly not the esoteric and censored expositions of Faith recorded in later monastic sources but instead an interface of the spiritual and the vernacular and with such power to attract that they rivalled that contemporary 'learning on the job' which filled the workaday week. One wonders whether the 'new', post-Conquest, French clergy who gradually replaced the English oral tradition after 1066 had anything half as good to offer, anything half so attractive. There must often have been an additional language barrier. Still, what mattered to the post-Conquest Church was doctrinal conformity, the acknowledgement of the importance of the Church, of Rome and of St Benedict. The peasantry, it appears, were there to serve them and not the other way about!

So what of the more academic pre-Conquest teachings which trickled down from monastic seclusion and isolation into the filter and catalyst which we say was provided by the local preaching priest in England?

How sound, comprehensive and informed was this 'higher education'? Its quality is important if we are to understand these people of 1066 (and before) for scholastic education is presented by exemplars, whereas pragmatism instructs the informal delivery, yet we are really attempting to understand the synthesis of the two and preferably without the handicap of our own implanted and later prejudices and instilled beliefs. Ælfric, Abbot of Eynsham, was a very influential scholar and in his 'Die Temporibus Anni' of *c*. 993 we encounter an interesting, potentially misleading, amalgam of biblical and Classical teachings with which to blend contemporary, secular, pragmatism by 1066.[22] He teaches that God created this (His) world and so all that is in it and around it, the Cosmology, is His and being omnicompetent He can effect whatever He pleases. Standard doctrinal delivery of course, but no doubt taken more literally then than it is now? Yet the view our scholar presents of the natural functioning of the earth and its surrounding 'stars' (we cannot put modern words like 'planets' into his mouth) is wholly indebted to Roman scholarship, as informed by the Greek philosophers. It is Classical. God, it seems, becomes the capricious element within an order and set of rules He has created!

All other spheres, Ælfric says, move around the earth for it is the centre of His Cosmography (or universe) but Ælfric slips in the information that the earth is <u>round</u>. The stars, he says, are much bigger than they appear to be because they are so distant: he therefore invokes perspective in his literary vehicle when visual artists would not employ it for another 500 years! Now, we must be circumspect. We cannot implant foreknowledge of modern scientific discoveries onto this text by some process of abiogenesis or Divine revelation. I have no idea how he could have explained the necessary physical theories, such as gravity or space teaching matter how to curve. In spite of what some people have written I believe his concept of 'round' was discoidal and not a sphere. I certainly doubt that the scientific theories propounded by some (long-dead) Greeks were known to him, the Latin manuscript versions by then available to him had been corrupted in the intervening centuries by too many copyists.

He was certainly familiar with Isidorus of Seville's 'De Natura Rerum' but he was also borrowing from the scholarship of the Venerable Bede and so his exposition of the firmament, at first view, does read surprisingly well to our modern age and modern minds. Thus 'Seo heofan, and sae, ond eorðe sind gehatene middangeard' – 'The Heavens and the sea and the earth are called middle-earth' – and he goes on to say that the firmament turns always about us, both under this earth and above it, with unmeasured space between it and the earth. He also speaks of 'ðaere eorðan sine wealtnysse', which is said to be translated as 'the earth's roundness' (presumably from 'sinewealt'?).

Could he possibly have meant that the earth was a sphere, I think not, so we should ask just how far did he understand the texts he had read and how far did these exemplars, upon whom he drew, understand what they in their turn had read in even older sources? Simple fables, of course, were much easier to understand but, even so, the sources available then were not as comprehensive as they later became, nor were the fabulous elements of the available bestiaries quite as fanciful as they later became (when fabulous journeys became popular with the literate laity).[23] These Church-trained English, pre-Conquest, scholars preached what they believed from their own comprehension in academe and they and their lay audiences together compounded such information with what they had observed in life. In this way they pragmatically created a comprehensive and satisfying foundation of knowledge within which belief, rather than evidence, sometimes helped them to comprehend the world around them. Without televisions or iPads they nevertheless created a happy synthesis which enabled them to form beguiling fantasies on the back of harsh realities of existence. This made for a psychologically comforting world and though we do not share the same synthesis of knowledge we do share this dependency.

They also had the religious assurance that angels moved among and around them unseen while legions of devils lurked in bush, brake and briar to tempt them. What they could not explain often became folklore, itself often based on older and pagan beliefs not approved by the Church. These elemental aspects of knowledge, these beliefs, we should however separate from the practical knowledge we have discussed, from practical applications such as measuring, counting and calculating though, of course, imagination is as important to literary achievement (at times) as the ability to express it. We see no such comprehensive parallels among

Continental or Scandinavian populations, though the latter created their own literary traditions.

Most telling of all, to my mind, is the existence of the 'hide' unit in England, a unique unit of comprehensive area, for without it the ability to survey could not have existed. The mathematical ability which made this possible surely formed the foundation of England's successful economy while the existence of such a unit made an equitable specie-only taxation possible. This piece of fiscal magic (the geld) initially brought nothing but mischief to England until, through the perception and single-minded application of William I, it was redeployed as the key element of defence. Finally, once security from external forces could be assured, the same monarch emplaced the machinery of internal security, resulting (eventually) in a stability that allowed a national identity, pride and consciousness to evolve under his posterity. Had it not been for the institutions and polity of pre-Conquest England, themselves consequential upon the country's education and wealth, this process could never have begun.

Appreciation of land uses and the calculation of areas, of course, were alike pragmatic and represented 'the inevitability of gradualness'. We know of no surveying instruments so the accumulation of areal units, of hides, must have been the result of thousands of individuals all visually discerning acres, just as William Cobbett was still doing (with amazing accuracy) in the early nineteenth century, or as Columella had advocated in his first-century treatises on agriculture.[24] We see the same process at work in those Domesday shires which measured their pastures or woodlands by leagues and furlongs rather than in acreages, so much by so much. The Anglian 'extents' are identical compilations made on areas occupied by inhabitants maybe a century before 1066, maybe even older.[25]

Some men clearly thought of measuring things in one way, others in another, but to have commercial viability each of these individual systems had to have acceptance over a given locale, district or region. In Domesday Book we find men in one shire defining 'meadows' or 'pastures' in one way while their neighbours, the other side of a river, defined them in another.[26] The units they used to express such land uses were matched to their local evaluations, so that high-quality (thus high-value) land might be expressed in small, precise, parcels (such as acres) while those communities with tracts of (to them) less valuable land (which they defined with the same noun) used larger units (such as furlongs by furlongs). Woodlands, whose extent the eye cannot easily encompass, are easier to express in linear measurements than in acres though small arable fields, open to the eye, are easily encompassed. We are also assisted in our comprehension of their thinking by lexical reciprocity, which means that arable, pasture and meadow will always be present over a hundred, wapentake or shire, even if one of them is omitted from the written record, for sometimes we find communities putting meadow and pasture together (for example) or even conflating pastures (untilled land) with plough lands (tillage). Well, how would you define the difference say between pasture and scrubby common, meadow grass and grazings, even the difference between fallow (resting tilth) and tilth (arable)? Even today such things are still evasive in law as well as in everyday speech.

It would appear that among the peasantry there was a common appreciation of the area of an acre, of 22 x 220yd or (as later termed) 'an acre-shot', which is (of course) descriptive of an eleven-score bowshot distance. The ability to aggregate such visualised units seems to have had universal application. The common objection (by historians) to accepting such evidence is that such people would not have had a 'standard' foot or yard by which to work, but such standards are not difficult to enforce, in fact they even commend themselves. They are considerably less precise than the standards applied to the production and regulation of contemporary specie coinage and far less arcane than the knowledge required to produce steel in a world without any chemical knowledge or microscopic examination.[27] As to repeated accuracy, I would refer doubters to the exacting thirteenth-century standards set for the Assizes of bread and ale, or the practical application that could create a clincher built ship capable of crossing the North Sea and rounding Rattray Head and Cape Wroth to Ireland (let alone crossing to North America), not to mention the navigational problems involved. One failure in repeated accuracy might be your last!

If some of these skills were relatively commonly distributed across Europe and Scandinavia, skills such as steel-making and ship-building and sailing, it is all the more remarkable that only in England do we encounter surveying and comprehensive land-survey units; a system (or series of linked systems) for the definition of land usage with the ability to create both mathematical formulae and arithmetical (coded) messages. With such achievements in mind, very possibly unique achievements, the capacity of England to create desirable material objects and so to generate trade favourable to wealth creation is not, perhaps, surprising.

For the peasantry their basic numeracy was apparently based on very simple concepts, mainly on aggregation of visualised parcels of land, though they seem to have had some ability to count stock as well and, at times, paid in-kind rents in large quantities (e.g. eel rents). This is not really surprising for even the educated clerks must have done their arithmetic in a similar way and a very ancient, universal way. Just as speech and language can exist independent of reading and writing so counting and numbers can be independent of any system of documentary numeration. Thus our universal system of algorithm, otherwise known as 'Arabic numerals', that is the ability to create columnar calculation through the abstract of a number which 'is' and yet does not exist (that is '0') in combination with numerals 1–9, was not employed. I used to tell children that 'cypher', zero, is a magic number, for so it would have seemed in 1066 or 1086, so it did seem several centuries later, being simultaneously something and nothing. As far as we know Western scholars, let alone the mass of the population, did not yet have this system. Instead they employed Roman numeration, a system used to express products rather than processes: MDCLXVI (=1666). This was the universal numerical system for documents in Europe. For process they used counters (later termed jettons) which were cast (jetter) on a board ('chequer board') or table divided into columns of notional value, an abacus process which was intelligible alike to accountant and to observers. The term 'ex-chequer' means 'out of the counting-house', the place where the royal chequer board was kept. We can say that the everyday process of arithmetic was therefore visual, just like the picture-writing of the Bayeux Tapestry. Being so, the carter on his side of the board or table could read the figures just as well as the clerk who was casting the account.

Of course, the process of transferring visualised and pictorial language to a written language (like Latin) was open to mistakes, both mistakes in perception of the handwriting and in spelling. The alphabet and calligraphy employed for Latin could also prove misleading, especially when ligatured (as it is throughout Domesday Book) and combined with Roman numeration. Thus a cursive series of 'IIIIII' might stand for 'i', 'I', 'm', 'n' or 'u' and at times even for 'o'![28] The transfer of columns of counters on a 'chequer' was also open to error when drawn up (or set down) as a product on parchment in combinations of 'i', 'v', 'x', 'I' or 'c', simply because the outcome could be altered by a slip of the pen.[29]

So we do, but only very occasionally, detect errors of this sort in the Domesday records, though we only rarely discover that the actual areas measured are incongruent (when we are able to check or verify them by comparison with known values). In later and less important local documents, such as Compotus Rolls, we often encounter the replication of the 'chequer' process in the margins in the form of dots as the accountant checked the arithmetic against the expressed outcome. In such everyday cases the Roman numeration is often deleted and corrected, but we do not see such emendations in Domesday Book – these entries were apparently double-checked before being engrossed in epitome! So we can say that systems were less than satisfactory but basic education was adequate for purpose, which only increases our admiration for their achievements.

It would indeed have been surprising if education had not played a major part in creating, sustaining and deploying the wealth and the bounteous resources of England. This education was not some esoteric, scholastic learning confined to and then handed down by a tiny cadre of supermen and clerical intellectuals, as we have so often been told in the past. It was, as we have now seen, a long way from that closed religious world which was so often restricted to Holy relics, corrupted classical references and Divine revelations. It was instead practical, comprehensive and contemporary, it was common, everyday and fit for purpose in the English world. Moreover it was this educational and educated resource which then made the Norman invaders themselves successful and which has ever since, to the uncritical eye, made them look so efficient. Indeed, with hindsight the Anglo-Norman world seems so much more efficient, organised and certainly cohesive than that of their Franco-Norman brethren over the water. Is it not strange that this comparison has not been made before now?

Chapter 12

The Attraction of England in 1066

H istorians do, so often, seem to assume that money grows on trees, or at least in fields, perhaps because it is so difficult for modern minds to grasp the essential nature of a medieval subsistence society? So writers such as Arnold have written of 'the land's wealth' of the Anglo-Saxon kingdoms mainly in terms of food and pottery production and settlement types.[1] Well be the surplus of food you produce never so great, you still have to sell (or barter) it to someone else in order to profit from the excess and then they have to have the means to buy, buy both in guaranteed specie and low denominations. If there is no one to purchase it and it does not keep, then it does not sell, so what is the point of producing it? Food production is not the simple answer to wealth-generation, rather it is marketing it that earns value and demand and distribution govern marketing. The best one can achieve without outlets is to present the excess (over subsistence), in kind to a powerful elite, to those who do not participate in creating it but offer you land on which to produce it. This means that they have acquired controlling rights over the land, usually by force.

Although not strictly 'feudal', English society in 1066 was definitely hierarchical: as the Indian proverb had it, 'mankind belongs to God, the land to the government and power to the powerful rulers'. A land-owning English aristocracy held estates from the Crown, which was a kingship ratified and advised by a council or Witan of the powerful and rich. Anyone else who wished for a share in the landscape had to provide services in return. For most people this sub-owning stratum (the tenantry) had limited property interests which were not automatically heritable and in return for their land grant they had to support themselves on it while creating a surplus for their landowner. This was subsistence. Thus the landowner had guaranteed sustenance and service plus whatever else he or she (in England it included women) could find or create from the several assets at their disposal. Defence of one's overlord was of paramount importance and politically this was manifested in defence of the realm (the kingdom) or of the lord's private interests. The two did not always coincide. Paradoxically, such coincidence was to be an Anglo-Norman achievement, yet it was one created in England which was then exported to Europe and is now called 'feudalism'.

This basic subsistence model meant that the most important assets any lord possessed were his tenantry, those who produced for him. He protected them and his enemies (whoever, pro tempore) tried to wipe them out, unless aiming to take them over as sub-tenants. If they wished for his lands it would be prudent to preserve the sub-tenants, the producers, if not, these were expendable. Aggression might aim to eliminate a landholding family or interest, or it might aim to eliminate their 'assets' and so beggar them. At the bottom of the social heap were slaves (a notch below serfdom), the marketable, absolute property of their owner and so assets worth acquiring and usually with no economic loyalties at all. These might once have been criminals, refugees, debtors or simply prisoners-of-war and had no merit outside the labour they could provide. They could be used for the worst types of work but, as they had a market value, it was sensible to treat them with some small consideration. As in the Classical World, some may have possessed valuable skills and so possibly able to ameliorate their lot. Among the Saxon/English stories of skilled slaves, 'Weland smith' comes to mind.

We have established that it is the lure of wealth, in some form and generally as bullion, that attracts invaders and conquerors. Yet this economic structure does not seem to be well understood and many modern people do not seem to have an appreciation of the mechanics involved. Perhaps it is worth establishing the fundamentals before we go on to discuss wealth generation and accumulation. In the 1950s there was a proposition that if one built 'a better mousetrap, then the world would beat a path to your door', so was that the case for Saxon England? Yes and no, the world has first to know that you have built a better mousetrap and that involves publicity and demonstration. Note also that it has to <u>be</u> a better mousetrap than anyone else can build <u>and</u> that we are talking of selling something.

Sales of any commodities require 'vehicles' to move them and some form of acceptable exchange, something 'fungible'. That England possessed desirable and known wealth by 1066 is undeniable but this was the result of a long process, it did not happen by itself or overnight. Ultimately England could even run to luxury goods such as exceptional textiles. The Bayeux Tapestry may not be a 'treasure' of the OPUS ANGLICANUM type but, though vernacular and unpretentious in materials, its very sophistication and size and the fact that it was the creation of a skilled workshop made it a luxury (viz. a non-essential but desirable) product.[2] Before we reach the stage where such workshops are sustainable we have first to establish a flourishing economy and social structure. We have to begin with more ordinary and essential commodities before we reach such a stage.

Let us take this step by step in order to obtain a clear picture. The problem with commodities was in finding markets for them, for without markets they are still not fungible. Luxury goods were desirable, armaments essential, therefore the skills and knowledge involved in these fields were valued. The peasantry could produce food, the rich and powerful could enjoy it and feed their servants on it, but who was there to buy the surplus? Answer, who else but those who produce luxuries rather than food. Money, specie, therefore took second place to skills and commodities: money was fungible (capable of unitary exchange) given a socio-economic structure to employ it and given the means of creating and circulating it, but you couldn't eat it, sail in it, wear it or fight with it. Before you can make use of money, even precious metal money (specie) you first need markets and markets require that people without something you have will trade what you want for what you possess. Now, with everyone producing foodstuffs (or being presented with them) the opportunities for food exchange (outside military needs) are limited to regional specialisations (e.g. those resulting from ecology or topography) and to personal taste. You need non-subsistence producers to purchase either your excess or your specialities in order to benefit from surplus produce and they cannot exist outside a service economy of some sort, one generally based on commodities. Then we can say that the tanner ('knowledge' of chemistry plus skills) will tan when it is more profitable to do so than to subsistence farm, the shipwright will build ships if it is more lucrative than fishing and farming: here we enter the realm of industry. Even agriculture can become a service industry when it supports other industrial outputs, especially those concerned with conflict. Industries, in a subsistence economy, are the key commodity generators. Welcome to the world of Adam Smith.

In the tenurial structure of a medieval local economy sustainability, for each individual, would ultimately depend on whether the land could be apportioned equitably for unitary exchange, for it also has to be 'fungible'. For land to be fungible it must avoid unitary ambivalence, which means that there must be standard measurements of area, for only then can it become, in financial terms, 'liquid'. It also has to be conformable to purpose and purposes require their own specialisations. Ploughing is a specialisation and a skill and without it there is no grain. The fungibility of produce, which is certainly present in grain (as in money) and might also be said to exist in tenurial services, is incentivised (gains added value) by productivity, provided there is also access to markets, and this productivity will be the result not only of land quality/suitability to given outputs (grain, meat, fish) but also of enterprise (incentive output) and effort (input) and these depend on skill sets. Roman Britain had possessed measured landscapes, markets and also a specie currency (coin of an intrinsic value guaranteed by the government, in this case because it was part of an Imperial or 'universal'/global economy). If these things were entirely lost at the Migration and under Anglo–Saxon occupation, as appears to have been the case, then it would take time and some alternative stimulus to that of an empire to incentivise their reinstatement. They would need to grow and develop organically, but according to some new economic model which did not require either an empire or a global economy.

The Romans had once created markets but, as Hodder observed, the non-random pattern of Romano–British towns, so that each area with a market was founded on a fort serving variously military and economic functions, and providing administrative and other training, was something that took perhaps 200 years to create.[3] If these had all disappeared by the sixth century, then the process had to begin again and in a very different way for there was no state and there was no army by which to justify markets or money, or even to train vocations. As long as a man can feed, clothe and house his family his immediate incentives are gratified. At this basic level grain may be fungible but this fungibility will be limited by demand. In order to develop (or employ) other skills a man requires assurance of greater reward. Only then will he actually sacrifice his subsistence independence.

Finer food, clothes and accommodation may mean social status but only fungibility can guarantee any real stimulus. Specie coinage is the fungible concomitant of specialisation and so of industry and commodities, though someone powerful also has to produce and guarantee it. In an industrialised society we have now taken away the security of subsistence but for medieval man the incentive, to abandon subsistence and trust to a capricious and precarious survival, had to be the lure of some comprehensive fungibility, and only bullion can guarantee that and only specie coinage can make bullion generally liquid. Even then it will not permeate society until transactions are reduced from the major to many minor scales. The silver penny of Saxon England gave specie liquidity only for higher value goods and communities dependent on individual warlords for protection were compact enough to self-supply smaller payments in kind, and therefore had no need of coinage at the local level. For lack of an Imperial state and an army it was then necessary to make the massive evolutionary jump to an urban pattern without that (convenient) intervening military occupation stage which the Roman model (like all colonial powers) had included.

Sutton Hoo and the Staffordshire Hoard point to an age of gold, of treasure rather than of currency, mirroring the obsession of Beowulf, so where did it come from and is it an indicator of the general economy? Well bullion, even when used as specie, has fungibility not liquidity, it is still difficult to divide among recipients. It is treasure in its most obvious form but treasure, though desirable, has to have fungible value through liquidity to be of general use. Gold only had fungibility among the most affluent in the society. Other 'treasures', such as manuscripts, needed an agreed buyer (in default of intrinsic value) before the proceeds of acquisition could be enjoyed, they therefore could not be readily traded or divided even among the wealthy. Gold and silver objects could more easily be hacked into crude shares, but for true liquidity one needed not only a relatively moderate value coinage, that is a silver coinage of guaranteed content, but also its general distribution across society. Trading in luxury imports and in exports was difficult to transact in gold so silver coins, though still equivalent to our higher denomination banknotes, came into wider use among those with the resources to acquire them. For unless one was mining the bullion or receiving it in return for luxuries and manufactures, silver pennies were themselves restricted to the rich.

To convert agricultural surplus to cash one needed markets, markets only existed in towns and even townsmen tilled the fields around them in order to lessen their dependence on money purchases.[4] In times of dearth it became easier for country dwellers to acquire silver pennies because the more isolated town dwellers, traders and artisans had no choice but to pay high prices for essentials, they were vulnerable, but at the subsistence level of the peasantry there was no real need for specie transactions, so liquidity was still restricted, even long after the Conquest. Peasant communities did not usually starve, whatever novelists believe and it would be a foolish landlord who oppressed them to the point of debility. His was the greater loss. Ploughmen do not grow on trees and lordlings do not have the peasant's practical expertise or his inclination to work. Peasant societies are invariably composed of knowledgeable specialists upon whom others depend.

Even when there was access to a market – and for many people there was not – one had to sell a lot of eggs in order to qualify for one penny! Subsistence peasants can rarely have been in the position to sell dozens of eggs in one batch and their modest surplus was generally accounted in gifts of eggs (or other commodities) to their landlord. He alone then had the quantity (if his household did not consume them) to trade in eggs, but only when he had a market readily available. He too paid his overlord, even the King, in butter, eggs, bread and ambers of ale, as required. The world of everyday rural transactions relied on foodstuffs and labour (sometimes on carrying service) in return for the tenancy of a subsistence holding. Not that such holdings were always small, though population pressures could eat away at tenancies: villeins were very like eighteenth-century tenant farmers, maybe with 60, 120, 240 (or sometimes more) acres. They could not work such sizeable units alone (so a family was essential) and, as in later centuries, holdings of this size, once established, were capable of providing very comfortable subsistence.

There needed to be some stimulus for urbanisation and this urbanisation (and attendant industries) was only likely to emerge with the evolution of comprehensive kingship. Warlords are the enemies of urbanisation and the 'castles' and townships necessary to develop markets and trade links only become organic under secure conditions. The more comprehensive the power of kingship the greater the stability, the greater the stability the stronger becomes the incentive for the craftsman to relinquish subsistence alone and to transfer into a money economy via specialisation. When King William established a network of 'castles' in the North and the North Midlands he effectively created the old Roman model of fort, garrison and market and this in itself encouraged specialisation and enterprise, stimulating growth of the money economy over a wide area.

The pre-Conquest villein, like other tenants, held his land and home 'at the will of the lord' and if he could not meet his obligations, his in-kind rent, he was dispossessed. Only the landholder, the land's lord, had a little more security, provided he discharged his duties of provision and civil and military service to those above him and as long as his peasant tenants survived and thrived to provide provisions. This militated against their arbitrary dispossession. While the peasantry, who were the vast majority of the population, relied on subsistence, self-sufficiency and barter, their lord needed arms and armour and status luxuries which <u>had</u> to be purchased and, when required, the 'lord' and landholder had also to provide 'treasure' for the support of his lord. Those lords who supported (we are told) Duke William in 1066 were required to contribute twice the normal amount of treasure to his cause. It is extremely unlikely that the true peasantry ever possessed or used specie.

For a start, money was struck by moneyers at a limited number of centres guaranteeing quality, and those who required pennies brought their own silver and paid the moneyer a commission; he, in turn, paid the King for coin dies. There was no central, royal mint (though there was central royal control of coinage in England), it was all enterprise. We can hardly imagine the peasantry carrying pieces of silver or travelling miles to a moneyer. Specie was for the rich. Kings taxed the moneyers, so adding to the value of the coinage made from the silver presented to each artisan.[5] If the burghs then became marketplaces we can make sense of Edward the Elder's tenth-century fine for buying outside any market (the later crime of 'forestalling'), though the goods involved are generally likely to have been luxuries. Thus the moneyers would be established in burghs, for trade and for their own security, in such places as Pevensey, Winchester, Wallingford or London with their ready made defences, places producing coins in order to pay the market tolls and other indirect forms of taxation attached to burghs and to supply the burghers who traded within them.[6] William, of course, effectively enlarged this network of secure bases when he developed numbers of smaller burghs or 'castles'.

Before the advent of the 'Vikings' ('pirates'), Norse raiders and invaders, trade with the Continent had been conducted by merchants landing at specific 'emporia'. These have been defined as 'an expression of administered long-distance trade' and their rationale was 'to import rather than export, the converse of our modern long-distance trading system', thus a model only possible in a subsistence society.[7] Nevertheless merchants came to trade their luxury goods for other luxury and high-value commodities and not for basic foodstuffs, so they formed a basis for industrial constructs, a stimulus in many fields. 'The implications for Kingship were considerable, it had to adapt itself to a new socio-economic environment', observed Hodges and in this the Anglo-Saxon Kings were successful.[8] Tolls were levied in the eighth century on ships at London and elsewhere, an incentive encouraging commerce. Were these adaptations of the Roman PORTARIUM or were they later introductions? 'The possibility of Roman influence cannot be dismissed', says Sawyer, so continuity may even have created trading opportunities long before the creation of specific emporia.[9] The name EMPORIUM itself came from the Greek EMPOROS, a merchant or one coming to port after crossing the sea. It was as aspecific in the Anglo-Saxon as it had been in the Roman world. We cannot, therefore, say how many emporia there were or whether unrecorded havens such as Pevensey were ever Emporia. 'Commercial affairs as such have no special term; they cannot be positively identified ... the reason is that ... it was an occupation which did not (traditionally) correspond to any of the hallowed, traditional activities'.[10]

So there we have it, the needs of most people, whether within or without the Roman Empire (and then also in Saxon England) were met from local resources: the rich had their own vast estates with their own servants and craftsmen. Even 'their dependent freemen also had rights in the varied common resources of these estates', including communal building enterprises, and there were also probably some travelling craftsmen.[11] A specie economy, therefore, though of great potential to kings (if they were aware of such models), was hardly, easily, realisable outside the realms of a very rich minority of subjects and quite unnecessary to the vast majority of the peasant population. Coinage, as opposed to treasure transfers, had to await greater urbanisation than just emporia or burghs and then, of course, the pirates got in the way.

The change from small gold coins, really just bullion reserves, to silver 'sceattas' seems to have happened at the end of the seventh century and the 'penny' appeared in the late eighth. Edgar reformed the coinage in 973 but the southern foci, the mints, were still London, Canterbury, Rochester and Southampton or Winchester: by now Ipswich seems to have withdrawn. The profitability of the moneying business probably accounts for the large numbers of moneyers at work, normally about sixty of them in Æthelred's reign, but undoubtedly the greatest stimulus to specie and coinage was the imposition in his reign of the specie-only taxation: 'gafol', heregeld, danegeld or simply 'geld'. As a result probably millions of pennies were eventually struck to finance the increasingly heavy ransoms demanded by Viking armies, holding the kingdom to ransom, and as a result more English pennies have been found in Scandinavian hoards than in England. The taxation, the geld, as I have said, was equitably assessed by linking it to the known estates of the landowners, estates assessed in 'hides' in England (proper) and in 'carucates' in the Danelaw districts, that area agreed between Ælfred and Guthrum at Wedmore.[12] Thus the Danish element settled in England was as much a victim of the Vikings as anyone else. There were probably about 4,000 major landowners we might say 'freemen', with minor 'free' tenants (such as socmen) under them. So a simplistic division of a geld of £16,000 (or 3,840,000*d*.), as paid in 994, would average-out at £4 per landholder (or 960*d*.) with the largest landholders paying most. What would this be in recent purchasing power is impossible to say, perhaps £29,000 (minimum) each, maybe even £48,000 or more, levied on an averaged out estate (if we ignore non-paying terra regis) of 6,000 acres per taxpayer. Anything (in broad theory) from 1/25 to 1/40 of income perhaps?

Of course, this use of specie (as opposed to bullion) not only made collection/contribution more equitable (and certain) it also made disbursement among the Viking armies so much easier. In this way it also stimulated the use of specie for Vikings were spending pennies not haggling over scrap-metal barter, hence the growth in moneyers for they alone could regulate and maintain the value of the pennies (the weight and purity) which they struck. It must also have given a big kick to both mining and manufacturing for, assuredly, England did not yet export foodstuffs. No common market (such as the Romans had enjoyed) demanded food for urban conurbations, so the cash required didn't grow in the fields, it had to come from under the ground or by refining foreign coins. One of the attractions of England for the many contemporary 'mafias' was her mineral wealth. She was mining lead, tin, copper, iron, silver and gold in Derbyshire, Devon, Cornwall, the Forest of Dean and the Weald and also had an established cloth trade in at least Devon and on the Essex-Suffolk border.[13] Now let us consider the 'geld', heregeld, danegeld or 'gafol' in greater detail.

As it was put by Green, this danegeld was the first system of national land taxation to reappear in Western Europe since the collapse of the Roman Empire in the West.[14] My own researches have determined that it was an equitably assessed land tax (CAPITATIO TERRENA) and that the Domesday Surveys of 1086 went even further, gathering the full information for the CAPITATIO TERRENA, ANIMALIUM ET HUMANA, which then developed into a comprehensive audit. This administrative knowledge base was therefore and in itself unique among the kingdoms of the West, presumably resulting from an insular survival of numeracy and bureaucracy in Anglo-Saxon England only made possible by the unique, English, 'hide' unit. In Europe this unit was unknown.

The first such 'gafol' (tribute) was £10,000 paid over after the Battle of Maldon, presumably to save London and the south coast from Viking depredations once Britnoð's death had demoralised the English defenders. This was probably in the region of 3,300 kilos (64.9577cwts or 7,275lb averdupois), 2,400,000d. Sadly this expedient then operated like a magnet. Between 991 and 1012 it has been estimated that £132,000 were paid (in instalments) to various raiders, a staggering total of 31,680,000[d]. equivalent to 857.4417cwts or 42.872 tons of silver. Where did it all come from and is it any wonder that the silver content was finally debased as Viking demands grew ever more greedy? Over the course of twenty-one years the simplistic average for each major landholder (each one of 4,000) was therefore a theoretic 24lb, viz. 1lb (and more) of silver for each year on each 6,000 acres (theoretical) holding.

Now consider, if you will, the miscalculation made by both William of Normandy and his major lords for, after the Conquest, the 4,000 major Saxon landowners reduced (yes, went down) to about 180 adventurers ('chief tenants') giving these new nobles vast estates. Yet if their holdings were (on average) almost 22¼ times greater than their antecessors, so was the tax liability which they then theoretically inherited! Given the liabilities attending scale, the evasions possible by sub-tenants and the vicarious nature of markets, finding 1lb of silver a year would then seem trifling compared with a possible liability for a theoretic 22¼lb of silver pennies, yet King Edward (and possibly Canute) had started even worse mischief with his many exemptions to favourites and religious houses. I think there can be no doubt that the Franco–Norman invasion in 1066 was originally intended as a means of extorting 'gafol' or tribute and that when the throne was offered (accidentally one might say) to the victors the entire enterprise changed. The prospect of taking the whole 'kitty' must have seemed incredible, but at that point the full implications were unknown to the victors.

King William became the enemy of his own coterie and cadre when he rewarded his joint stockholders without lifting their liability, for the nation was soon crying out (as so often before) for mercenaries and defences by which to defend her from other avaricious outsiders who could see, only too clearly, the inexhaustible wealth of this nation. Like us and like the Normans they might be perplexed by the economic foundations of this but the proof was in the extortion: demands had increased from £10,000 (991), to £24,000 (1002), to £48,000 (1012) and finally £82,000 (1018) but they were met and by 1066 this had not been forgotten.[15] That is when realities came home to the victors; from then on they were disabused and probably often disillusioned. In the 1070s King William began to build impregnable stone castles at London and at Colchester but was forced to call a halt to both because his exhausted lords were cheating him of taxes, hence (as we have seen) the Domesday Surveys (audit), designed to identify the traitors and the missing revenues.[16]

Some English landholders, of course, remained and for them the payment of geld was not such a shock, only Waltheof seems to have become greedy enough to throw in his lot with the foreigners. Initially, for the many dispossessed English former landowners (men we have afterwards re-allocated to hearth-troops) those who had survived Battle but whose lands were forfeited, certainly for their families, this gigantic re-distribution of property was a disaster. The conventional view is that somehow they faded away into the landscape, perhaps as maquisard Robin Hood characters, not to be heard of again. More discerning historians have noted that English miles, knights or sergeants, were serving with the Normans by the end of the century.[17] Certainly some of the fyrdmen who turned out to support first King William in his campaigns and afterwards served King William 'Rufus' (against the rebellion led by Odo in 1087) were men of the select fyrd, professional soldiers, otherwise they could not have overcome Bishop Odo's French knights, vikings or the western men. What other trade could they follow who had been trained from birth in skill of arms? Early in the next century (the twelfth century) we begin to notice many minor subinfeudations, the consequences of retained 'King's thegns' (as Domesday sometimes termed them) or even new men, also we see evidence of their taxation.[18] These were subinfeudations of minor men with unknown French or Norman names, men now living in the countryside.[19] It seems that families like these, at least those who two centuries later survived the Black Death, often remained to become the country squires of later centuries. Their roots may well have been English rather than French, fyrdmen turned hearth-troops.

So it seems to me that those who were dispossessed in 1066 and yet who had never had any absolute certainty of inheritance under pre-feudal (English) social arrangements were (after 1066) relieved alike of both the burdens of tax and of service. It seems likely that many took the opportunity, in a newly expanding and defence-fuelled specie economy, to seek financial security rather than landholding liability, for one did not pay geld on cash transactions.[20] Whether these Englishmen became some sort of entrepreneurs, or perhaps freelances (mercenaries and hearth-troops), it was certainly in their interest to adopt French names (if only, for example, as 'Richard fitz William') and so become 'French' (in law), and they then escaped any tax liability until and unless they accepted modest, manorial, sub-enfeofments. If they did not, then they enjoyed the profits of their labours until such time as the tax system caught up with the rest of society, which was (in 1066–86) some way off in the future. The full separation of legal 'realty' and 'interest', and then the management of both aspects, equitably for tax purposes, took time to evolve. For some time land remained the sine qua non of taxation.

So the socio-economic structure which the Normans initially acquired was a partly developed specie economy only, but one to be stimulated by defensive activities and the establishment of 'castles' and then again, after 1086, by much stricter application of the specie-only land tax. The larger element of society not paying tax was mainly the one which had no need of specie; Collis' Hypothesis says that coinage spreads downwards on the social scale, modifying its value as it descends (from specific and often luxury functions) until only one group is left, a group for whom it answers no needs.[21] Thus coinage had originated as a primitive valuable used for status, compensation (e.g. weregeld, a legal convenience) and warfare, passing next to the stage where it was a medium also in peripheral market exchange, usually when bartering for high-value commodities or manufactures and it finally descended to specie (coinage) payment of taxes and, ultimately, fines and market exchange.[22] From possessing specific functions money became multi-purpose, though still (as specie) retaining a bullion value, still as yet unsuitable for small-value transactions.

Because marketing systems are conditioned by statehood and because the appearance of coinage pre-dated levels of social development encouraging its universal adoption, the spread of specie coinage down to the lowest social level did not occur until well after the Conquest, yet the emergence of a dispossessed post-Conquest land-owning class, forced to enter upon a full money economy and benefitting substantially thereby, surely helped to diffuse this leaving only the peasant, or bond tenant, level outside the coinage (and so outside this early tax) system. The archaeological evidence of coinage (other than in hoards) increases as the distribution of specie coinage extends down the social scale and, also, as the standard penny gradually eroded in value into the thirteenth century.

As Barlow put it, 'it is, however, the coinage which is the most impressive – and enigmatic – memorial to the financial expertise of the Old-English royal government'.[23] However linking specie coinage to the geld would now seem to divide such laurels and to help explain the process.[24] It was also the case that in England there was only one coinage, royal coinage, quite unlike France and Germany where there were Comital and Episcopal units with fluctuating standards.[25] King Edward, however, added to the number of mint units in operation (presumably to facilitate striking of specie for the geld, for under Æthelred there had already been more than seventy mints) and he did tamper with coin weight, see-sawing from 17 to 27 grains of silver, which naturally affected relative values. William inherited 21.5 and raised this to 22.5 grains in 1080 (which further increased the burden of the geld). 'The silver penny had a purchasing power somewhat similar to that of a gold half sovereign before World War II' it has been claimed and so changes in grain weight and in purity were important considerations.[26]

Such changes do not, however, encourage the general use of a specie coinage and it is to Edwards' credit that he did not seriously tamper with purity as his predecessors had done, but then he was not paying the pirates. Neither did King William tamper with purity, even though his Normandy coinage was miserable by comparison. Clearly he appreciated that the maintenance of the specie value of English pennies gave him (as well as his traders) a great advantage when hiring mercenaries or other material of war: the real value (quality) of silver was very persuasive in all transactions, so that those who challenged English purchasing power were always at a disadvantage when English purity remained high. Some of us remember the broadly analogous situation when London sale rooms still permitted bids in guineas as well as pounds.

I know I have probably appeared to labour the subject of economics and taxation but it is essential to eliminate those foolish conjectures, so commonly repeated, that the peasantry were forced to pay the taxes of the rich, because the rich were exempted. This Robin Hood fantasy just does not and cannot be made to hold water. Time and again Domesday Book tells us that landowners were cheating on their taxes and had been, progressively, cheating for years because it was no-longer a national ransom ('gafol') but a (regular) royal tax. Some claimed exemptions made by Cnut, others (very many) exemptions made by Edward, former royal estates claimed that they should not have to pay when devolved to other landholders (for the Crown does not tax itself, but of course others should pay), churches claimed exemptions (which had at times been vicariously permitted), probably relying on the ancient precedent and claims made in Roman times and scotched by Constantine (in order to prevent the creation of tax havens under ecclesiastical patronage).[27] Many landholders simply altered their tax liability on an incremental, diminishing scale (which tells us they were both devious and not subjected to an audit prior to 1086), others seized on commutation to claim that the land was FORIS DIVISIONIS, and thereby they retained dominium and cash without the (tax) burden of proprietas.[28]

Truly creative accountants (stewards) fudged the units, mixing up those used in hidated shires with those used in carucated shires.[29] They were detected by the Domesday clerks (as we have seen) and I have called the coded directions applied by these royal clerks to such detections 'scribal apothegms'. It is worth repeating this particular example. At Melton Mowbray in 1086 an estate was deponed as 7 hides, 1 carucate and 1 bovate (viz. 1,830 acres, presumably hoping that such confusion would resemble complexity) but a suave royal scribe in 1086 noted that 'in each hide are fourteen and a half carucates', which gives us 12,330 acres instead, in all 19 square miles of land. The aggregated total of all the separate assets and berewicks set down in this shires' Domesday record then confirmed this total liability and if we place them all on the map, and then also total the area with more modern survey records for further comparison, we also in each case accumulate 19 square miles![30] A clever attempt by an unknown estate accountant at evasion of taxes, but one detected by the royal auditors and so recorded in 1086. As I have said, there were others.

The point is that peasants did not have pennies for taxes, they just did not need them and they also had no way of obtaining them with their limited means of production, so they <u>couldn't</u> pay, but their lords received (from them) massive (aggregated) resources in kind which they then either consumed or converted into silver. For example, Richard of Tonbridge could convert his in-kind food rents by selling them to Wealden iron masters, who needed to feed their workforces. To do this lordlings needed markets and (of course) industries employing artisans and labourers who did not have the security of subsistence farming, for such workforces had to feed themselves by other means, ultimately by their industry alone. 'Coinage appears to be a function of long distance trade as it becomes regularised and more formally organised' and this trade concerned manufactures and commodities, luxuries and high-value goods which made the prosecution of profitable ventures easier.[31] The sinews of war are a good example of such goods, but not the only one. Luxury jewellery might be another. Of the more ordinary, everyday industries or manufactures, those local specialisations required in ordinary agricultural villages we know nothing certain, Domesday Book makes only intermittent reference to smiths, millers and the essential tradesmen of the vills, sometimes we hear of fishermen; very rarely we even hear of doctors and embroiderers.

At this very ordinary level we should still expect to find in-kind payments (for example, payments in grain to the miller) and not coins, though the 'gold embroideress' was clearly a producer and a purchaser of luxuries. We must keep Domesday Book properly in focus, it was an audit of the land tax, not (as some think) a census or a comprehensive survey. It did not record cash (outside references to evasion) because there was no tax on cash. It primarily wanted to know who was concealing land (tax being conceptually raised on land) and the consequences for such concealment after 1086, for doing this, could be severe.[32] Interest had not yet been defined in law, so interest raised on realty (such as cash payment for renting out land) was seen as an evasion of realty and punished accordingly. Such a refusal to support the King with treasure, when in need, was treason.

This need for liquidity by landholders was, of course, an incentive. We do not know the extent of mining for lead and silver in Derbyshire (though it was presumably centred in Wirksworth Wapentake), nor of iron in the Forest of Dean or in the Weald, while intermittent references in Domesday Book to bog iron do not reveal the scope of this resource either. However, such accidental inclusions in Domesday Book do tell us that these resources existed and were being exploited, that such enterprise existed. There are no direct references to the stanneries or stannery districts of Cornwall and Devon but analysis of the indirect evidence, the incidence of over population in under ploughed localities with plenty of arable, those then surrounded by a ring of over producing agricultural settlements, all accompanied by massive claims to rights over (and therefore under) the soil, reveal an extensive picture of mining activity, presumably for tin, copper and silver, with corroboratory evidence of tin-streaming in the archaeological record.[33] Within a hundred years of Domesday the Crown itself had acquired these stanneries and was taxing them. I think we might point to Domesday Book as the instrument which revealed, at the least, the extent of this 'black economy', and maybe its very existence to the Crown.

In Essex and along the Essex–Suffolk borderlands there was a vigorous emphasis on wool together with clear evidence of early activity in places subsequently famed (in later centuries) for spinning and cloth production; many of them also having surviving evidence of rich Saxon church artefacts, emphasising their early affluence. Once again these are places betrayed by pockets of non-agricultural workers ringed by over producing (agricultural) service industries.[34] We also can discern a clear distinction between socmen and freemen in this area, the former being (it appears) the craftsmen and the latter the entrepreneurs and sheepmasters. Were perhaps some of the latter dispossessed thegns after 1066? Moreover we have a name from Domesday Book for one powerful factor in this trade, a man called Siward of Maldon, which tells us of at least one point of seaborne trade. Nor is this cloth trade on its own for in Devon we have very similar, if less detailed evidence[35] of cloth production. The 'golden fleece' of East Anglia (and elsewhere), first noted in Roman times and surfacing in Carolingian records, then becoming so prominent in the later medieval period, was therefore flourishing in 1066–86, though its precise foci did shift at times down the centuries, with the passage of time.[36] Up to now its existence in 1066–86 has gone entirely unnoticed by historians.

Another very important but often overlooked industry, one that was coastally widespread along the littoral, was salt. Salt was essential for the preservation of vegetables and meat and also butter and cheese production and, of course, as a flavouring. Nor should we forget fish,

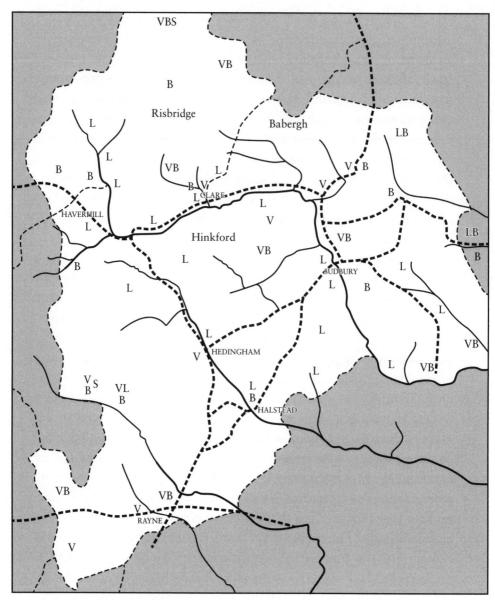

Map 8: Industry on the Essex–Suffolk border in 1086.

for although we know little of the stockfish trade from abroad in this pre-Conquest period we do have records which allow us to assess local catches and so establish a need for English salt at source.[37] The evidence of Domesday Book strongly indicates that the establishment of fisheries

Map 8: Industry on the Essex–Suffolk Border in 1086
The Hundreds of Hinkford, Risbridge and Babergh, with roads and rivers running through this ancient and valuable textile-producing area, are shown on Map 8. Communities in this area comprised farmers (V = villeins), workers (B = bordars) and serfs (S) with 'freemen' and 'freewomen' (L) as the presumed industrial workforces. Among the 'freemen' group the socman class was abnormally numerous in this area. These 'free' communities of workers seem to have been supported by the surrounding farmers, workers and serfs and to have made extensive use of local waterways to move their products eastward to the coast. (Roads are conjectural.) It also appears from pre-Conquest records that this industrial area had been in active contact with the Carolingian Empire which suggests that there may also have been some continuity from the Roman textile industries of Britain long ago.

went hand-in-hand with proximate 'salinae' wherever the necessary fuel was to be found, whether in Lincolnshire, Suffolk, the Isle of Wight, Sussex or Eastbourne and Pevensey.[38] Moreover salt was itself a currency for it could be traded as either a large or a small transaction, it did not depend on specie (pennies) and being fungible could even replace money altogether for most purposes.[39] Ælfric's Colloquy bears witness to the essential nature of salt and for most of the south and east coast regions its production depended on salt water rather than on the remote rock salt of Cheshire during the medieval period, even more so than in the archaeologically well-attested Roman period. These 'salinae' (salt houses) in turn depended on very local fuel supplies, thus essentially on fenny wet lands or maybe even from some proximate heaths with supplies of sedge or furze.

Although we may marvel at the amount of shipping plying the waters of north-western Europe in *c*. 1000 it was not comparable with that of 700 years before, either in individual size or in overall volume and neither were the economic conditions the same. The merchant bottoms were smaller, the transit security was weaker by far and such main contractors as the Roman armed forces had long since ceased to exist, so that for everyday commodities local supply sufficed. Even inland trade was inevitably less, due to the absence of good (paved) roads and maintained highways, though not of trackways (which Rackham estimated to be possibly greater in number than later road systems), while the urban demand for commodities was minute by comparison with the Roman period.[40] For all these reasons England was certainly not increasing her wealth by exporting what other subsistence communities across the Channel could produce for themselves.

In order to transport anything in quantity one also requires the right vessel (container) and although wine can be carried in barrels and stowed reasonably successfully either in a small-hold vessel or as supercargo, commodities such as hides and wheat or barley require watertight, large compartments if the ballast ratio and centre of stability of a ship are to be safely maintained. Some shipping of hides and goods in dry ('slack') cooperage may have been possible from the emporia, when they were in operation, but Viking piracy soon put an end to most such trade centres and for a while even perhaps to trade itself. Londenwic (the Strand) contracted in the ninth century to be abandoned around the mid-century, probably as a result of Viking attacks in 842 and 851, and to their over wintering in 871. Hamwic (Southampton) declined at the end of the same century after attacks in 840 and 842 and, in the southern part of England, only Ipswich seems to have continued into the tenth century. In 980 Hamwic was sacked again and Thanet attacked and in 991 Folkestone, Sandwich, Ipswich and Maldon. In 1009 Thorkel's army landed at Sandwich. Under such conditions emporia and trading stations, where foreign traders could land and safely do business, found it impossible to operate.[41] The cross-Channel trade between Hamwic, Londenwic and Thanet, Rouen, Amiens and Quentovic, even though possibly stimulated by Offa's coinage and Alfred's, seems to have been almost destroyed by the later tenth century.[42] Vikings may sometimes have been traders, but their camps and seaways lacked the stability required by established emporoi and such places lacked any overall control or command by which to guarantee consistent behaviour and security.

From a very early date Kent, especially Thanet, seems to have had a near monopoly of luxury imports.[43] What was it that was being exchanged here for the island's imports of gold, garnets, glass and mercury?[44] I believe that residual craftsmanship and industries were responsible, luxury productions whose necessary skills had been inherited from the Romans, though I know this flies in the face of much received wisdom and a belief in wholesale destruction by 'primitive invaders' during the Migration Period. Looking back from Domesday Book's evidence I have already drawn attention to the probable cloth trade of north Essex and the Suffolk border in 1066 together with the very convenient (and reciprocal) tidal flows along the Essex coast down to Thanet and then to the occurrence in archaeological contexts of early metalwork associated with Kent into Essex, which could have moved on the return tide.[45] I have more recently proposed that the Roman iron-working enterprises of the Weald were also perpetuated so and survived even up to the Conquest.[46] The very name may even be an indicator for the O.E. 'Weald', from 'Wealdan', is an indicator of control, dominion or power and need not necessarily be a derivative of 'weald/wolde'. ('Wolde' itself comes from 'willan' an anomalous, athematic verb indicating wish, desire or will.) Such a specialised arms industry would certainly require very careful control.

It was Thanet's location which presumably gave her a monopoly of trade. Quite apart from the convenient reversal of tidal flow along the Essex coast and down to the Kent shore the prevailing tides all along the Channel would be to her advantage carrying ships from west to east. The tidal flow would be least at the widest point and strongest in the narrow straits of Dover, abating after the North Foreland. This would encourage shipping to stand well off from the Goodwin Sands but then able to manoeuvre eastwards into the lee of Thanet and so drop down either to the northern inlet of the Wantsum or onto the Reculver coastline. Given also that the prevailing winds during ten months of the year are from the south and south-west this would make sailing large from Brittany and Normandy (and also from Quentovic) to any point east of Beachey Head (e.g. Pevensey, Romney and the later Cinque Ports) far more attractive than attempting to sail directly west in a beam sea. The return journey to France is, therefore, (for most ships) most likely to have been from the Kent-Sussex coast (sea area Dover) due east, in order to hug and hop the Contentin coast when returning southwards. It also follows that most of the shipping accessing the English coast from sea area Wight would be from much further south and west along the French coast (e.g. Gascony and Bordeaux) while shipping from Wight and Southampton could access the entire northern coast of France. These were considerable natural advantages for English traders and carriers. They also gave English military expeditions distinct military advantages.

Cloth and clothing from Anglia, weapons and perhaps pattern-welded swords from Kent, would make high-value trade goods, luxuries (in return for luxuries) when traded internally or coastally and such a trade would merit close (royal) control, but then we know that Kent was a rich kingdom at an early date. The same tidal flow would link Sutton Hoo and Rendlesham with Thanet and there we also find silver imported from the eastern Mediterranean (if not residual) and conclusive evidence of skill in luxury jewellery manufacture, skill which perhaps may also have been exported. Perhaps Thanet, at the mouth of the Thames, waxed as Roman London waned and then, eventually waned when London waxed once again. Thanet would certainly become the most vulnerable of these two locations once Viking raids became regular. Before which we might expect most of her imports to have been landed from the Thames estuary onto her northern shore.

It is, of course, possible that the wealth accumulated by the two Roman provinces of Britannia, due to the international nature of Imperial trading over several centuries, was one of the natural resources acquired by the incoming Angles, Saxons, Frisians and Jutes, though not all at once. Even in the twentieth century we have been astonished by chance finds of gold and especially silver 'troves' (for example the Hoxne Hoard and the Mildenhall Treasure) and there is no reason to suppose that previous generations were less serendipitous in their turn. In this context it is amusing to see the drawing of ants digging up gold in the Tiberius Calendar.[47] Of course silver may also have been extracted along with copper and especially lead mining. We know that lead (as used on the roof of York Minster *c.* 700) was exported, for example to the Abbey of Ferrières in 852.[48] Silver may therefore have been extracted even this early from such ores. The acquisition of silver, once a society is reasonably settled, is moreover cumulative, the coins of a previous reign being melted down for its successor's use. Apart from what 'lies in the earth ... useless to men' (as Beowulf's author put it), what is in circulation, especially with bullion, is likely to be circulated again and again and I think we can add to this resource both the results of industry and, one might say, of agriculture or inquisitiveness, ants delving in the earth.

England, ex-Britannia, seems to have had a headstart in the use of gold, not only the metal but in metal working, so a continuation of Romano-British craftsmanship is (I suggest) not improbable. Anglo-Saxon decorative metalwork was also exported, for it is found in Dutch cemeteries.[49] The Tassilo Chalice, given to Kronssmünster Abbey in Austria *c*. 780, is a superb example of Saxon (English) mixed metalwork which has been attributed to Northumbrian craftsmen and it seems improbable that this was the only centre of such craftsmanship, rather we should assume that it flourished throughout Anglo-Saxon England. Let us remember that the metals used to construct it certainly came north from elsewhere in Anglo-Saxon England. Finally the use of lead for roofing requires not only metal extraction but plumbing technology and where would that have come from in the Anglo-Saxon period if not from some surviving tradition of Roman engineers? There was certainly no plumbing at Flogeln or Feddersen Wierde in the Saxon homelands and Terps! We find none at Mucking or West Stow.

'These (English Saxons) were not the exploited, overworked peasants who suffered the hardships so vividly described by cultural anthropologists ... nor were they the feudalised communities of Carolingia'.[50] Their estimated yields of cereals were good, possibly better than we could raise today on our depleted soils and without chemical assistance, enabling them to support more people than those working the land.[51] So we discover very specialised crafts, such as the making of lyres, and very unusual (possibly associated) tools, such as the Saare (Thanet) plane (a unique find from this period and itself of distinctive Roman pattern), as well as makers of jewellery, sword furniture, superb helmets and probably the sword blades themselves.

Metal analyses of silver alloy brooches suggest that both silver and copper (Anglo-Saxon) alloys were very similar to Roman contents with similar findings for copper objects.[52] England was rich in resources and such similarities could be evidence of continued metalworking traditions or of reused materials. Yet we can say that even some of the raw materials seem to have come from elsewhere in England, to be used and possibly finished in Kent: whetstones from the north-west Pennines and the Lake District of sand-silt greywacke, glauconitic limestones from Northamptonshire which went to Hampshire, while assay touchstones found in Kent were of flinty jasper or fine crystalline quartz from south-west England and Wales or Cumbria.[53]

Something of the wealth of pre-Conquest England may be proposed from more recent silver hoards found here, let alone in Scandinavia: the largest yet was probably the Cuerdale Hoard from Lancashire, of 7,500 coins along with another 35 kilos of hack-silver dated to 905–10, though the Sedlescombe Hoard from East Sussex (of *c*. 1066) was also enormous. Such wealth was presumably founded on the metallic resources of the Anglo-Saxon kingdoms and the wealth they also then generated, through subsequent international trading, all of which together made England an apparently inexhaustible source of wealth. And note that although the emporia had gone long before the Conquest, there was still a seaborne trade (for example in Anglian woollens) apparently able to avoid at least some of the Channel pirates in 1066. Surely that argues for some naval parity with the pirates?

The wealth of London, as a trading centre, probably accounts for Duke William's indirect approach to its capitulation. No sensible aspirant to ransom or to kingship would wish to see its sack and to attempt as much would possibly have been to presage Charles I's inequal struggle between military and economic forces.[54] The capitulation of the city seems to speak volumes for (as Adam Smith put it) 'the mean, monopolising spirit of merchants', men with a higher regard for profit than for political factions. I intend no censure of this response, it is pragmatic on either side. Nor would it have been prudent to sack Winchester, with the almost certain destruction of its ancient archive and geld records, so we may guess that William possibly had intelligences in this area of administration and wealth generation, as well as in that military sphere which had caused him to land at Pevensey.[55] Both Canterbury and Winchester seem to have gained in prestige and importance during the tenth and early eleventh centuries and both (we should note) were quick to surrender in 1066 and so, one surmises, they saved themselves and benefitted thereby.

Though it is presently presumed that by Æthelstan's death in 939 the royal school founded by Alfred at Winchester had become less important than the monastic, monastery based, religious schools, nevertheless Æthelstan's court was well known for visits made by foreign scholars and those seeking charters and law codes.[56] This bureaucratic competence tempts me to speculate that Alfred's Winchester School had in fact evolved away from being a purely religious foundation and syllabus into the basis of an administrative unit based at the royal palace of Winchester. It is a thought, for both the Domesday Surveys (Domesday Book) and our embryo civil service and royal exchequer came from somewhere, stimulated by a specie-only taxation, itself made possible only by the combination of great accumulated wealth and of a measured <u>and recorded</u> land survey conducted long before 1066 or 1086, by some highly competent body.[57] Indeed this last was truly a 'long before', one which certainly predated Alfred, but also one which he then appears to have regularised and augmented.[58] He would have needed an administrative unit in order to accomplish his collection and review of data and such an 'office' would then have helped secure the subsequent survival of such early records as both muniments and exemplars.

Finally we need to touch on slavery for this was certainly a source of wealth for the Danish and Viking raiders and we have Anglo-Saxon records of both the class and the trade. As late as the Conquest we hear mention of slaves at Bristol from Wulfstan of Worcester (*c.* 1008–95), though these may well have been Welsh captives. Perhaps the Welsh did not count as Christians if only because they certainly did keep and take slaves themselves? Internal English slaving would be surprising by 1066, given the Church's prohibition of slavery, so perhaps these people were destined for the Irish market? Alfred's laws had certainly placed restrictions on the killing of slaves and unfree servants (Laws of Alfred, Preface, cap. 17), deeming it murder, and if a man blinded his slave in one eye or struck out a tooth he was required to free the slave (male or female). Christian slaves should be freed after six years and a daughter sold into slavery was to be better treated than other slaves and her master could not sell her abroad, only free her to go abroad (Laws of Alfred, Preface, cap. 12).[59] This is early evidence of a more enlightened attitude to this class. Wales and Ireland may not have been so enlightened.

Substantial numbers of slaves seem to have been freed on their owner's deaths in tenth-century Anglia and manumissions are recorded as early as 681, while Wihtred of Kent's legal Code of 695 had already required this act to be done in a church (MANUMISSIO IN SACROSANCTIS ECCLESIIS), so linking manumission with the approval of the Church and reinforcing the presumption of redemption for the former owner.[60] There was certainly a perception that manumission of Christian slaves benefitted the owner before God (this, as previously noted, at a time long before the concept of Purgatory or the 'bosom of Abraham', had been invented, therefore represented a rare opportunity to purchase Paradise) and so one consequently supposes that the practice of slavery was rapidly failing in England even well before the Norman Conquest.

Domesday Book includes a curious entry for Lewes. Here the port reeve was entitled to a penny each from the vendor and from the purchaser of a horse, half a penny for an ox and four pence for a man. This does not have to mean that there was still a slave market in 1086, only that there had once been one there, or it may mean that a man who sold himself into serfdom had to be witnessed by this official who was after all responsible for witnessing all financial transactions. Either way, serf or slave, his obvious English destination would be at one of the Wealden iron industries and if he was a slave and the entry was not just historic, then it gives the lie to the claim that the Normans freed all slaves. On the other hand it seems that some captives, possibly Welsh, were traded over to Irish slave-masters, for the Crown had a 'cut' of this traffic and, we are told, it was Archbishop Lanfranc who persuaded King William to proscribe such exports during the 1070s. This entry also tells us, through the tariff involved, that men were <u>very</u> expensive to 'buy', so one would need deep pockets in order to work them to death! Slaves also (and obviously) tied up overseers and so increased expenses; in the final analysis serfs would be cheaper than slaves, another reason for manumission!

In the past slaves had certainly had some property rights, dwellings and often families but there is a general confusion (even among historians) between slaves and serfs, especially as post-Conquest jurists, even years after the Conquest, sought to eliminate free status and reduce as many of the peasantry as possible to bond status, including reducing villeins to generic 'serfs'.[61] It is probably in this sense that we should interpret the entries in the Exeter Book which date from the 1130s and mention 'slaves', perhaps these are no more than crude attempts to disadvantage the defenceless?[62] De Zulueta remarked on similar attempts by jurists of this generation to reduce the East Anglian peasantry to absolute serfdom.[63] Nevertheless, there are historians who seek to credit the Normans with the abolition of slavery in spite of such evidence. I suppose it might be part of the 'supermen' image they wish to promote, though the facts are dead against them, while such elaborations of the sparse evidence available certainly pander to popular tastes in sadism and sensationalism and also make the past licentiously attractive?

The concept of slavery seems to be deeply attractive and so, it has to be admitted, it is difficult for the ordinary modern psyche to relinquish the wish when fantasising the past. The SERVI (serfs) of Domesday Book are often glossed as 'slaves', but if this was so then why not use an English name (as was done for bordars and cottars) and where then would we find the serf-class, for it is separately entered in 1086 when (specific) slaves are not and is certainly attested afterwards? Had all the slaves been made into serfs in response to the Church's (pre-Conquest) proscription of slavery or were residual slaves unrecorded for, after all, Domesday Book was really concerned with the land and so, if there were landless slaves (for example in unpleasant industries), there would surely be no reason to record them at all?

The Norman conquerors could indeed have been less altruistic than their admirers would wish and the money economy was certainly not a matter of record in 1086. Yet I feel that had there been such a true slave class then, if only sporadically and accidentally (like commuted services and quirky occupations), they would have accidentally found their way into the surveys. So it seems that by 1066 slaves , per se, were <u>not</u> part of the English internal economy, if only because unity as a single kingdom made all men a part of the polity, leaving true enslavement as only to be feared from Viking, Irish, Scots or Welsh raiders? What then happened (I wonder) to those who had formerly been enslaved for criminality (including for debt)? I can only speculate that either they were absorbed into the serf class, or they suffered rather more severe penalties, being now denied the option of life by Christian sentiments? Maybe they were executed, maybe we have created similar paradoxes today, 'on the road to Hell'?

Yet there is something more which we can glean concerning the English economy from this well documented serf class. If we look at Sir Henry Ellis' famous analysis of Domesday Book[64] we can see that some shires had far more tenants in serfdom than others and this is perplexing if it was, in truth, a 'universal condition'. Some writers have made the whole feudal system dependent on universal serfdom but this is pure fantasy and devoid of evidence for they are only ever a small minority in the Domesday records. In Yorkshire <u>no</u> serfs were returned, for whatever reason and there could be several. Surely this is surprising in such a Danish, even supposedly Viking-sympathetic, area when Vikings believed in slaves and slaving? In Huntingdonshire, Lincolnshire and Rutland we find none, in Norfolk only 3½ per cent of the population were serfs, in Suffolk only 4 per cent and in Staffordshire only 6½ per cent. Over the total of thirty-four English shires Ellis only recorded an average of 9 per cent (25,156 ex-283,242 households), the same percentage as were socmen, but some shires seem to have had surprising numbers of serfs. Kent was still low at 9 per cent, Essex and Hertfordshire each had 11 per cent and Surrey 10 per cent. Clearly serfs were not invariably the general (and abused) lowest agricultural stratum, as historians so often present them, or they would be more numerous and better distributed in the records? Warwickshire rose to 13 per cent, Worcestershire 14½ per cent, Oxford to 14 per cent, Somerset and Wiltshire each 15 per cent. Surprisingly, perhaps, Hampshire had 16 per cent and Shropshire 17 per cent. Devon recorded 19 per cent, Wight 20 per cent, Cornwall 21 per cent and Gloucestershire 24 per cent, this last in spite of an apparently sylvan landscape much of which (superficially) could have had little need of forced labour.[65]

Why were there no serfs in Yorkshire? Had they all been taken as slaves by Vikings, Northumbrians and Scots, had they all run away southwards in 1068–70, had they all changed status when they returned to devastated farmsteads in 1070–1? So, why none in Lincolnshire, Huntingdonshire and Rutland? Why then so many serfs in Shropshire, always vulnerable to Welsh incursions, why so many in Cornwall, open to coastal raids by Vikings and Irish slavers? Perhaps all the Yorkshire serfs, without exception, died of starvation and exposure? Is this really likely? Let us consider the problem laterally. We have said that in 1086 there was no contemporary definition of villeinage, the immense variety and variation of recorded wealth and landholding of this (supposed) class, as seen in Domesday Book, renders definition impossible.[66] The same is true of bordars and cottars. Presumably the same is true of serfs?

The problem is the phantasy world created in the past by writers, especially that sociological orientation which seeks to produce a history of serfdom. These people have regularly conflated villeins, cottars and serfs, in fact all peasants, as 'serfs' without regard to the contracts they held or the use of a pejorative. Legally and colloquially it then becomes easy simply to dismiss the complex structures of peasant societies. These fantasies have no evidence in Domesday Book and so no relationship to the mass of the English population in 1066–86. The serf of Domesday Book was not 'manorial', neither was there a 'feudal system' to which he belonged and which repressed him. What the title really represented and represents have never been explored, maybe simple absolutes (even when untrue) require no expenditure of effort, yet the failure to explain the shire-to-shire differences in numbers of serfs bears absolute testimony to this negligence on the part of historians.

What if 'serfdom' in 1086 merely represented the lowest stratum of the bond-tenant peasantry, presumably the landless? These would truly be the 'day labourers' and 'seasonal workers', the 'landless men', who, without even a garden for vegetables and a pig, would need to work for others in order to earn their daily bread and a shelter. Thus the dispossessed peasantry of Shropshire, burnt out by Welsh raiders, would have to take ad-hoc work because their service contracts had ended when their lords were ruined or slain, the Cornish serf-peasantry might be involved in industry of some sort after losing their (maybe Dumnonian) holdings to Anglo-Norman conquest or the post-Conquest fighting.

The serfs of Yorkshire, however, would find themselves suddenly translated to another class as the need for new service-contract tenantry became critical, in order to produce for and supply the military columns and the numerous castles which characterised the northern shires after 1070. We should have a care when we attempt to reduce a vague title of 'serf' to a pejorative and in order to avoid applying ourselves to the available evidence.

Now, returning to Hampshire and Gloucestershire, they were notably shires replete with 'forest' and 'parks', hunting heavens frequented by lords temporal and spiritual, as well as by the Crown, also with extensive fish reserves. Wight probably had much hawking in the passage season but was also closely linked to the repeated assembly and shipment of armies as well as an undocumented but possibly incidentally recorded fishing industry. Shropshire was certainly good hunting and hawking territory and therefore involved many interests from lords spiritual, though it was a little remote for the Crown, and I do wonder if we should associate her sometime inclusion of (separately defined) 'Welshmen' with this serf class, as the lowest social stratum. Devon was streaming tin and no doubt fishing and was also on the edge of the Cornish mining area. Cornwall seems to have already developed several unofficial stannaries (and probably other minerals as well) to account for forced labour while Gloucestershire did include the Forest of Dean, where we can surmise an iron industry (with charcoal burning, never an attractive occupation) was probably in full swing, using roasted Limonite-ores (low in phosphorus and sulphur).[67]

But if the Forest of Dean needed semi-slave labour for this industry, then why not the Weald as well? Well, it seems that the Weald was a very well disguised and also an ancient area of iron working not dependent on mass production and if it had highly technical production, like sword blades, and its special ferrous ores (spathic iron roasting to haematite) were not so onerous to recover, it might not have had historic traditions of slave labour which it felt compelled to follow. Remember 'Wealdan', as indicative of control, dominion and power? There were certainly no defined freemen in control here, but there were many villeins operating under someone's control and doing something specialised. On the other hand, maybe slaves were still being used here, for so much else is omitted from the records? It is interesting that these suspected specialists within the Weald were neither free nor socmen but villeins, a sensible military precaution but also an indicator (perhaps) of ancient royal control and monopoly, maybe from the 'days of Thanet' and the Kentish kings? Conditions in the mines of the Forest of Dean and Cornwall and on the tin streams of Devon may not have been so congenial as in the ancient Weald and so, perhaps, these others had been acquired more recently, or maybe had even once been ancient slave colonies.

Yet I think there was a difference which we should remark between Hampshire and Wight. In Hampshire it was not only the Crown that kept serfs for the Bishop of Winchester had numbers of them. Given the Church's proscription of slavery <u>this</u> of all arguments seems the strongest possible evidence that serfs were <u>not</u> slaves. Anyway, at Alresford he had thirty-one though the ploughs employed were only half in number to the villeins available to use them, so the good bishop was engaging men of all degrees in some other, profitable, activity. Indeed in the whole of the Fawley Hundred of Hampshire he had seventy-seven serfs and far more villeins and bordars than the plough totals would justify. However, on the Isle of Wight we have a different picture with the majority of serfs engaged by the Crown and, once again, more bordars than would be required for arable production. Significantly these royal estates covered the south-east and east sides of the island as far inland as Arreton, Brading and Woolverton and especially the coast from Bambridge Point right 'round to Blackgang and Atherfield Point.

We have no obvious references to extensive fisheries or salt-making here and, indeed, there is no proper supply of fuel here for salt-making, though there is on the mainland opposite where we have records of salt being made and presumably fish were keddled. Salt was certainly being made in quantities further east in the Pevensey Lagoon. This leads me to suggest that the large number of bordars on East Wight might have included 'bordars super aquam' (as the entry reads for Leigh-on-Sea in Essex), viz. fishermen: fishermen not just keddling in fish weirs but men going out upon the waters for pelagic fish. If so, then the serfs could be the processors, gutting and salt-barrelling large quantities for provision when an army gathered, or for the daily needs of the royal household at nearby Winchester. Such a solution would indicate that the serfs of the Hampshire/New Forest hinterland were also processing and preserving both littoral fish (keddled in the Havant and Hayling areas) and maybe also the viands of preference taken from both private and from the royal hunting preserves further inland. These preserved foods could then be loaded onto eastward-bound vessels for onwards shipping to London and the south-east of England. And as Wight was the traditional point of assembly for armies bound overseas, maybe such armies had sporadic need of stevedores, camp followers and low-skilled manual labourers, men who need not be retained when surplus to requirements and who could then be left to find work as 'bratters'.

So, to conclude: the historic and aggregated wealth of England, her inheritance once derived from Britannia, was one attraction in 1066, even (maybe) with 'ants' delving in the earth to locate treasure, her ancient and established industries yet another, the skills these represented yet a further incentive, and her fecund agriculture and fisheries the underpinning and sustaining factor for all such allurements. Then there is one more thing: kings and nobles not only enjoyed hunting, they also relied on it for their viands of preference so that when they were personally inactive in venery and occupied with real business, their foresters and huntsmen were not idle. Hunting, however enjoyable for kings, barons and prelates, was not just an idle pastime, it filled the Epicurean larders of the rich and that is why royal foresters and huntsmen continued to hunt for the King in his absence. Add to this picture hawking, falconry, the only means of taking birds on the wing and especially those larger species which could not be limed, and you have a further incentive for the acquisition of an England rich in passage habitats. Domesday Book also tells us of 'hawk's eyries' further north, the sources of such valuable raptors as peregrine falcons, for other species were less valued, more widespread and it appears that only peregrine habitats were enrolled. The environmental diversity and riches of England were a part of her surprising portfolio of assets. Indeed we may say that England <u>was</u> in so many ways 'Merlin's isle of Gramarye', the biggest prize in Europe. It was a magnet for every military leader who could raise an invasion force and much of her treasure was portable. Holding on to such a kingdom and prize was an even more major challenge, especially after Duke William had proved in 1066 that English infantry were not invulnerable. King William's multitude of problems in the twenty years succeeding his invasion were, in an expiatory sense, a condign punishment!

Notes and Sources

Chapter 1: Eliminating Fantasy

1. F.M. Stenton, *The First Century of Feudalism (1066–1166)* (1932).
2. H.R. Loyn, *The Middle Ages, A Concise Encyclopaedia* (1989), p. 129.
3. W.C. Sellars and R.J. Yeatman, *1066 And All That* (1930), pp. 17–18.
4. Ibidem, p. 17.
5. F.L. Ganshof, *Feudalism* (3rd English edn, 1961 and 1964), p. 67.
6. Marc Bloch, 'Feudal Society' (trans. L.A. Manyon, 1961).
7. Stenton (1932), p. 214. On p. 215, 'mere abstraction to apply the adjective "feudal" to a society which had never adopted the private fortress nor developed the art of fighting on horseback'.
8. For the superb English infantry see the account of the Battle of Hastings in Arthur Wright, *Decoding the Bayeux Tapestry* (2019), pp. 66–85.
9. Ibidem, pp. 38–42. Arthur Wright, 'The Mottes of Old England', *Wiðowinde*, 180 (2016), pp. 35–40 and *Wiðowinde*, 181 (2017), pp. 38–40.
10. H.A.C. Sturgess and A.R. Hewitt, *A Dictionary of Legal Terms and Citations* (1934), p. 44.
11. For which see Chapter 2 (below).
12. J.R. Collins, 'Functional and Theoretical Interpretations of British Coinage' in *World Archaeology*, No. 3 (1971–2), pp. 71–84.
13. D.C. Douglas, *William the Conqueror* (1964), pp. 49–51.
14. Ganshof (1961 and 1964).
15. Stenton (1932), p. 213 (for example): 'the Norman Kings appear as strong rulers … while the barons form a body of militant aristocrats aiming at independence which might at any time become anarchy'.
16. Wright (2019), p. 126 and the tirades of Wulfstan of York. Arthur Wright, *Domesday Book Beyond the Censors* (2017), pp. 154.
17. D.M. Stenton, *English Justice Between the Norman Conquest and the Great Charter, 1066–1215* (1965), pp. 31–2 and note 23.
18. Arthur Wright, 'The Myth of Magna Carta', *Wiðowinde*, 173 (2015), pp. 36–8.

Chapter 2: The Jackpot

1. Wright (2019), pp. 66–89.
2. Ibidem, p. 76.

3. Ibidem, pp. 50–5 and 101–8.
4. Wright (2017), pp. 81–5.
5. Ibidem, p. 43, also Wright (2016), pp. 35–40.
6. Wright (2017), pp. 30–3.
7. Arthur Wright, *'Fools or Charlatans' The Reading of Domesday Book* (2014), p. 109; the geld lay as an obligation upon the land as Maitland observed in *Domesday Book and Beyond* (1897), though many historians seem to have overlooked this
8. Wright (2017), pp. 82–3.
9. 'The Anglo-Saxon Chronicles' detail the event, the calculations are provided by 'The Burghal Hidage' for which see Wright (2014), pp. 122–3 and tabulation on p. 124.
10. 'The Anglo Saxon Chronicles', also Andrew Bridgeford, *1066 The Hidden History of the Bayeux Tapestry* (2004), p. 154, also Marc Morris, *The Norman Conquest* (2012), pp. 195–6.
11. Wright (2019), pp. 92–3.
12. See Bridgeford (2004), pp. 204–5 for a discussion of the origin and fate of this 'nepos', though he assumes that this person only became a hostage in 1067.
13. The *Carmen de Hastingae Proelio* written by a kinsman of Count Eustace, makes him the hero but William of Poitiers dubbed him a coward in the *Gesta Guillelmi Ducis*.

Chapter 3: 'Blood, Toil, Tears and Sweat'

1. Tacitus, 'Nationis nomen, non gentis evaluit', *Agricola and Germania*, cap. 2, 'so what was the name of people not a race gradually prevailed'.
2. Douglas (1964).
3. Wright (2014), pp. 118–20 after Cyril Hart, *The Tribal Hidage*, Transactions of the Royal Historical Society (1971) 5th series, 21, pp. 135–57, and H. Vierk and W. Davies, *The Contents of the Tribal Hidage* (1974), Frumittelalterlich Studien, 8.
4. Bridgeford (2004), pp. 200–2 and pp. 187–8 for the grudge which had begun in 1051 and which therefore dismisses William of Poitiers' account.
5. Wright (2019), pp. 92–3 and 95.
6. Ibidem, pp. 96–7.
7. Ibidem, pp. 90, 97 and 138–9.
8. Wright (2017), pp. 67–72; also Wright (2014), pp. 360–2 and 371.
9. Morris (2012), p. 213, quoting Orderic Vitalis and John of Worcester.
10. Wright (2014), pp. 160–1; also Douglas (1964), pp. 97–8 and 273–4.
11. Wright (2019), pp. 31–3 and 92, for the background to 'Harold's mission'.
12. Ibidem, pp. 46–9, for the building of William's fleet,

13. The Isle of Axholme was entered in Domesday Book as 'marsh 10 x 3 leagues' which would be 120,000 acres, some of it fens and some parts the 'Island'. Today the area is bounded by Bawtry, Gainsborough, Scunthorpe and the River Humber, an area of 153,600 acres in all and now reclaimed. It therefore seems that the *c.* 1070 'marsh' covered much of this low ground and not just the 47,000 acres given for it in 1911.

14. Wright (2014), pp. 23–6: as already noted, Maitland observed that the geld did not lie upon the cultivator but upon the lord of a land.

15. Ibidem, pp. 132–4 and 25–6.

16. Ibidem, pp. 158, 358–9 and 371–3.

17. Ibidem, pp. 138–9.

18. For which see H.C. Darby and I.S. Maxwell, *The Domesday Geography of Northern England* (1962 and 1979), pp. 144–5.

19. Ibidem, p. 217 and fig. 55 on p. 219.

20. An ancient earthwork found here is christened 'the Dane's Dyke' in spite of its prehistoric origin, so the name might well embody a folk-memory of this dyke's reuse at a later date?

21. For which see H.C. Darby, *The Domesday Geography of Eastern England* (1952 and 1957), p. 73, fig. 17.

22. Ian Crockatt (trans.), *Crimsoning the Eagle's Claw: the Viking Poems of Rognvaldr Kali Kolsson, Earl of Orkney* (2014) and also 'Orkneyinga Saga' set down *c.* 1200 from an oral tradition.

23. William E. Kapelle, *The Norman Conquest of the North* (1979), p. 114.

24. Douglas (1964), p. 359, for a reference and to be found more fully in the Monk of Caen's and Ordericus Vitalis' accounts 'De Obitu Willelmi' and 'Historia Ecclesiastica'.

25. Wright (2014), pp. 141–3.

26. Even today gathering such widely dispersed and difficult to attribute deaths would be open to dispute and error but in 1070 where were the survey teams which would be required, how did they operate, to whom did they report and where were their records stored? Also, in the absence of the Internet, how did a French monk writing sixty years later access records (which we must suppose were) stored in England? This statistic is a rhetorical invention.

27. The defenders of Alençon had taunted William with this in 1051: when he captured the town he cut off their hands and feet in retribution!

28. There are, of course, many sources available but I would recommend Frances Stonor Saunders, *Hawkwood, Diabolical Englishman* (2004).

Chapter 4: Strategic Acumen

1. Morris (2012), p. 233. Clearly its inhabitants were not prepared to join the Welsh and the bandits outside their walls.

2. Ibidem, Morris dramatises with 'probably tens of thousands killed' but where do such estimates come from? Where is the evidence?

3. And where had they come from, had Normandy been depopulated in order to subjugate England? Surely that would be a God-given gift to surrounding (French) Comital factions?

4. The 'Penitential Ordinance' in *English Historical Documents* (1953), Vol. ii, pp. 606–7.

5. See Morris (2012), pp. 237–40.

6. Bishop Æthelwine seems to have been a regular contributor to St Cuthbert's miracles as later collected and recorded by Symeon of Durham.

7. John Grehan and Martin Mace, *The Battle of Hastings 1066, the Uncomfortable Truth* (2012), pp. 92–4 in particular.

8. Wright (2019), pp. 59 and 65.

9. Morris (2012), pp. 240–2.

10. Wright (2014), pp. 122–8.

11. Wright (2019), pp. 38–42, also Wright (2016), pp. 35–40 and Wright (2017), *Wiðowinde*, pp. 38–40.

12. C. Warren-Hollister, *Anglo-Saxon Military Institutions on the Eve of the Norman Conquest* (1964). Part of the 'Trinoda Necessitas', for which see M. Lapidge, J. Blair, S. Keynes and D. Scragg (eds), *The Blackwell Encyclopaedia of Anglo-Saxon England* (1999 and 2001), pp. 456–7.

13. As disclosed by the 'Winchester Domesday', for which see Wright (2014), pp. 286–9

14. Ibidem, pp. 126–7.

15. See the map of 'Wasted' entries in Darby (1952 and 1957), p. 73, fig. 17 (for example, Addlethorpe and Saltfleetby).

16. Claimed by Morris (2012), p. 243. Here he does indeed cast doubt on all but a very few elements in the late twelfth-century *Gesta Herewardi*.

17. Ibidem, p. 244.

18. The 'two hundreds' being somewhat intermixed, Darby (1952 and 1957) sorted them into northern and southern parishes (q.v. p. 294) and I think we can say that it probably reflects the vast amount of fenland with islets that then comprised the northern half.

19. Wright (2014), pp. 54–6.

20. If we suppose this to represent a tythe of some sort of average catch then we are looking at an estimated haul of 962,830 eels, broadly 1 million eels!

21. Morris (2012), p. 246 drawing on the *Gesta*, but it seems plausible enough.

22. Between the *Gesta Herewardi* and the *Liber Eliensis* there is some confusion as to actual events but I think we can accept that King William took personal command

23. Wright (2019), pp. 56–60 and 101–8.

24. Wright (2014), pp. 138–9, explaining 'Ðe DomesDæge'.

25. 'and went in with the ship force on the sea side': see Anne Savage, *The Anglo-Saxon Chronicles*, p. 204 (1982).
26. Out of 10,000 we are probably looking at a minimum of 25 per cent and possibly something approaching twice that percentage.
27. 'Anglo-Saxon Chronicles'.
28. Kapelle (1979), pp. 128–32.
29. 'surrounded that land on the sea-side with ships' says the Anglo-Saxon Chronicles and also see Kapelle (1979), pp. 125–7. As well as a supply fleet this sounds like a determined attempt to smoke out pirates and prevent an attack on the rear of the army.
30. Kapelle, p. 128: not the least of St Cuthbert's (and Symeon of Durham's) miracles!
31. Letters to Pope Alexander II, Morris (2012), p. 263.
32. Anglo-Saxon Chronicles: apparently the English contingent in particular did great damage in the province of Maine.
33. Fear of King William's anger when he should finally return may now have influenced Waltheof's subsequent disastrous liaisons.

Chapter 5: Keeping Faith
1. Ganshof (1961 and 1964), pp. 24–5.
2. For example the Battle of Maldon in 991. This incomplete poem (B.L. Cotton, Otho A xii) clearly extolls the virtue of old retainers like Byrhtwold, who chose to die alongside his dead lord, fighting to the end, while condemning Godrich and the other sons of Odda for their demoralising (cowardly) flight. Such was the English heroic tradition.
3. Ganshof (1961 and 1964), pp. 24, 26–8.
4. Ibidem, pp. 35, 84–5. See Chapter 1, note 11, which states that 'collusion' involves fraud but here we are speaking of English loyalty to the King, of co-operation and 'covine'.
5. Wright (2014), pp. 133–4.
6. Frank Barlow, *Edward the Confessor* (1970 and 1979), p. 183.
7. The 'Keeping Cheeses' always require labour and skill, as well as special facilities, for their production, so that anything that would keep was always expensive. It is a common fallacy (factoid) that cheese of this sort is cheaper than meat and easy to produce under 'cottage industry' conditions. See Arthur Wright, *Cantles of Tart and Pungete, a History of Essex Cheese* (2004); also Wright (2014), p. 253.
8. Wright (2019), pp. 59–60. For example the royal stud located in the Park of Rayleigh (Essex) which subsequently absorbed the old castle site, q.v. L. Helliwell and D.G. McLeod, 'Rayleigh Castle', Rayleigh Mount Local Committee of the National Trust, (1981), pp. 6–8. There was a park here in 1086 and the Parson's tythe would appear to carry the stud aspect back before the thirteenth century.

9. Wright (2014), pp. 38–9, 251 and 253.
10. Ibidem, pp. 38–44 and 166.
11. Wright (2019), p. 96; Morris (2012), pp. 202–4.
12. Wright (2014), pp. 113–31, 292–300 and 302; Wright (2017), pp. 161–3.
13. Kapelle (1979), pp. 134–5.
14. Douglas (1964), p. 232.
15. Wright (2014), pp. 373–88.
16. R.W. Southern, 'Ranulf Flambard and the Early Anglo-Norman Administration', *Transactions of the Royal Historical Society*, Vol. 16, series 4 (1933).

Chapter 6: Husbanding Resources
1. Trevor Rowley, *The Man Behind the Bayeux Tapestry* (2013), pp. 121–2.
2. Wright (2014), pp. 118–21.
3. Ibidem, p. 119.
4. Ibidem, p. 37. Many historians have laid great emphasis on the '5-hide' unit and it may, therefore, be a 'fossil' from an earlier period.
5. Ibidem, pp. 122–6.
6. Wright (2019), pp. 55, 59–60 and 105–6.
7. Wright (2014), pp. 114–17.
8. This is the invariable social structure recorded in Domesday Book and for centuries to come.
9. Wright (2014), p. 163 after T.F. Tout, *Chapters in the Administrative History of Medieval England* (1920, 1937 and 1967), Vol. 1, particularly pp. 93–6.
10. This is where Domesday Book itself was originally housed and we can hardly doubt that the earlier records were then elsewhere.
11. Martin Biddle, Frank Barlow, Olof von Feilitzen and D.J. Keene, *Winchester Studies 1, Winchester in the Early Middle Ages, An Edition and Discussion of the Winton Domesday* (1976).
12. See Giraldus Cambrensis' 'Vita San Remigio', cap. 27 'Opera', ed. J.F. Dimock (1877).
13. Was this deliberate arson by 'the old fox' Henry of Blois who subsequently demolished the Old Palace (claimed Gerald of Wales) to enlarge his cathedral precinct and who reused the materials for his own residence – see Biddle et al. (1976), pp. 295–300.

Chapter 7: Growing Suspicions
1. Douglas (1964), pp. 292–7.
2. Ibidem, pp. 284–5.
3. In the first instance large tracts were granted, as for example Kent or the Rapes of Sussex (which James Tait, 'Placenames of Sussex', English Place-Name Society, 1.9, proposed as castellaries), but subsequent grants

(prudently) mirrored the previous scattered estate holdings of English magnates.

4. Douglas (1964), p. 298.
5. Ibidem, p. 293.
6. R.J. Ivens tabled the English lands held in chief by Odo and made a total of 1,697.3 hides with only 274.5 hides held in demesne, thus only 65,880 acres out of a grand total of 407,352 acres, an undoubted inducement to redirect tax liability. (Incidentally in the first case the valuation was 6.7 acres per shilling and in the second 6.2 acres per shilling.) Ivens' 'Dedington Castle Oxfordshire and the English Honour of Odo of Bayeux', *Oxoniensia*, 49 (1984), quoted by Rowley (2013), p. 118.
7. Wright (2014), pp. 173 and 272–5.
8. See W.E. Wightman, *The Lacey Family in England and Normandy, 1066–1194* (1966) and also Kapelle (1979), pp. 144–6.
9. Rowley (2013), pp. 134–5 and 139–41.
10. So said Ordericus Vitalis; see Morris (2012), p. 302, Douglas (1964), p. 243.
11. Arthur Wright, *Hoax! The Domesday Hide* (2007, expanded 2014 and supplemented 2017).
12. Wright (2017,) pp. 79–86.
13. Wright (2014), pp. 156–61, 292 and Wright (2017), pp. 73–9.
14. Tout (1920, 1937 and 1967).
15. Wright (2014), pp. 165, 292, 298–302; Southern (1933).
16. See Wright (2017), pp. 67–8, 70, 85, 109–10, 117 (and elsewhere in Wright (2014), pp. 287–8, 372, 384–7) for examples of industries being discharged by villeins in some cases and by socmen and freemen in others.

Chapter 8: Crisis and Resolution

1. Wright (2019), pp. 48–9 and 146–7.
2. Ibidem, pp. 79–80 (citing the *Carmen de Hastingae Proelio*) and also 119–20.
3. Anglo-Saxon Chronicles, 'a severe and heavy tax … seventy-two pence for each hide of land'.
4. Wright (2017), pp. 54–7.
5. Ibidem, pp. 58 and 61.
6. Wright (2014), pp. 373–80; Wright (2017), pp. 61–2.
7. Thomas Tusser, 'Five Hundred Points of Good Husbandry' (1571): 'Maies Husbandry', Chapter 40, 3rd verse. Tusser was an Essex farmer.
8. Wright (2019), pp. 50–2.
9. Morris (2012), p. 306 says he dismissed some mercenaries but retained others.
10. Wright (2014), pp. 323–40 speculating on eight good reasons for Gloucester.
11. Ibidem, same place for the procedure and logic which were presumably involved in this process.

12. The 'Inquisitio Eliensis' lays emphasis on these men and they were, of course, principal money generators even though not major landholders. Clearly King William was interested (as the source says) in 'if <u>more</u> can be had'.

13. Wright (2017), Chapters 2, 3, and 4 for the skill with which a flexible lexicon was devised, so enabling comprehensive statistical comparisons.

14. Ibidem, pp. 120–1.

15. Ibidem, Chapters 9 and 10, for the value of 'extents'. All of these put together provided a comprehensive 'map' but one in the form of a contemporary 'terrier' or territorial description (rather than a picture).

16. Wright (2014), pp. 319–23.

17. Such as occupations found in the money economy or local topographic details expressed in regional units.

18. For an analysis of the evidence see Wright (2014), pp. 137–9.

19. Viz. Tout's 'camerarii' and Douglas' 'chaplains', as he calls them (on p. 592).

20. Wright (2014), pp. 152–3.

21. Ibidem, pp. 154–5 and also consider the case from 1279/80 (pp. 227–9) examined by Sheila Raban, for this ability to amass and then deploy statistics for specific audit purposes.

22. Wright (2014), p. 204. So at Corston in Wiltshire he paid the due geld even though he could have safely claimed he owed much less. Such camerarii relied absolutely on royal favour for their security because they were hated by all the aristocracy.

Chapter 9: The Legacy

1. Anglo-Saxon Chronicle, especially under 1087 (obituary), also Orderic Vitalis (reflecting the attitudes of the Church and of the nobility).

2. Wright (2014), p. 342.

3. Ibidem, pp. 256–7 and 290.

4. Ibidem, p. 130.

5. Barlow (1970 and 1979), p. 183.

6. The Anglo-Saxon Chronicles, the Peterborough Chronicle 'ealle þa gewritta þeron gebroht to him syððan'.

7. Patrick Wormald, 'Lex Scripta and Verbum Regis: Legislation and German Kingship from Euric to Cnut', in P.H. Sawyer and I.N. Wood (eds), *Early Medieval Kingship* (1977), p. 115. The legal aspect of what follows is also testified by the Peterborough (Anglo-Saxon) Chronicle 'and there came to him his Witan and all the land-owning men of any account … whose soever men they were and all bowed down to him and became his men'.

8. Some were 'commended' to a mesne lord before 1086 but this class was relatively 'free' though without strictly military obligations. They often

appear to best represent the money economy rather than some small free-holding class, see Wright (2014), pp. 180, 190–1, 305 and 378–9.

9. Words of the 'Inquisitio Eliensis'.

10. Douglas (1964), pp. 356–7 and note 2 citing T.A.M. Bishop and P. Chaplais, 'English Royal Writs to A.D. 1100' (1957) for a possible 1086–7 Christmas in England. As Morris (2012) puts it, 'Domesday Survey ... gave William and his successors the means to manage their aristocracy more effectively than other rulers in Europe ...', p. 325, but this also meant that in spite of the King's apparently serious stomach problems it was essential for him to continually manage both major spheres.

11. Mantes is 30 miles from Paris and this suggestion was made by Douglas (1964), p. 358. Perhaps, as at Rye in 1066, his savagery here was intended as a warning (to Paris) not to resist his coming?

12. In formal ceremonies he moved and presented with great pomp and display, as was expected of a powerful king, and he built impressive palaces. Regal *savoir faire* would have helped negate both his humble origins and any stereotyping as a warrior prince.

13. The Monk of Caen, writing soon after his death, gave him a formidable good character including 'temperate in eating and drinking, especially was he moderate in drinking for he abhorred drunkenness in all men ... particularly in himself ... sparing in his use of wine and other drink that after his meal he rarely drank more than thrice ... If his voice was harsh, what he said was always suited to the occasion'. Douglas (1964), p. 370 who also quotes Southern's 'lapidary conclusion'.

14. See Morris (2012), p. 347, he was a competent publicist, p. 340, a son of the Church who resented surrendering its wealth, p. 178, though not above bending the truth of Hastings to suit his purpose.

15. Another offspring of mixed marriage, he it is who tells us that to be accepted one had to be 'French' and not 'English' but his assertion that the English 'did not know arrows' and Duke William's supposed contemptuous dismissal of English military prowess are obviously, alike, falsifications.

16. See Wright (2019), pp. 95–9, 126–7, 136–7; Wright (2014), pp. 160–2 and 201; also Wright (2017), pp. 73, 77 and 83–5.

17. See Rowley (2013), pp. 124–8.

18. Wright (2014), p. 272, quoting 'Dialogus de Scaccario', I, xi, q.v. W. Stubbs, *Select Charters and Other Illustrations of English Constitutional History* (1870 and 1913), ed. H.W.C. Davis.

19. Eadmer's 'Historia Novorum in Anglia', trans. G. Bosanquet (1964).

20. See F.R.H. du Boulay, *The Lordship of Canterbury* (1966), pp. 240–6.

21. See Loyn (1989), p. 180 for overview and Douglas (1964), pp. 257–9 for William I's involvement.

22. See note 20 above.
23. Kapelle (1979), p. 149.
24. Ibidem, pp. 150–3.
25. Wright (2014), pp. 299–302.
26. Southern (1933).
27. For William's strategy in 1066 and the advantages of Pevensey see Wright (2019).
28. For the contributions of such men as deLucy, Bracton and Glanville see Richard Barber, *Henry Plantagenet* (1964) and Stenton (1965); also Stubbs (1870 and 1913). 'There was less need to reconstruct than to set in motion again the processes of administration and to make them effective. This was speedily done', Barber (1964) p. 82.

Chapter 11: What Had Made It Possible?

1. An early voice 'crying in the wilderness' here was Fraser who commended the superiority of the Scottish 'shieling' (transhumance) economy which once supported more cattle and more people than was possible in the 1960s, see Alan Fraser, *Animal Husbandry Heresies* (1960), p. 148 and his general acknowledgement of peasant wisdom, p. 154 (also in Wright 2014, p. 254). Now we are beginning to appreciate that the baulks and 'Jack's pieces' of medieval fields were not wasted space but biological beetle-banks, though rejuvenative practices will certainly require major attitudinal changes in modern agronomy. See also H.J. Massingham, *The Wisdom of the Fields* (1945) and other works.
2. See Wright (2019), pp. 3–8.
3. See Wright (2014), pp. 63–85 and Wright (2017), pp. 87–111 and 41–50 in particular
4. 'postgradchronicles.org' have made this claim despite the fact that the evidence they rely on depends on woven wool grounds and soumak weave, silk threads and decorative borders, all of which are the opposite of the Bayeux Tapestry, q.v. Arthur Wright, 'Ærendgewritu', *Wiðowinde*, 187 (2018), p. 46.
5. See Wright (2019), pp. 9–17.
6. Ibidem, pp. 2–5.
7. See Chapter 8 above.
8. L.J.M. Columella's *De Re Rustica*, book II, xvi.3, trans. H.B. Ash, Loeb (1941 and 1967), also xvii.
9. The 'arpent' was a French measurement usually (in England) applied to vineyards and equivalent to 1½ acres (q.v. M. Devèze, *La Vie de la Forêt Française au XVIe Siècle* (1961), Tome 2). In folio 74v Richard held Burbage with 'two arpents of meadow', at Shalbourne he had another 'three arpents of meadow' and at Marten Robert had 'two arpents of meadow', whereas

(in the same section, 'LXVIII – Land of the King's Servants') Theobold and Humphrey held Alton with 'eight acres of meadow' (the usual unit employed in this shire). See the Alecto Editions' *Domesday Book, A Complete Translation* (1992), p. 196.

10. See Wright (2019), p. 21.
11. Wright (2014), p. 284.
12. Ibidem, pp. 38–9, 43–4, 279, 284 and Wright (2019), pp. 26 and 133.
13. Ibidem (2014) pp. 124–7.
14. See Bridgeford (2004), pp. 233–8 and 239–44 linking him to both Guy of Ponthieu and to Eustace and also connecting the *Chanson du Rolande* and the *Carmen de Hastingae Proelio* (as proposed by D.D.R. Owen in 'The Epic and History', *Medium Ævum*, 11, 1982).
15. Domesday Book incidentally mentions professional embroiderers and such works generally appear to have covered a whole field (or ground) in expensive silks and bullion. Examples and fragments are known from Durham, Maaseik (Belgium), Sutton Hoo, Dover, Durham, York and Icklingham. For the *Liber Eliensis* see Capitulum 62 in E.O. Blake (ed.), Royal Historical Society, Camden 3rd series, Vol. XCII (1962), pp. 133–6.
16. Wright (2019), pp. 7, 134–6.
17. Ibidem, pp. 23, 38–41, 109–20, 133–4.
18. David Dumville, 'Kingship, Genealogies and Regnal Lists', in Sawyer and Wood (eds), *Early Medieval Kingship* (1977), pp. 102–3.
19. Wormold (1977), p. 105.
20. Ibidem, p. 115.
21. Wright (2019), pp. 12–17 and 151–7.
22. See the entry in Lapidge et al. (eds) (1999 and 2001), pp. 8–9. He was another millennialist and fervent preacher of the coming of the Antichrist.
23. Such as the 'Travels of Sir John de Mandeville' written *c.* 1370 by an author who may never have travelled anywhere, but which became a very popular work.
24. See William Cobbett's *Rural Rides* (1821–32) for numerous examples. *Supra*, note 8: book V, i–iii.
25. See Wright (2017), Chapters 9 and 10 in particular.
26. See Wright (2014), pp. 199–210, as with Surrey and Middlesex.
27. See Barlow (1970 and 1979), pp. 182–3; Lapidge et al. (eds) (1999 and 2001), pp. 113–15; 'the Normans inherited from the Anglo-Saxons an elaborate system of coinage assessment and collection and storage of revenue', said Henry Loyn in *The Norman Conquest* (1965), p. 149.
28. For an extreme example see B.L. Ullman, 'Abecedaria and their Purpose', in *Transactions of the Cambridge Bibliographical Society*, III, No. 3 (1961), illustrated by Marc Drogin in *Medieval Calligraphy, its History and Technique* (1980), p. 67.

29. Anyone with experience of such records will recognise that the inability to process in tabular form (as is done with algorithms) means that to check and express the result one has to return to the casting counter.

Chapter 12: The Attraction of England in 1066

1. C.J. Arnold, *An Archaeology of the Early Anglo-Saxon Kingdoms* (1988), pp. 17–93.
2. Wright (2019), Chapter 11 in particular.
3. Ian Hodder, 'Locational Models and the Study of Romano-British Settlement', in D. Clarke (ed.), *Models and Archaeology* (1972), pp. 887–909.
4. F.W. Maitland, 'Township and Borough', being the Ford Lectures delivered in the University of Oxford in the October term of 1897 (1898).
5. See Daniel Sinclair *The Pound, A Biography* (2000), especially pp. 53–68; also M.A.S. Blackburn, 'Moniers', pp. 324–5 and 'Mints and Minting', pp. 317–18 in Lapidge et al. (eds) (1999 and 2000).
6. F.L. Attenborough, *The Laws of the Earliest English Kings* (1922).
7. Richard Hodges, *Dark Age Economics, the Origins of Towns and Trade A.D. 600–1000* (1982 and 1989), p. 65.
8. Ibidem.
9. P.H. Sawyer, 'Kings and Merchants', in Sawyer and Woods (eds), *Early Medieval Kingship* (1977), pp. 143–4.
10. E. Beneviste, *Indo European Language and Society* (1973), trans. Elizabeth Palmer.
11. Sawyer (1977), p. 147.
12. Wright (2014), pp. 38–43.
13. Ibidem, pp. 373–89, also Wright (2017), pp. 70–2.
14. J.A. Green, 'The Last Century of Danegeld', *English Historical Review 1996*, No. 319 (1981), p. 241.
15. Martin J. Ryan, 'The Age of Æthelred', in Nicholas Higham and Martin Ryan, *The Anglo-Saxon World* (2013 and 2015), p. 345.
16. Wright (2017), p. 185, also Wright (2016), pp. 40 and 179, 'Men and Supermen, the Norman Myth', *Wiðowinde*, 179 (2016), pp. 19–22.
17. Stenton (1965), pp. 8 and 58.
18. Wright (2014), pp. 247–9.
19. Wright (2017), p. 154. Landholders had a double incentive to maximise sub-infeudations by Henry I's reign for he not only required geld but initially he held back and instead invented a whole range of new 'feudal reliefs'. (Chief tenants then began to make similar demands of mesne lordships, so boosting the evolution of a money economy.)
20. Wright (2014), pp. 133–4 and 150, 156–60.
21. J.R. Collis, 'Functional and Theoretical Interpretations of British Coinage', *World Archaeology*, No. 3 (1971–2), pp. 71–84.

22. G. Dalton, 'Aboriginal Economies in Stateless Societies', in T.K. Carle and J. Ericson (eds), *Exchange Systems in Pre History* (1971), pp. 191–212.
23. Barlow (1970 and 1979), p. 180.
24. See Wright (2014 and 2017) in general; also R.H.M. Dolley and D. Metcalfe, 'The Reform of the Coinage Under Eadgar', in *Anglo-Saxon Case Studies Presented to F M Stenton* (1961), p. 154.
25. See H.R. Loyn, 'Boroughs and Mints, A.D. 900–1066', in Dolley and Metcalfe (supra, 1961), pp. 136–68.
26. An assessment made in Barlow (1970 and 1979), p. 183.
27. Wright (2017), p. 121, quoting Joseph Bingham, *Origines Ecclesiasticae* (1840).
28. Wright (2014), pp. 146–7 and 157–8; for deliberate omissions see Wright (2017), pp. 75–8.
29. Wright (2014), particularly pp. 151–2 where I call this scribal litotes (that is using a footnote to mark a disguised evasion), the 'scribal apothegm'. For the recognition of 'concealed land' as early as the reign of Cnut see Wright (2017), pp. 77–8.
30. Wright (2014), pp. 152–3.
31. Hodges (1982 and 1989), p. 105; Wright (2014), pp. 158–9.
32. Wright (2004), p. 159, quoting the 'Dialogus de Scaccario', II, xii and xvi, that to be in the King's mercy is to risk forfeit of all goods, estates and 'all his money', this to include those who 'deal with wares' by hiding money not made directly from agriculture and also including those who coerce tenants to offer sureties for their lord. See also Wright (2017), pp. 77–8 and p. 145, 'Dialogus …' L, xi, in Wright (2014), p. 272, quoting I, xi, Bishop Nigel (for the Crown) versus Earl Robert of Leicester.
33. Wright (2014), pp. 358–73; Wright (2017), pp. 67–9 and p. 371, see aerial photograph in M.W. Beresford and J.K.S. St Joseph, *Medieval England* (1979), p. 261, fig. 110.
34. Wright (2014), pp. 373–80 and 382–8.
35. Wright (2017), pp. 70–1 (in addition to Wright (2014), pp. 374–7).
36. Wright (2014), pp. 387–9 and p. 380 (Offa's export of English cloaks to Francia).
37. Ibidem, p. 180. If the herring renders of Suffolk represented a tything of an average catch then over 1,420,000 p.a. were landed on this coast alone. See also Anne Hagan, *Anglo-Saxon Food and Drink* (1995), p. 160.
38. For the latter see Wright (2019), pp. 102–3, 105–6, 108, 149.
39. See Higham and Ryan (2013), pp. 181 and 422. For food as a medium of exchange see Hagan (1995), p. 363.
40. Oliver Rackham, 'The History of the Countryside' (1986 and 1995), p. 263; for Anglo-Saxon 'highways' see pp. 257–63.

41. Hodges (1982 and 1989), pp. 23–5, 40–86 (gazeteer, 'in Ottar's footsteps'), 122–5, 141–9, 171–5 and 193–7. Also see K. Polanyi, 'The Economy as an Instituted Process', in K. Polanyi, C. Arensburg and H. Pearson (eds), *Trade and Markets in the Early Empires* (1957).

42. Hodges (1982 and 1989), pp. 45, 165 and see Higham and Ryan (2013), pp. 343–4.

43. Arnold (1988), p. 92.

44. Mercury was an essential adjunct to 'fire gilding', though I have seen a fragment of a South Midlands brooch (Southend Museum) using the much rarer overlay gilding process.

45. Wright (2014), pp. 373–89.

46. Wright (2017), pp. 82–6, also Wright (2019), pp. 102 and 106–7.

47. Tiberius 'B' Calendar, British Library.

48. Hodges (1982 and 1989), pp. 127 and 88, quoting J. Dhondt, 'Les Problems de Quentovic', *Studi in Omere di Aminture Fanfari* (1962).

49. Hodges (1982 and 1989), p. 118, quoting J. Ipey 'Fundstucke mit Anglo-Karolingische Tierornamentil in Niederlandischen Sammlungen', *Berichten van der Rijksdienst vorr het Oudheikundig Bodemonderzoek*, 18 (1968).

50. Hodges (1982 and 1989), p. 138.

51. Ibidem, pp. 136–8, quoting G. Barber and D. Webley's calculations from Roman Somerset in K. Branigan, *Gatcombe Roman Villa*, BAR, 44 (1977). Also P. Sawyer, *Medieval Settlement: Introduction to Early Medieval English Settlement* (1976). We should not assume that Saxon/English agriculturalists were less capable than their Romano-British counterparts.

52. Arnold (1988), p. 84, quoting D. Leigh, 'The Square-headed Brooches of 6th Century Kent' (D. Phil thesis, Cardiff, 1980), p. 188ff.; J. Mauser, 'A Technological Study of the "Bronze" Brooches Excavated at Spong Hill, Norfolk, 1972–76' (dissertation, London, 1977), pp. 22–3.

53. Arnold (1988), pp. 180, 161–80, quoting S.M. Davies, 'Excavations at Old Down Farm, Andover, Part I: Saxon', *Proceedings of the Hampshire Field Club Archaeological Society*, No. 36, 81, quoting D.T. Moore and W.A. Oddy, 'Touchstones: some Aspects of their Nomenclature, Petrography and Provenance', *Journal of Archaeological Science*, No. 12 (1985), pp. 58–80.

54. When we consider that in 1016–18 London paid £10,500 on top of the £72,000 paid by thirty-four shires (England) then she was worth 14½ per cent of the rest of the kingdom, a prospect of finding ready cash in one (small) location and so critical for the payment of mercenaries. Securing London, therefore, deprived any opposition of the sinews of war.

55. Winchester's lucky escape might be attributed to Queen Edith as a pawn (apparently in residence) and/or to the gifts which 'primates urbis' offered the Conqueror in November 1066. Its compliance facilitated William's strategic accumulations and opened the way to Wallingford and London.

I also suspect that he might have known something of the archives kept there; see Wright (2019) citing the evidence of the Bayeux Tapestry.

56. M. Lapidge, 'Schools', in Lapidge et al. (eds) (1999 and 2001), pp. 407–9 and Sean Miller, 'Aethelstan', p. 16

57. Wright (2014), pp. 113–31 and 346–7, also Wright (2017), pp. 162–4 and 175–6.

58. Wright (2017), pp. 87–103; also Arthur Wright, 'English Surveyors and Surveys, the "Extents" of Norfolk in Domesday Book', *Wiðowinde*, 176 (2015), pp. 37–40.

59. See Bill Griffiths, *An Introduction to Early English Law* (1995), pp. 45–8.

60. David A.E. Pelteret in Lapidge et al. (eds) (1999 and 2001), pp. 423 and 301–2.

61. See F. de Zulueta, *English Monasteries on the Eve of the Dissolution Patronage in the Later Empire*, Oxford Studies in Social and Legal History, Vol. 1 (1927) and D.C. Douglas, *The Social Structure of East Anglia*, Oxford Studies in Social and Legal History, Vol. 9 (1927). For feudal concepts of vassalage and benefice see Ganshof (1964).

62. Highlighted by Pelteret in Lapidge et al. (eds) (1999 and 2001), p. 302. Such alterations appear to evidence the confusion between reality and wish-fulfilment on the part of the victors.

63. See de Zulueta (1927).

64. Sir Henry Ellis, *A General Introduction to Domesday Book* (1833, repr. 1971), Vol. II, 'Summary Tables'.

65. See Wright (2017), pp. 126–43 for a general analysis of the economic picture in Oxfordshire and Gloucestershire. In the latter, 'based on evidence from other shires I would speculate that the handful of freemen and coliberts were quite likely the entrepreneurs while a number of the villeins and radmen were operating an intensive agricultural service industry supporting them. Mining seems the obvious enterprise and the occupation of the serfs', p. 142.

66. We have already seen that the ferrous metallurgy of the Weald appears to have been run by 'villeins', probably for security reasons. There is a similar anomalous hierarchy in Devonshire where we see 'villeins' holding manors, or even 'ad firman', with 'villeins' as part of the money economy and at Kenton and Ottery St Mary even swineherds were paying in cash! One wonders what 'villein' status really meant in this shire. See Wright (2017), pp. 67–8.

67. See Wright (2014), pp. 358–73 and Wright (2017), pp. 68–72.

Index